PROJECT: Two RPO cars you can't buy 58

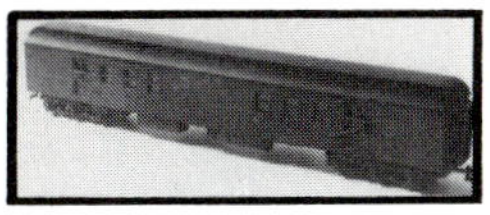

7 Kitbashing locomotives 62

PROJECT: An E8 B unit 66

PROJECT: Updating an American 70

8 Structure kitbashing 74

PROJECT: Low-relief background buildings 76

PROJECT: Kitbashed Victorian station 82

9 Advanced finishing 86

TOOLBOX: Airbrush care and troubleshooting 90

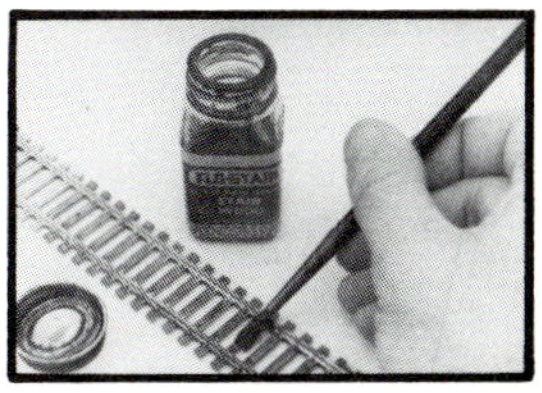

PROJECT: Adding realism to plastic track 92

10 Advanced kitbashing 95

TOOLBOX: Using motor tools 96

PROJECT: A tall steel trestle 98

Glossary and Index 102

ART DIRECTOR: Lawrence Luser
CONTINUITY: Burr Angle, Mike Schafer
LAYOUT AND COVER DESIGN: Bill Scholz
PHOTOGRAPHY: Robert Schleicher and A.L. Schmidt except as noted.

KALMBACH BOOKS

Published by Kalmbach Publishing Co., 1027 North Seventh Street, Milwaukee, WI 53233. Printed in U.S.A. Library of Congress Catalog Card Number: 79-84874. ISBN: 0-89024-540-1.

Introduction

Break out of the straight-from-the-box variety of model railroading!

MODEL RAILROADING TODAY is a richer and more fascinating hobby than any other, and much of its richness and variety is a result of the use of plastics. Because plastic products have made it possible for one man to accomplish a great deal in a relatively short time and at low cost, many modelers have built stunning—and near-complete—layouts in only a few years, and many others are following their example.

The plastic track, kits, and ready-to-run equipment in today's model railroad marketplace are well detailed and, considering their wealth of detail, extremely low priced. The molding process used to make these models is capable of reproducing nearly microscopic details, and items as tiny as rivet heads appear in scale size with the round-head contour of the real thing—features often missing on even the most expensive imported brass models. Mechanically, plastic models are usually at least as good as their high-priced metal brothers, and correcting an occasional flaw such as oversize wheel flanges puts them in flawless operating condition.

If one or two details are revised and one or two minor mechanical matters corrected, virtually any plastic item can rival the realism of contest-quality scratchbuilt models. The parts you'll need to upgrade plastic cars are inexpensive, and you'll find that a "loaded" (detailed and reworked) plastic car often costs less than a comparable item built from a craftsman-style wood, metal, and cardstock kit.

In fact, from the standpoint of some modelers, plastic models have *too much* detail! That sounds impossible, since most of us strive to reproduce every nut and bolt of the prototype. The problem is that brake piping, handrails, ladders, grab irons, drain piping, and electrical conduits are molded into the surface of the models. Upon close inspection, this kind of detail lacks the fully rounded, free-standing look of the real thing, and it's often difficult to paint neatly. In this book you'll learn how to cleanly remove unwanted cast-on detail and replace it with wire or individual parts.

One valid complaint about plastic railroad models is that, being mass-produced, the models are too common. When they are used straight from the box, they are exact duplicates of models found on thousands of other layouts. Naturally, you want your railroad to look—and be—different from your neighbor's pike. This book provides you with the techniques you'll need to make your plastic models unique. With just a little extra work, you can make your one-of-ten-thousand plastic model one of a kind, even more distinctive than a limited-run brass import.

Fig. 1-1. This HO work car was built from an MDC old-time refrigerator car. You can easily do the same; the detailed project starts on page 46.

Replacing the molded grab irons, adding brake hoses, and repainting transformed this AHM HO diesel into a realistic one-of-a-kind miniature.

Making your models unique. Space is too limited on model pikes to ever do the same thing twice, so the solution is to alter—either a little or a lot—any duplicate item on your railroad. The simplest alteration is to renumber any cars that have the same number. The resulting variety "expands" your layout. Next, you can make plastic models unique with simple paint-and-decal conversions. Even if engines and cars don't come lettered for your favorite railroad, you can *make* exactly what you want by using some of the thousands of available decal sets. The techniques for applying decals are fully explained in Chapter 4; once you've mastered them, the work is easy and fun, and the results are as good or better than out-of-the-box lettering.

Finally, there's something called *kitbashing*. This is the process of building unique models by modifying and rearranging kit parts. Plastic models are especially easy to modify because of their strength and simplified construction. An inexpensive diesel body, for example, may furnish the correct louvers, fans, and vents needed to modify another body to represent a specific engine or even an entirely different prototype. Blunt ends from two A-unit diesel bodies can provide the raw materials for building a B unit that you can't buy. An old, outdated refrigerator car can be converted to work train service, fig. 1-1, the same thing that real railroads do when they need rolling stock for maintenance-of-way duties. Even if you don't have the patience or skill to tackle wood and cardstock craftsman-type kits, you'll find plastic kitbashing easy.

How to use this book. To familiarize yourself with the information, read all the chapters, and study all the photographs. Read through the projects, too; you may not have the slightest interest in some of the models presented as examples, but you'll gain an appreciation of basic techniques and tricks that do apply to your modeling. The procedures used to build the RPO car in Chapter 6, for example, can be used to lengthen or shorten or combine any passenger cars. The techniques used to "think out" and build the large Victorian station in Chapter 8 are applicable to any structure—large or small—and the window, door, and grab iron replacement techniques used to convert the refrigerator car into a work car in Chapter 5 are the same ones you'll need to add doors or windows or grab irons to any piece of rolling stock.

Throughout the book you'll find "Toolboxes," short sidebars describing useful modeling tools, how to use them, and how they work best. These toolboxes explain basic tool information without getting in the way of the information in the text. The Index and Glossary is designed to help you find information rapidly. Too often in "How-to" books you'll find that information that you know is in the book *somewhere* isn't where you remember it or think it belongs. The Index is arranged by techniques—if you are looking for tips on cutting, just look up "Cutting" or "Sawing" and you'll find the techniques, tips, and hints that you need.

How plastic models are made. The kits we discuss in this book are made by forcing molten plastic under pressure into steel, brass, or aluminum molds. This is called injection molding. The plastics used are thermoplastics that become fluid at several hundred degrees. The plastic comes in bags of pea-sized pellets that are dumped into a hopper on the injection-molding machine, melted, and squirted into the mold.

The molds are filled with high-temperature plastic many times a minute, so they must be sturdy. Most are hardened steel. The reverse image—usually called the female—of the model parts is cut into the face of the mold using milling tools similar to those that the dentist uses on your teeth. This is an expensive precision machine-tool operation and there are no shortcuts; every sliver of steel has to be cut away and each feature of the finished model is the result of the mold maker's watchful eye and careful craftsmanship.

Most models begin life as a "master." This is the pattern that is followed to make the molds. In some cases this master pattern may be a relatively crude model in the same scale as the finished product will be, or even an existing kit with some modifications. For simple models, blueprints are made from the master, and the men that make the molds work from these blueprints.

When the finished model is a complicated one, such as a steam locomotive, the patternmaker will build a master many times larger than the finished product. If this pattern is twice the size of the model, the pattern is said to be "two up." It's common for patterns to be "five-up" or even "ten-up," particularly if there is a lot of fine detail. This pattern can be brass, aluminum, plaster, hardwood, or plastic. Every rivet, seam, crease, hinge, crack, and knot hole is included, all in full three-dimensional form.

Most mold cutting (also called diemaking) is done in a vertical milling machine, fig. 1-2. This sturdy machine holds the mold block firmly while a spinning milling tool cuts the reverse image of the model into it. Both the bed of the milling machine and the milling tool can be moved with micrometer precision so the cut can be controlled to within a thousandth of an inch in any direction.

Sometimes, a pantograph is used to guide the movements of the milling bit. This device is a set of four bars hinged to form a parallelogram. A stylus extends

Three N scale Rico stations (above) were used to kitbash a Southern Pacific combination depot (below). Similar conversions are possible in any scale.

from one of the arms and is used to trace over the master pattern, fig. 1-3. At the other end of the pantograph a milling bit cuts away material in the same path that the stylus traces on the master. The pantograph can be set to enlarge or reduce the size of the master. This is how our "two-up" pattern is reduced to final size.

When a complex mold is to be milled using a pantograph, the shape of the master must be converted into the reverse-image cavity that will be cut into the mold. This is usually done by pouring metal-filled epoxy over the master pattern.

The mold is completed by cutting paths that the molten plastic will follow to reach the cavity. These become the sprues (molding trees) in the finished kit. Finally, dozens of holes are added for alignment pins (these hold the parts of the mold in proper relation to one another) and ejection pins (these force the completed parts out of the mold), fig. 1-4.

Simple two-piece molds are used to make flat parts like structure walls and windows, separate boxcar roofs, and trim and detail items. Larger, more complex parts—freight and passenger car bodies, steam locomotive boilers and cabs, and diesel shells—are produced in molds that have three or four—or more—sections. The front, back, and end sections of these molds are called "slides," because they slide away from the part when the mold is opened. Most locomotive and car superstructure molds have a top, a bottom, and four slides, fig. 1-5. Pins and guide grooves are added so all six mold sections fit together snugly, and cams in the mold-

Fig. 1-2. A 3-D pantograph cutting a steel mold for Model Die Casting's HO handcar. The flat oversize master pattern is on the table beneath the patternmaker's right hand.

Fig. 1-3. The finished molded parts were made in the mold block at the left. The flat pattern at the right is the "five up" master for the handcar handle support frame.

This Arburg injection molding machine is typical of those used to make plastic kits. The hopper holds pea-sized plastic pellets that are melted and injected into the cavities of the mold.

ing machine automatically separate the slides and operate the push rods that eject parts from the mold, fig. 1-6.

Many models from a single mold. Obviously, injection molding is expensive; tooling up for a freight car or structure can cost tens of thousands of dollars, and locomotive models cost considerably more. This is far too costly for the manufacturer to use the tooling to produce only a single, specific kit, so molds are designed to produce parts that can be used in several models. One way to produce many models from a single set of tooling is to paint the models in as many different road names and color schemes as possible, fig. 1-7. Other ways of utilizing tooling to the maximum are to make kits with interchangeable parts, fig. 1-8, and to make molds with interchangeable slides.

The manufacturers use interchangeable mold slides to allow them to get more life out of their tooling. The Train-Miniature line of box cars and reefers is an example. Because many of the cars have the same overall shape, interchangeable mold slides can produce steel, outside-braced, or wood-sheathed ends on the same basic car body. The sides are interchangeable, too, so cars with identical roof, underframe, and end designs but different sides can be made without retooling the entire mold.

If you train yourself to recognize identical parts that have been "disguised" by different paint jobs or by use in different kits, you'll have taken a giant step in understanding the kitbashing process. Remember, where the manufacturers use only a few of the combinations possible with their parts—because they must use them as-is—we can attack the pieces with razor saws and files to make them fit in countless combinations, and we can even combine parts from competing firms!

Tooling Exchange. Sometimes when you go out to look for a specific kit to kitbash something you have in mind, you won't find it. Because the tooling for

Fig. 1-4. A completed mold has dozens of ejection and alignment pins. The ejection pins force the completed parts out of the mold cavities after the plastic cools.

Fig. 1-5. Complex moldings require multi-part molds with slides that can be moved to allow the part to be ejected. The master pattern is shown here with the mold for Model Die Casting's modern 50-foot box car.

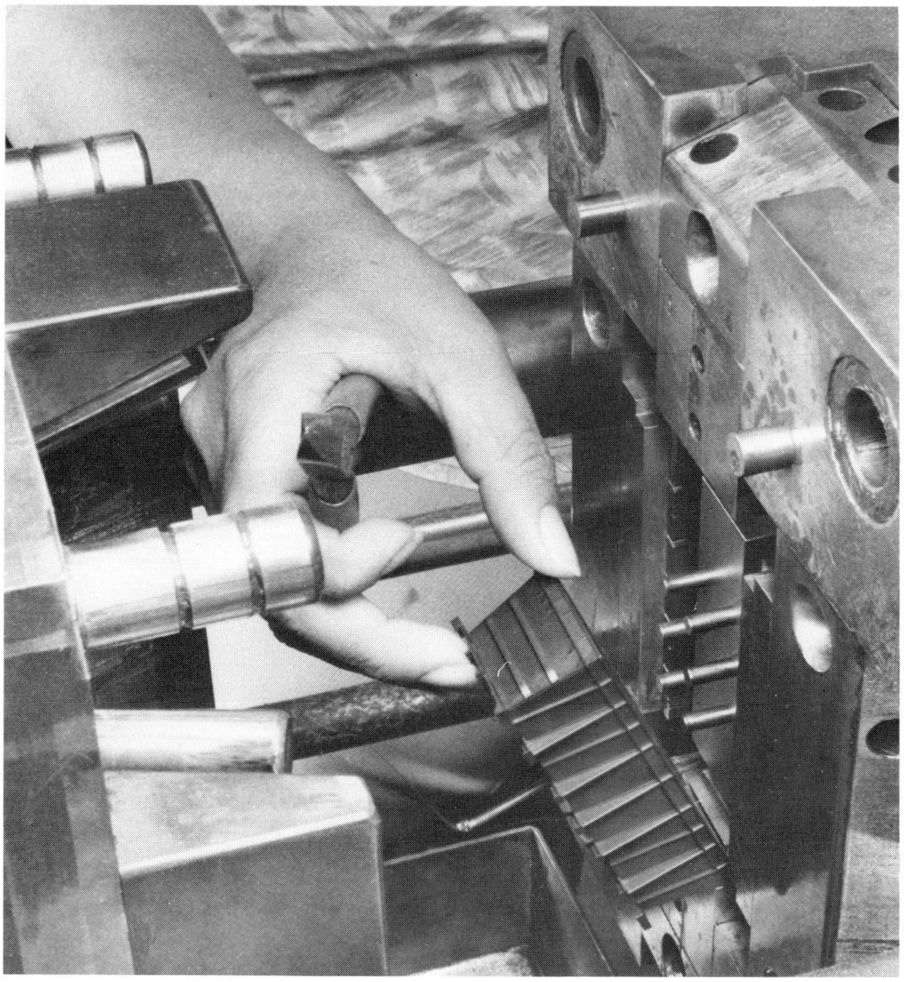

Fig. 1-6. After the hot plastic is injected, the mold sections are separated by air pressure and the ejection pins push the part from the mold.

Fig. 1-7. Here are several dozen Model Die Casting box cars just back from the paint shop. Colors are applied using a form-fitting fiberglass mask and the lettering added by a silk-screen process or precision rubber stamps.

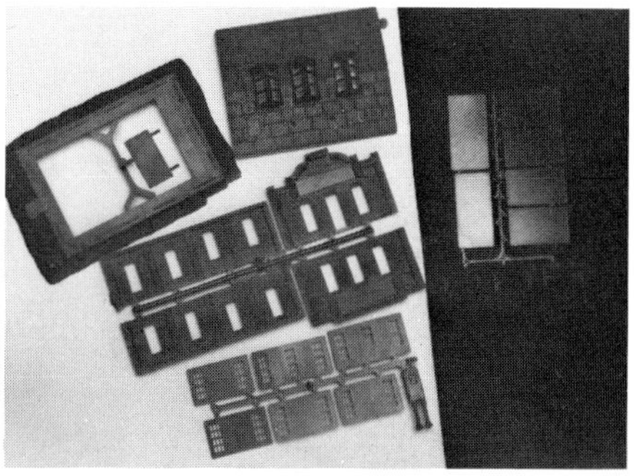

Fig 1-8. Some parts are used in several kits; these pieces from AHM's "Gruesome Casket Co." are a good example. Their interchangeability makes them especially suitable for kitbashing.

plastic kits is so expensive, it is rarely discarded or destroyed. Frequently, one manufacturer will sell molds to another, and the new owner will make minor changes, print a new box, and reissue virtually the same kit under his brand name. Watch for this, and talk over your needs with the man at the hobby shop—he makes it his business to help you find what you want and to keep track of changing product lines.

Finding what you need. Everything you need for plastic kitbuilding and kitbashing is readily available, either at a local hobby shop, hardware store, or art-supply house. Tools and where to find them are discussed in the Toolboxes.

Kits, plain and textured plastic sheet, strips, and structural shapes—the raw materials—and specific detail parts, paint colors, and decal sets may be difficult for your hobby shop to keep in stock simply because there are so many varieties. If you don't have a hobby shop nearby, check the catalogs offered by the large mail-order firms that advertise in MODEL RAILROADER magazine. There are dozens of manufacturers of kit and ready-built plastic cars, locomotives, and structures, and most will send you a current listing if you include a stamped, self-addressed envelope with your request.

Some of the firms that sell kits and ready-built items also have catalogs listing repair parts and separate components. These lists are treasure troves for kitbashing, since they mean you don't have to buy a complete locomotive when all you need is an extra body shell. Be sure to ask about repair parts lists when you write for catalogs.

Let's get started. So, how do you get started? If you haven't worked with plastic kits at all, first build a few kits as they were intended, following the kit instructions and the tips in Chapter 2. Try to do the best job you can at each step along the way, and try to do a better job on each model than you did on the last. Build a structure kit or freight car first—both are inexpensive and simple, and mistakes are easy to hide. Next, assemble a passenger car, and finally, a locomotive. Then, when you're ready, take on one of the basic kitbashing projects.

From left to right: Detail castings from A-W Miniatures, Grandt Line, and Model Masterpieces; ABS tubing (with end cap), rod, and channel from Plastruct; styrene strip and scribed sheet stock from Evergreen; and molded styrene cobblestone from Heljan.

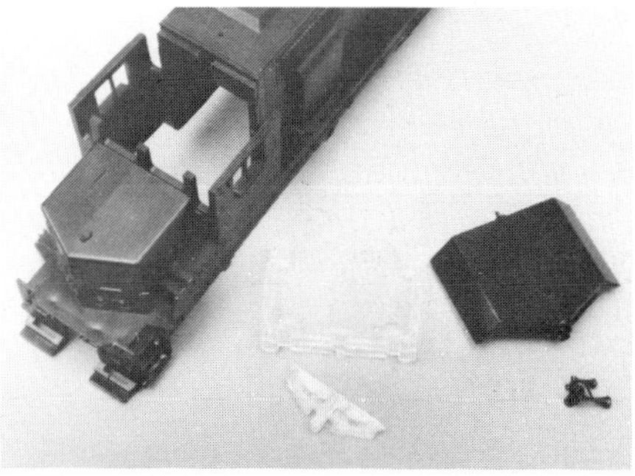

Many HO and N plastic locomotive and car shells are available undecorated (without paint or lettering). These are ideal for painting with your own special color scheme or for kitbashing.

Basic kitbuilding

Learn how to do the job right the first time!

KITBUILDING is the way to learn basic techniques, so be sure to build several stock kits before you plunge into kitbashing. When you've mastered the techniques needed to make a box of plastic pieces look like miniature wood, brick, stone, or steel, you're ready to call on plastic for any modeling need or situation. Regardless of price, no plastic kits and none of the so-called ready-to-run plastic models are truly ready to use. Every plastic part in a kit needs to be trimmed and tested for fit before assembly. Most of the work on ready-built models falls into the category of painting and lettering work, so for now let's concentrate on tips and techniques for doing above-average jobs on average kits.

The "secrets" of building better-than-average plastic models are the same as for building any model railroad kit: careful assembly and proper finishing. Too often, the pre-colored parts in a plastic kit offer an almost irresistible temptation to slap the kit together and forget about painting. Try to consider every plastic kit as just so many *parts* that require fitting, detailing, painting, lettering, and weathering to produce a presentable model. Take this approach and you'll find that your plastic models—and your modelwork in general—will improve. Never kid yourself that you'll assemble a model quickly to get it onto the layout temporarily—those "temporary" jobs usually last for years! Take the time NOW to do the job right.

About plastics. Several types of plastic are used to mold kits. Most are polystyrene or related compounds. This material is easy to work with, even easier than wood. You don't have to worry about grain or the strength of glued joints because the plastic is uniform throughout. Styrene works rapidly because most joints set almost instantly. The material is strong enough to be self-supporting in most model applications, and changes in humidity won't cause it to warp, so the extensive bracing required in wood or cardstock construction is not necessary. Excessive heat and ultraviolet light are the major enemies of completed plastic models. The heat of direct sunlight is strong enough to soften, warp, and buckle plastic in a random manner, and ultraviolet rays can embrittle the material and cause colors to fade.

Molded plastic is rigid, but soft enough that it can be cut easily using a razor saw, jeweler's saw, or motor tool. The work is neat—plastics take and hold crisp edges much better than wood or cardstock—and there is no sawdust, just tiny chips. Small pieces and thin sheet stock can be cut with a hobby knife or razor blade.

Basic tools for kit assembly. You may be surprised to learn that plastic kits require any tools at all for assembly. Some kits state right on the box that they snap together, and their pre-colored parts don't look altogether bad without paint or preparation. But if you want to convert those kits into realistic miniatures, you'll need to trim and file almost every part to eliminate casting flash and make the best possible joints, and you'll want to paint over the waxy, translucent plastic finish.

Here's a list of the basic tools you should have for kit assembly: a hobby knife (see the Toolbox on page 8); flat, round, and square needle files; fine-point tweezers; a small screwdriver; single-edge razor blades; steel scale rule; masking tape; chain-nose pliers; a No. 0 watercolor brush or precision needlepoint applicator; waxed paper; and a thick cardboard or hardboard working surface to prevent marring your desk or table top.

The hobby knife is a necessity, as is the packet of single-edge razor blades. You'll use the knife for trimming flash and for cutting parts from their sprues,

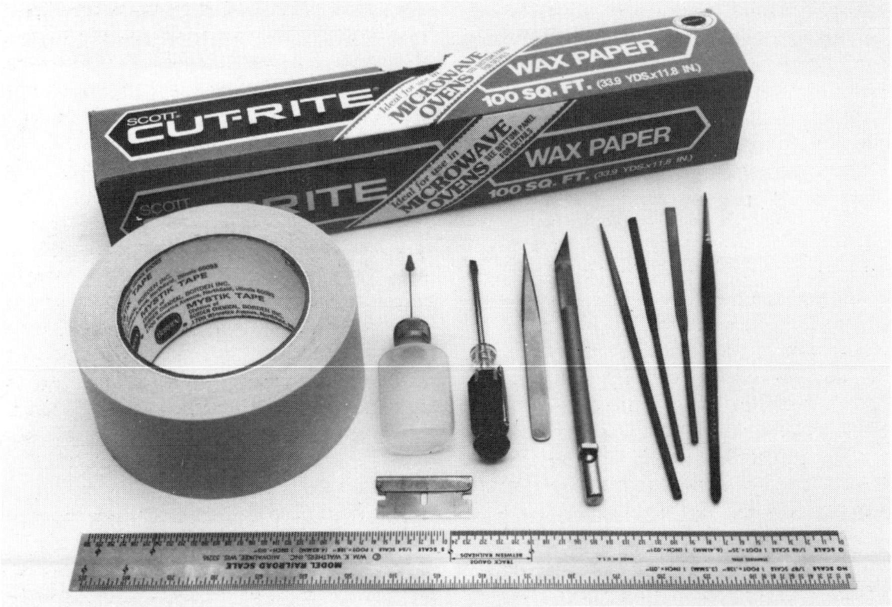

Basic kitbuilding tools: (left to right) waxed paper, wide masking tape, needlepoint cement applicator, small screwdriver, tweezers, knife, needle files, cement brush, single-edge razor blade, steel scale rule.

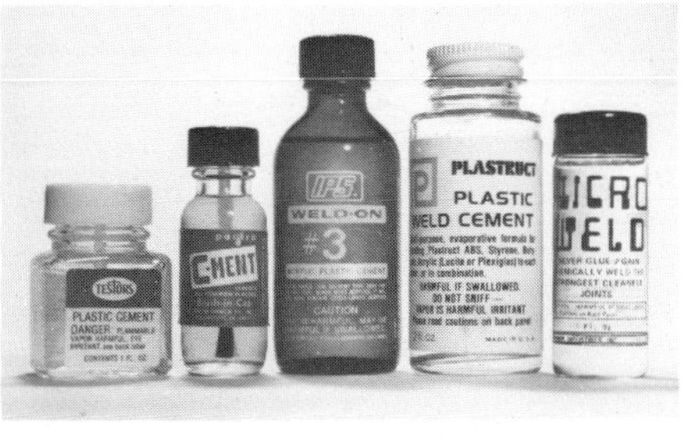

These liquid cements are all suitable for kitbuilding. Each has a different rate of evaporation, so experiment to find a brand you like.

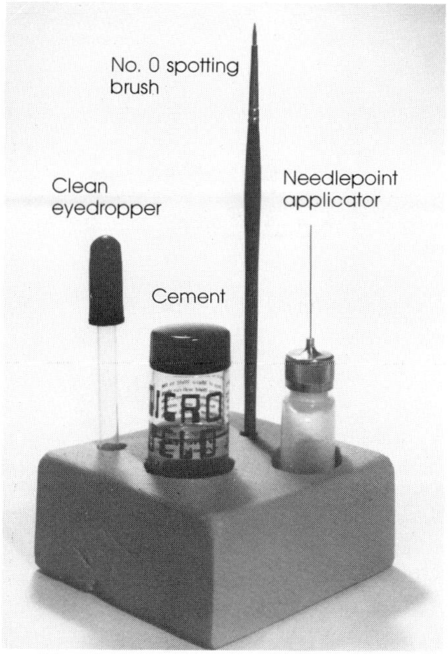

Fig. 2-1. This handy cement stand and tool organizer was made from scrap 2x4. It measures 3½" x 3½" and holds everything needed to apply liquid cement.

and the razor blades are handy for shaving away plastic in the same manner as a wood plane, for cutting sheet plastic, and for making vertical "chop" cuts such as removing unwanted mullions from a window casting. For files, choose one each of medium-cut (No. 0) or fine-cut (No. 2) jeweler's files in round, flat, and square shapes. These will reach into openings to remove flash where the knife will not fit.

You'll also need some clips and clamps to hold parts together while cemented joints set. An assortment of spring-action clothespins, rubber bands, and a roll of 2"-wide masking tape should be sufficient for most assembly jobs. A steel scale rule such as those made by Flint, General, or Walthers is used as a cutting and alignment guide as well as to make measurements in your scale.

Add a small screwdriver (blade about ⅛" wide), tweezers, and a pair of chain-nose pliers and your inventory of basic tools is complete. Not really a tool, but just as important, is a strong work light to eliminate eye strain and show you what you're *really* doing. Finally, give some thought to your working surface—it's a tool, too. You don't want to work on an unprotected table or desk, because spilled cement or paint will ruin furniture finishes. A thick sheet of glass with the edges smoothed or taped makes a good flat, non-stick surface for assembly work, as does a ¼" Masonite (pressed hardboard) rectangle about 12" x 18" with some waxed paper taped to it. Six to eight layers of newspaper make an excellent disposable protective covering.

Plastic cements. When you purchase cement to assemble your first kit, don't buy the kind that comes in a tube. What you need is the liquid cement for plastics that comes in a bottle. "Micro Weld," Pactra "C-ment," Plastruct "Plastic Weld," and Testors liquid "Plastic Cement" are brands that you'll find at your hobby shop. These cements look and flow like water, and their action on plastic seems slight if applied only to the surface like a glue. Liquid cement is a solvent that dissolves a thin layer of plastic on each mating part. The parts themselves become the "glue," and the joint is literally welded (fused) together. This solvent action slightly weakens the surrounding plastic, so the joints are only slightly less strong than an unbroken piece.

But why not use the plastic cement that comes in a tube? Well, these cements have plastic material dissolved in them that remains in the joint after the solvent has evaporated. This material thickens the cement, makes it more like a glue, and greatly increases the time it takes to dry. The disadvantages of tube cements are their tendency to ooze out of a joint onto the finished surface of a model, their tendency to form thin weblike strings which also mar model surfaces, and their slow setting. We'll use tube cement *only* where there is an extremely long joint or when parts cannot be fitted closely with knife and file work.

All plastic cements include powerful solvents, chemicals that can irritate your skin, lungs and eyes. Don't leave cement on your skin any longer than absolutely necessary, work with adequate ventilation, and keep your fingers away from your eyes when working with solvent cements. Perhaps the biggest hazard associated with liquid plastic cement is knocking over the bottle, flooding the bench with solvent and ruining any model parts that stand in the way. One way to stabilize the glue bottle is to cut a hole in a block of scrap wood to hold it, fig. 2-1. You can also glue the bottle into a small box top, or cut a foam doughnut to fit around the bottle.

Other adhesives. There's really no "stickiness" to plastic cements, and their solvent action works only on plastic, so you'll need to use other types of adhesives for attaching plastic parts to metal, paper, cardstock, or wood. A two-part, 5-minute-setting epoxy is a good general-purpose adhesive for use with any of these materials, and for attaching painted parts to painted surfaces. It's also a good "gap filler" glue where parts do not fit perfectly. Mix epoxy in small, manageable batches, and apply it sparingly. White glue is very handy for attaching clear plastic parts—it's valuable in several other applications, too, especially where you expect to remove parts later and want to do so without damaging the model.

Plastic cements won't work over paint, and they etch clear window parts. These adhesives offer alternatives for "problem" joints: (top row) rubber cement, Goodyear Pliobond, Dow Corning Urethane Bond, Devcon 5-minute epoxy, Elmer's epoxy; (bottom row) Wilhold white glue, Krazy Glue, Eastman 910.

White glue is especially good for attaching roofs to structures and rolling stock where you think you'd like to add interior detail later.

Thin cyanoacrylate "super glues" (ACC) are handy for attaching metal parts and for adding details to painted models. These cements require properly mated parts for good bonding strength. There are also a few gap-filling ACC adhesives capable of filling very small gaps where parts do not line up precisely. Most ACC's set extremely fast and are particularly well suited for adding wire parts such as handrails to your models. They *can* bond flesh, so be careful with them. ACC causes frosty white deposits on clear plastic glazing materials, so don't use it to attach windows or headlight lenses.

Assembly procedures. The advantages and disadvantages of plastic show up clearly when you focus on making a kit look like a complete building or locomotive or car, rather than a box of pieces that have been thrown together. The major advantage of molded plastic, of course, is that all fabrication work has been done for you—you bypass the tedious work of fitting hundreds of tiny pieces, of making thousands of individual rivets, of adding dozens of details one by one. Windows are a good example: The dozens of pieces that would be required to assemble a window from bits of wood and card are cast as a single piece in plastic structure kits, and, in some cases, they are molded right into the walls so you don't even have to fit them into their openings. The detail is there, and it's your job—the modeler's—to follow through with an assembly job that complements the diemakers' handiwork.

The first step in properly assembling any kit is to READ THE INSTRUCTIONS. That sounds *extremely* basic, but this step often makes the difference between a successful job and a model that never leaves the workbench. Study each step, and work with the pieces until you have a clear idea of how they

Modeling knives

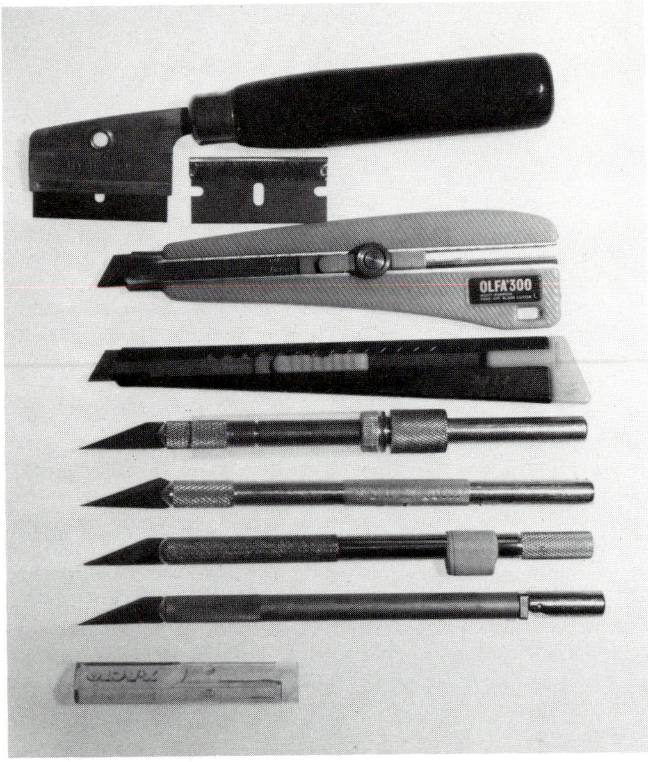

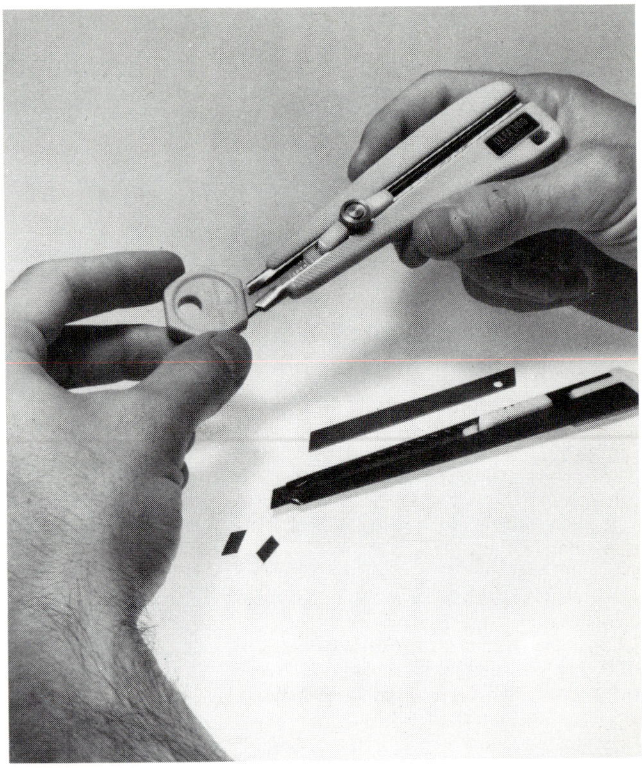

Knives with break-off blades feature a long blade that is extended and snapped off to make a new tip.

MODELING knives, also called hobby knives or craft knives, are the most basic of our modelbuilding tools. Most hobby shops and art-supply stores carry several brands and types of these knives. Dixon, E-Z-Loc, Grifhold, and PO Instrument are a few of the brand names you may find in your local store.

These knives are used for a wide variety of jobs: cutting parts from sprues, trimming flash, smoothing seams, scraping paint from edges to be cemented, cutting decals, and even holding parts during cementing. The knives can handle all sorts of punishment because the blade is replaceable.

HANDLES AND BLADE HOLDERS

Handles come in several sizes and shapes. Generally, the large, "fat" handles are for heavier work, but some modelers prefer them for all jobs. Most modelers use the thinner handles because they don't get in the way, and because they find themselves less likely to try to force the tool while using them. The knife handle should be comfortable in your hand, and a light handle is usually comfortable longer. The type of handle where you don't have to grip the blade collet near the cutting edge to change blades is preferable from a safety standpoint.

Most handles are round, and they can roll away even on a nearly level bench top. One solution is to tape a short section of sprue to the upper part of the knife handle as shown in the drawing.

Several handles are available that feature break-off blades. The blades are 2 or 3 inches long, with score marks to make them break cleanly when twisted. When you need a new cutting edge, you advance the blade in the handle and break off the worn portion.

Single-edge razor blades are just as sharp as modeling knife blades—and cheaper. They are also less convenient, but you'll find many places where you can use them. There are several types of razor-blade holders available, usually sold as wallpaper tools in hardware stores.

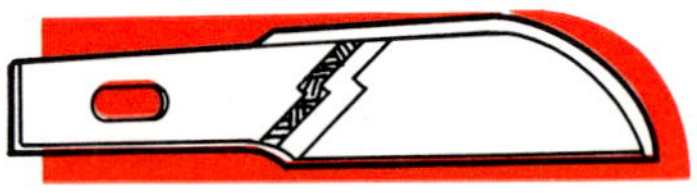

No. 10

Small cuts, fine cutting, carving. Cut or slice with rocking motion.

No. 11

General-purpose blade. Angled cutting, deep cuts, narrow spots.

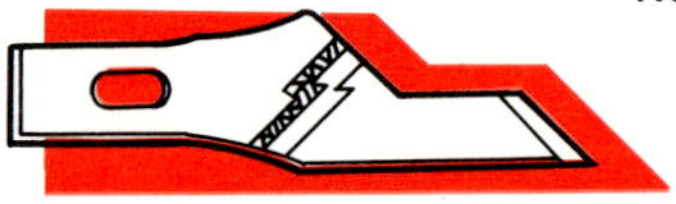

No. 16

Tight spots, small holes. Also good for scoring and scribing using back of blade tip.

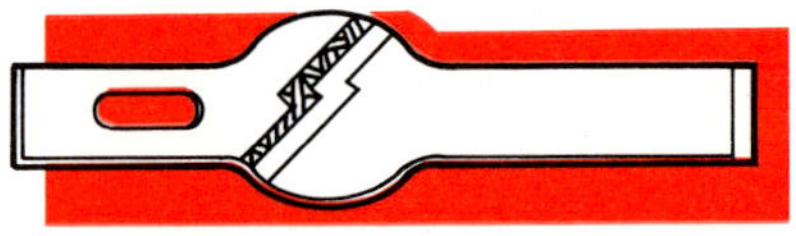

No. 17

¼"-wide chisel blade for narrow cuts on flat surfaces, removing unwanted detail.

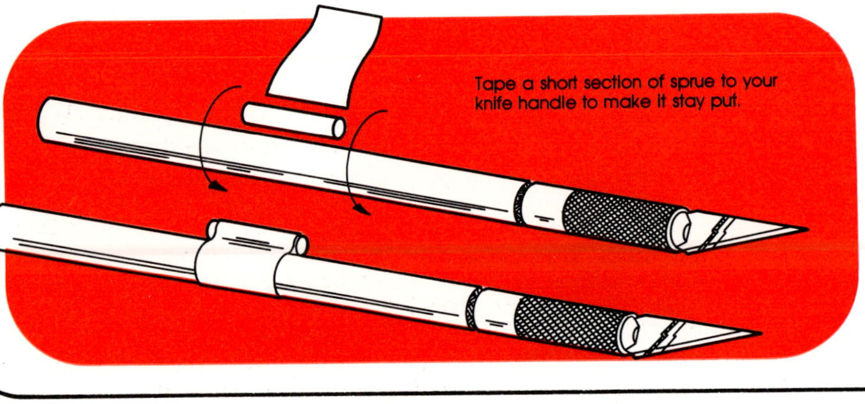

BLADES

When you purchase a knife, be sure to pick up a supply of extra blades. Some modelers work with two knives, keeping a brand-new blade in one for precision cutting, but allowing the blade in the other to become relatively dull for rough jobs. If you use this two-knife system, wrap some tape

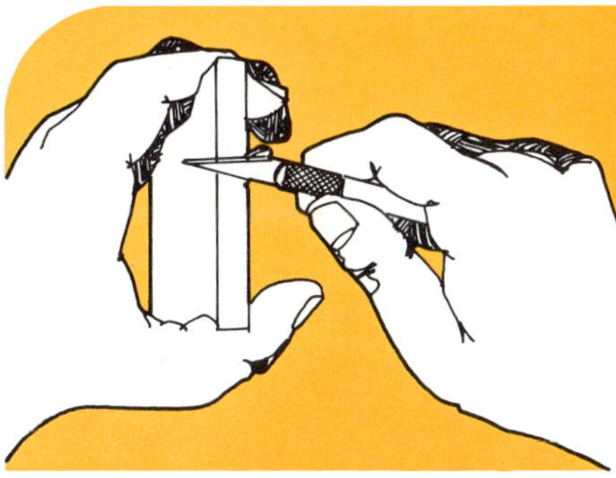

RIGHT — move the knife away from yourself.

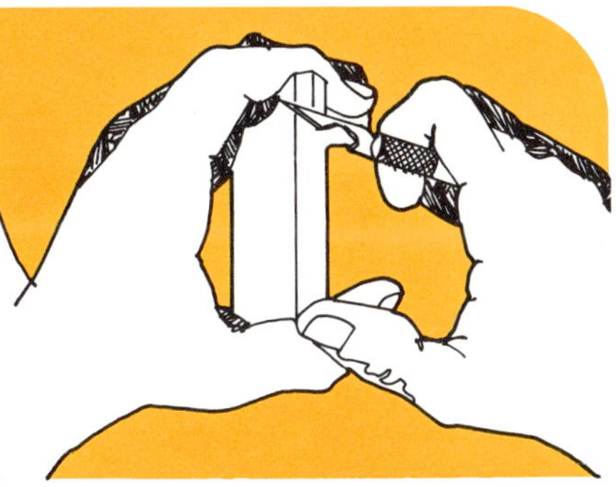

WRONG — a slip here means a nasty cut.

around one handle to earmark the sharper blade.

There are dozens of blade shapes available. The four most-useful shapes for modeling are shown in the drawing. The numbers are X-acto, but at least two other manufacturers use the same system. Knife blades usually come packaged with a translucent paper that is impregnated with a rust inhibitor. Keep the paper with the blades, and if you live in a damp climate, consider buying additional vapor-phase inhibitor (v.p.i.) paper to protect your blades.

Get industrial-quality single-edge razor blades. These are less expensive than the sterilized kind, but just as sharp. Boxes of 100 are usually available at hardware or art-supply stores. Whatever type of knife or blades you use, change blades frequently.

CUTTING OPERATIONS

To seat the blade properly, insert it into the handle as far as it will go. Don't over-tighten the knurled collar — it's easy to strip the threads and distort or crack the collar by tightening it more than necessary. Never use pliers or other tools to tighten the blade holder.

When cutting, move the knife away from your hand or body. Train yourself to look for where the knife blade will go if you slip — then make sure that "where" is safe. Keep the knife blade perpendicular to the surface of the stock being cut, and hold the knife in the same natural position that you would a pencil or pen. Use a cutting guide — a steel rule, or a template — wherever possible.

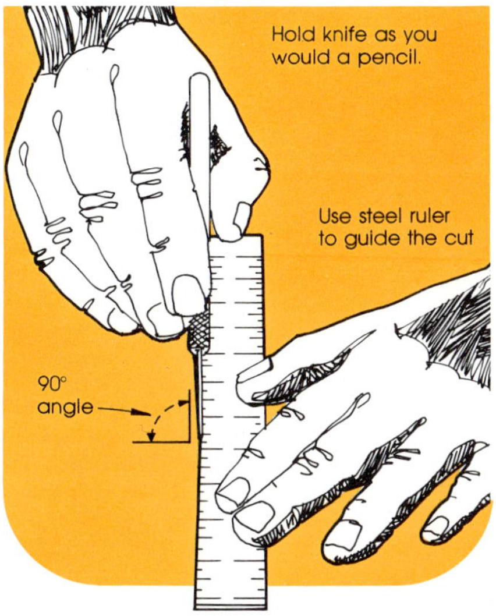

It is rarely necessary to press hard with a modeling knife; it will cut just as fast with light pressure. A series of light strokes is always preferable to a single heavy cut. Light strokes give you control, including the ability to stop and check that the cut is being made where you want it. Let the tool do the work while you guide it.

Sharpness simply can't be overstressed for ease and accuracy of cutting, and for safety. Don't try to get one or two more cuts out of a blade that you know is dull. When you use enough force to make a dull blade cut, you'll invariably slip and cut something you don't want to — either the model or yourself. The replacement parts or bandages will cost more than a package of new blades.

Razor blades have thinner blades than standard modeling knives. This feature makes razor blades especially valuable for cutting thin stock where you want the least possible deformation of the material on either side of the cut.

Cut sheet styrene or structure walls by scoring along the intended cut line once or twice, then bending and breaking the material along the scored line. Modeling knives are not made for cutting thick material. Anything thicker than about $^{1}/_{16}''$ should either be scored and broken or cut with a saw.

Your cutting surface is important, too. A wood or plywood surface has a definite grain that can catch the tip of the knife as it breaks through the stock and guide it off course. A rectangle of pressed hardboard (Masonite) is an excellent cutting surface, or, lacking that, a few layers of soft gray cardboard such as that found on the back of ruled writing pads will do.

SAFETY

Keep your mind on what you are doing while cutting. You should have a place to put the knife when not using it. A small slab of Styrofoam is a good place to stick knives to protect both the edge and you.

One of the first rules of workbench discipline is that you don't try to catch a knife as it rolls off the table top. Just get your feet out of the way and chase down the knife after it comes to rest.

Finally, if your household includes small children who are liable to rummage through the wastebasket in your work area, wrap all discarded blades in several layers of masking tape, or, better yet, put them aside and dispose of them where they don't present a hazard. Some blades come in a dispenser that has a slot for used blades.

fit together. Go over all of the illustrations. Make notes on the instruction sheet with a colored pen, and underline important steps and things you don't want to overlook.

Next, inspect the kit. Check to see that you have each part, and that all pieces are properly formed and not broken. Usually, the smaller pieces will be attached to the molding sprues; leave these parts attached until you're *absolutely* sure where they go. Sometimes it's difficult to tell where the part ends and the sprue begins until you determine just what the part is and how it's supposed to fit. In complex kits, many tiny parts are often similar, and the identifying numbers are cast into the sprues *near* the parts, rather than into the parts themselves. You'll find that some parts are easier to prepare if you leave them attached to the sprues, likewise, the sprues can provide "handles" for painting.

After you inspect the kit, but before you start working, put any clear plastic parts aside. These parts are the least-forgiving items in any kit; they scratch easily and frost if you put your cement applicator near them. Keep them out of harm's way until they are called for in assembly.

Preparing the parts. Now look over each part individually and inspect it for mold parting lines and flash. Parting lines are where the sections of the molds used to make the parts fit together. These lines run around the edges of thin parts such as building walls, and right down the middle of larger, more complex castings such as locomotive and car shells, fig. 2-2. Wisps of feather-like flash along the parting lines are formed when small amounts of plastic seep between the parts of the molds. Unless you trim off this flash before assembly, it will serve as an instant giveaway that the model is plastic. Some flash can interfere with a proper fit between parts. Work carefully so you don't remove any details or alignment pegs.

Use a sharp—that means inserting a new blade *often*—hobby knife to remove flash and parting lines. If you remove the parts from their molding sprues as you go along, be sure to cut, NOT break, the parts from the runners, fig. 2-3. One efficient way to do this is to clip the sprue near the part, using side cutting nippers, then carefully trim away the remaining bit of sprue with knife or razor blade. If you try to break parts from the sprues, you'll mar the part or leave some of the part attached to the sprue.

If you remove small parts from their sprues during cleanup, stick them to a strip of masking tape turned sticky side up and taped to the kit box top. Write the part numbers or identifying data on the tape with a ball-point pen. Often, you can paint the parts while they are attached to the tape.

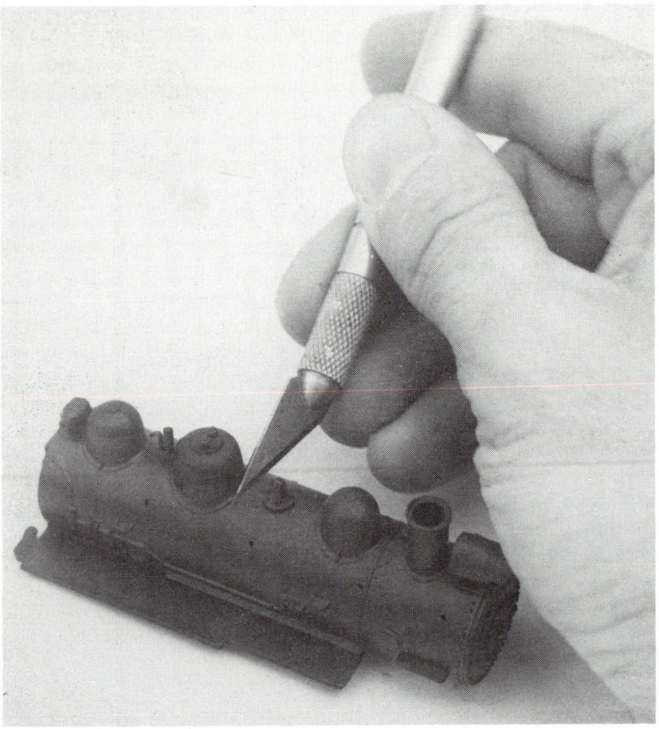

Fig. 2-3. Always cut parts from their runners – never break them off. Leave a little extra runner on the part and finish by trimming away the excess material.

Fig. 2-2. Use a sharp hobby knife to trim flash even with the surface of the model. Be careful that the blade does not dig in and gouge the surface. Use jeweler's files around details such as the bell and whistle.

Assembling your first car kit

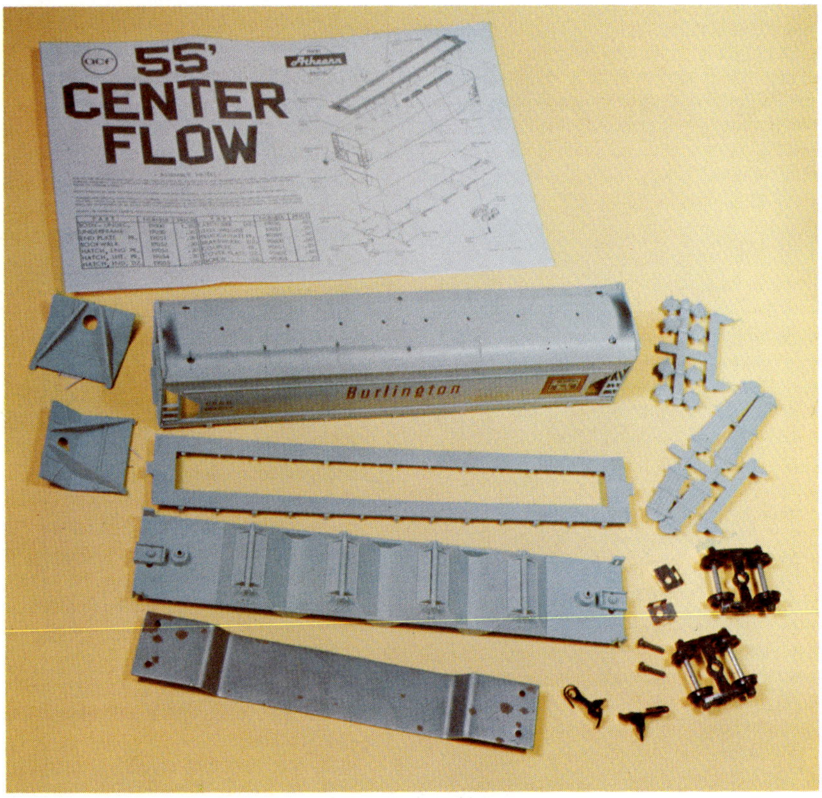

A. The first step in constructing any kit is to lay out the parts so you can go through a "dry run" of assembly according to the steps in the instructions. These are parts for an Athearn HO 55-foot ACF covered hopper.

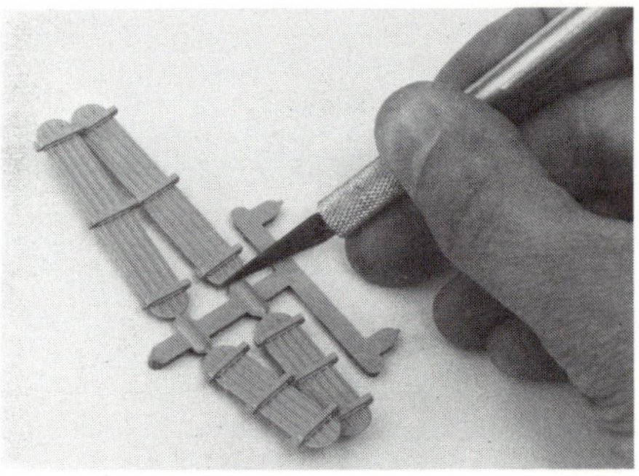

B. You have a choice of individual round hatch covers or these long trough covers in this kit. Carefully cut (never break) each part from the sprue.

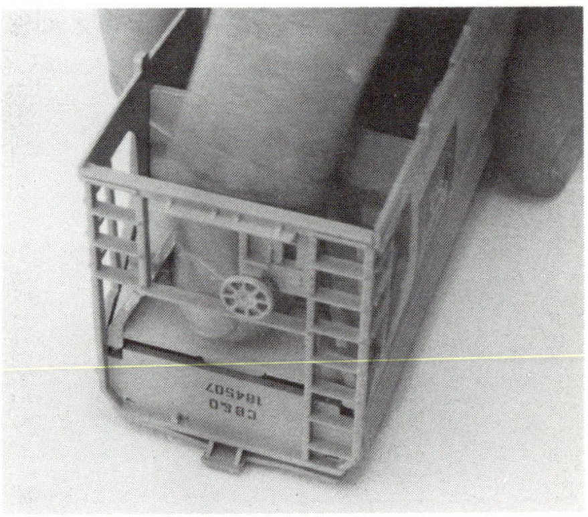

C. There's usually a minor problem area in every kit. In this one, the long center tabs on the two sloping end plates must be pushed in as you insert the end plates into the body so the end plates will snap into place properly.

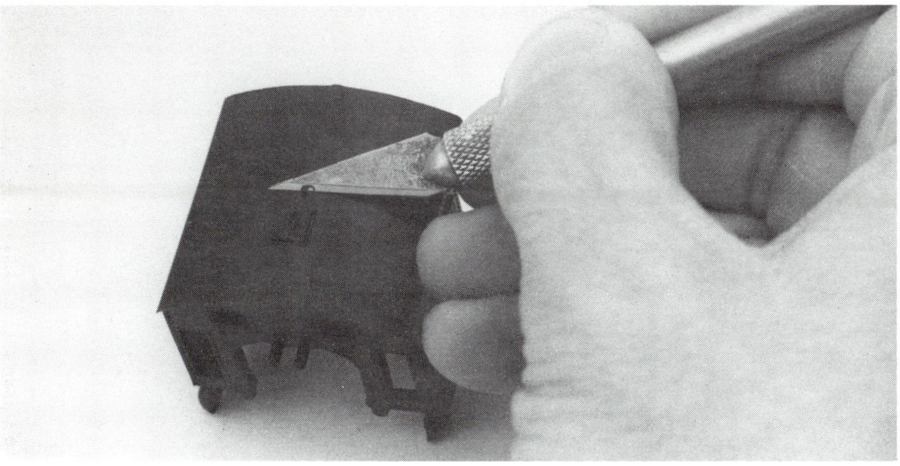

The mold parting line on this cab is a dead giveaway that the locomotive is plastic. After removing large flash, polish away the parting line with files.

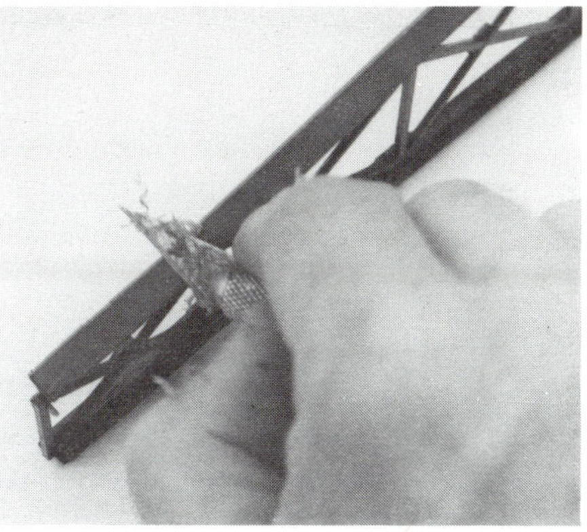

Fig. 2-4. Scraping is a method of rapid flash removal using the trailing edge of the hobby knife. Here, the parting line is being scraped from a plastic bridge support prior to assembly.

When removing flash, be careful with the knife blade—you don't want it to dig in and gouge a finished surface. Use jeweler's files around tiny details such as the bell and domes on steam locomotives. Where there is no surface detail to worry about damaging, you can remove flash by scraping the edge of the hobby knife over the unwanted material, fig. 2-4. This method is quicker than slicing, and there's less chance of the knife blade gouging. When you use this trailing-edge scraping technique, the unwanted plastic will curl away from the surface and look like the shavings from a wood plane.

Carefully examine the round parts to see if they are truly round. Because cer-

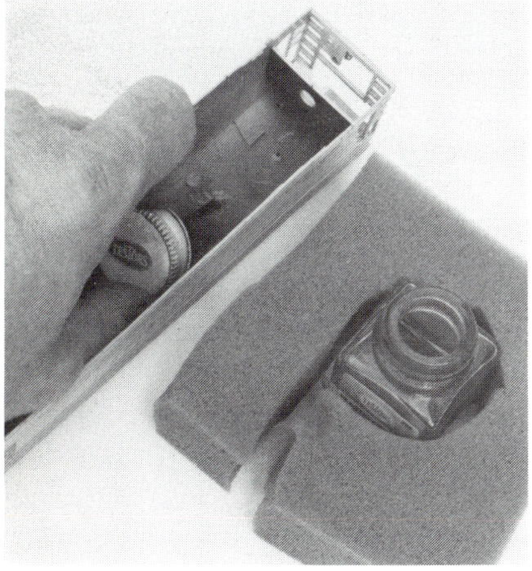

D. Install the hatches, roof walk, and end plates, and secure them with a dab of liquid cement applied from inside the body. Use just a drop so the cement doesn't run out onto the exterior of the car and ruin the paint.

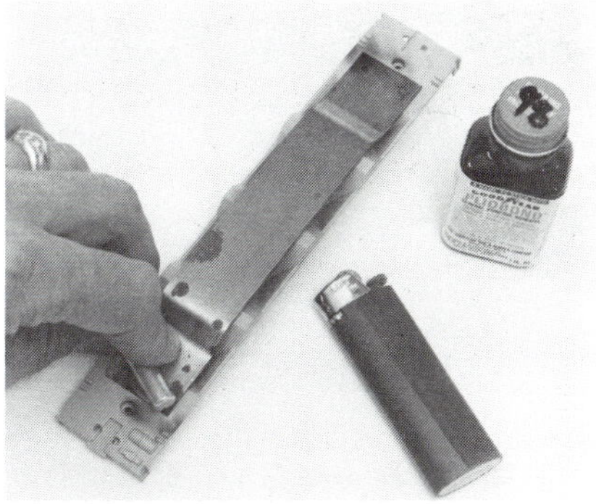

E. The stamped steel weight must be secured to the underframe or it will rattle inside the finished car. Soften the plastic weight-attaching pins with a match or cigarette lighter, and mash them into rivet heads with a screwdriver. If you don't want to take a chance on melting nearby plastic, glue the weight to the underframe with Goodyear Pliobond or Walthers' Goo.

F. Horn-hook couplers are provided with this kit, but many HO modelers prefer Kadee magnetic couplers (right). This is the time to decide whether or not to fit them. The Kadee No. 5 coupler and its bronze centering spring will fit this car. Read the coupler instructions carefully. File all burrs from the edges of the coupler pocket, the snap-on metal cover, and the spring before installing the couplers.

G. You may have to trim some flash from the inside edges of the truck mounting holes to give them a slight chamfer. Tighten the trucks so they swivel freely without rocking or side-to-side movement.

H. The trough hatches and the horn-hook couplers are leftover parts. Use a Kadee gauge to be certain the couplers are at the right height. This is the time to be sure everything works, before putting the car on the layout.

The thin flash inside these windows is typical of what you'll find in most plastic structure kits. Remove it carefully to avoid marring the window frames.

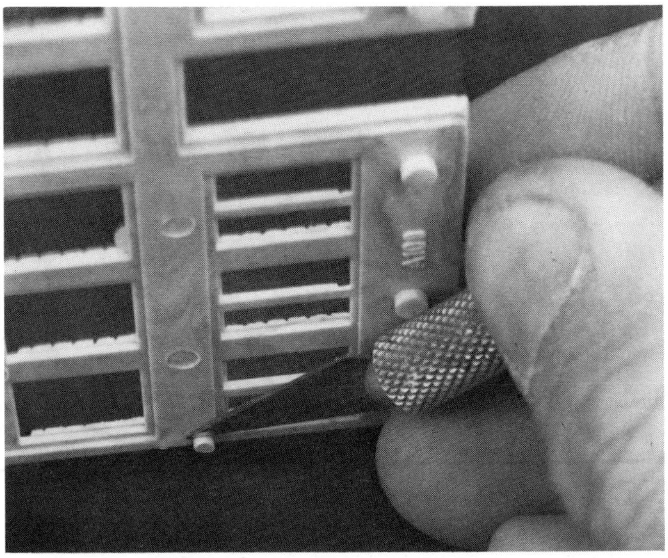

Fig. 2-5. Occasionally, removing the cast aligning lugs from kit parts allows a more precise fit between kit parts. Slice away the lugs a little at a time.

tain angles cannot be used if the parts are to eject smoothly from the molds, some parts will not be round but will have slanted sides. A little scraping with the sharp edge of the hobby knife will make these sections more realistic.

Test-fitting and dry assembly. The third step in kit assembly (note that there still hasn't been any cause to reach for the cement!) is testing the fit of all parts. Even with all flash removed, I have yet to encounter *any* plastic kit that fits together perfectly on the first try. Don't kid yourself that cement will correct minor faults in the fit of your parts—far too many models have been ruined by that kind of thinking. If you use enough cement to *make* the parts fit, you've used too much, and you've spent too little time working on the parts to get them to mate properly.

Use a flat file to smooth and trim joints between mating parts so they fit together flush along the entire length of the joint. For long straight joints, a large mill file helps to achieve a flat surface. Pre-assemble all parts that make up the main portions of the model—walls, body shell, underframe, roof, and so on—and check that there is no flash in or around the small aligning holes, pegs, and lugs to prevent parts from mating snugly. Check the lugs themselves—sometimes, you'll find that removing aligning lugs entirely allows more accurate fitting of the parts, fig. 2-5. With small parts, check the fit just before you're ready to glue them in place; they should remain on their sprues until the last possible moment.

Occasionally, you'll find large parts that are warped due to improper molding or heat encountered in shipping or storage. Where the parts are thin, assembly will eliminate the twist, but where the parts are thick, they will not mate properly. Some pieces simply have to be replaced, but in other instances you can gently heat the part to re-form it, or make several razor-saw cuts in the back of the piece to allow it to flex into the proper shape.

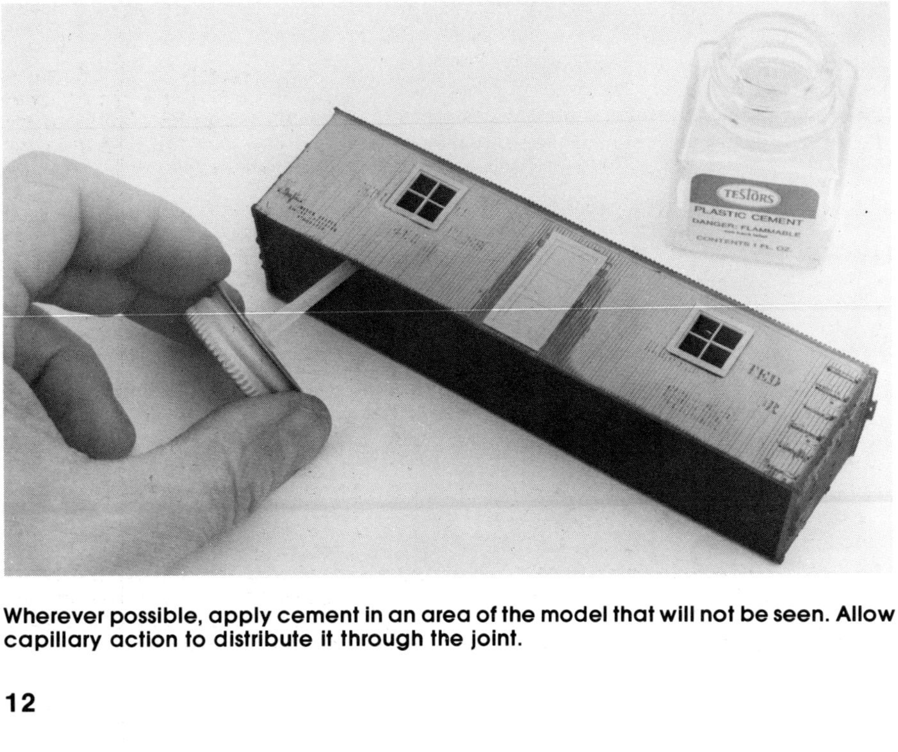

Wherever possible, apply cement in an area of the model that will not be seen. Allow capillary action to distribute it through the joint.

Painting before assembly. All of the superb molded-in detail and all your careful trimming and fitting will be wasted if you skip ahead to assembly without painting the parts, either before assembly or in sub-assembly units as you proceed with construction. Sure, the parts may be molded in three (or four, or more) colors, and the colors may be just the ones you'd paint the model anyway, but even with molded-in colors, raw plastic has a slight translucent quality—a "waxy" look. This immediately identifies your model as plastic instead of the board siding, or shingles, or masonry, or steel panels, or other material that the plastic represents.

Consider which parts you want to paint different colors from the rest of the model, and don't assemble those pieces until painting is complete and the paint is thoroughly dry. Many parts become nearly impossible to paint when the model is complete or semi-complete. It's far easier, for example, to paint the windows of a structure *before* they are glued in place than to try to paint them a contrasting color with a tiny brush after they have been installed.

The biggest reason for painting parts before assembly is neatness. No other way—certainly not by masking—can you achieve crisp separation of painted parts as by painting them first and joining them together afterwards. Painting before assembly also means that the

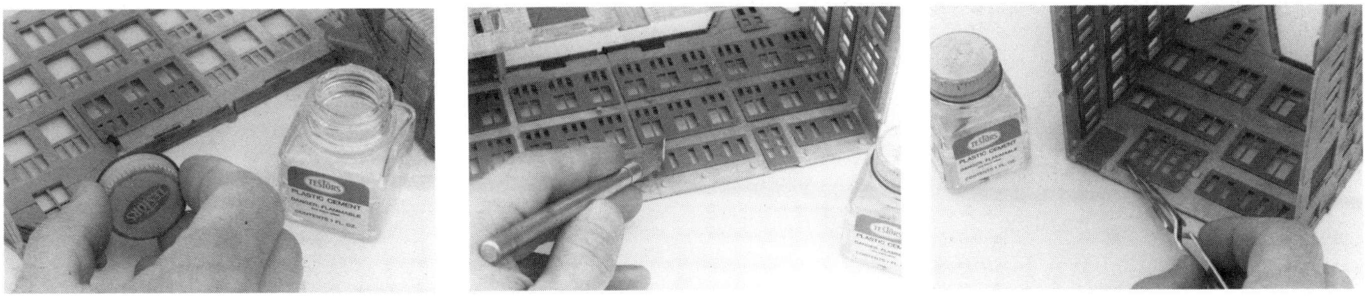

It's important to keep your fingers away from joints and other areas while cementing. Loose-fitting parts can be dropped in place, cement applied, and the parts held with a knife or tweezers while the cement evaporates.

parts you handle during painting are smaller, less awkward, and less likely to slip, drop, knock over the paint, and ruin the entire model.

The surface of many plastics is softened and etched by the thinners in most model railroad paints, but there are coatings available to prepare plastic surfaces so that any type of paint can be used, and there are special types of paint formulated specially for plastic models. Skip ahead to Chapter 3 for information on types of paint and painting techniques.

Final assembly and cementing techniques. Cementing the parts together is the final step in kit construction. Usually, you'll be able to follow the assembly sequence shown in the kit instructions. When you pre-paint parts or subassemblies, some steps will, of necessity, be out of order; as long as you understand *how* the parts go together, you won't run into trouble. The walls and roof parts on a structure, for example, should be assembled and painted before installing window frames and skylights, also pre-painted. Clear plastic windows come next, and small details such as awnings, railings, downspouts, and lights—all pre-painted—are added last so there's as little chance as possible for them to be broken off in handling the model. Consider this final assembly sequence before starting to cement parts together so that you can plan—before it's too late—to leave some of the parts *off* the model until the walls, or body, or boiler are painted. With experience, you'll learn to look at each model as several logical *subassemblies*.

Now—after what seems like an awful lot of thought and preparation—it's time for final assembly. To join parts, hold or clamp them together and apply a small amount of liquid cement to the *back* of the joint. Capillary action, the tendency of a thin liquid to creep along a crack, will draw the cement into and distribute it throughout the length and width of the joint. Here's where careful trimming and fitting pay off—the better the fit of the joint, the easier it is for the cement to spread. Touch the cement to several locations along the back of a long joint to ensure a strong bond.

When cementing thin sections, be stingy with the cement. Too much solvent on thin parts and thin sheet stock can cause sags, blisters and sunken areas, so too little is better than too much in this case. If you pre-painted parts, you must scrape the paint away from the cementing areas. A light scraping action with the edge of the hobby knife held perpendicular to the surface will usually do the trick.

The real key to success in plastic assembly is neatness. Keep your fingers away from the joints so there's no chance of getting cement on your fingers and spreading it to other areas of the model. The solvent action of liquid cement etches plastic surfaces, and this etching can obliterate details and destroy finished surfaces if the cement flows out of the joint. Softened surfaces take the impression of anything pressed against them, so it's extremely important that you use only the minimum amount of solvent required for bonding, and that you keep the cement in the joint until it evaporates.

Don't hold parts with your fingers where you can avoid it. Tweezers—once you get used to them—are easy to use, and they don't leave ugly fingerprints if the solvent leaks out and seeps between the tweezers and the surface of the work. For small details, try pushing the tip of a brand-new hobby-knife blade into the back or edge of the part and using the knife as a handle to hold it while the joint sets up, fig. 2-6. Pull the knife tip out after the part is bonded into place. When necessary, prod parts with a toothpick, tweezers, or screwdriver, all of which leave impressions if they touch plastic softened by solvent action, but none of which leave fingerprints.

Cement applicators. To apply cement, use a No. 0 or 00 watercolor brush, a ruling pen, or a precision needlepoint applicator, depending on what works best for you. Some liquid cements come with a brush in the cap, but you'll find this is usually too coarse—it applies too much liquid—for joints where neatness is important. Wrap masking tape around the handle of a brand new, quality watercolor brush to earmark it as your cement applicator so you won't inadvertently contaminate cement with paint.

Many modelers use needlepoint

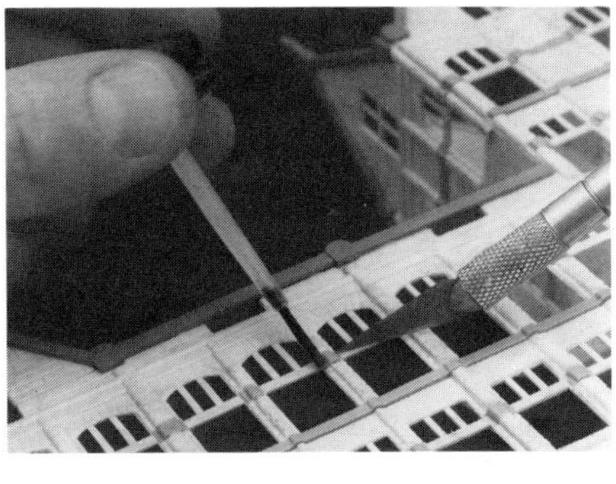

Fig. 2-6. Use the tip of a sharp knife to position tiny details while cementing. When the cement dries, pull the knife tip out of the part.

Fig. 2-7. Squeeze-bottle applicators with hollow steel needle points are an alternative to applying liquid cement with a small brush. Many different needle diameters are available.

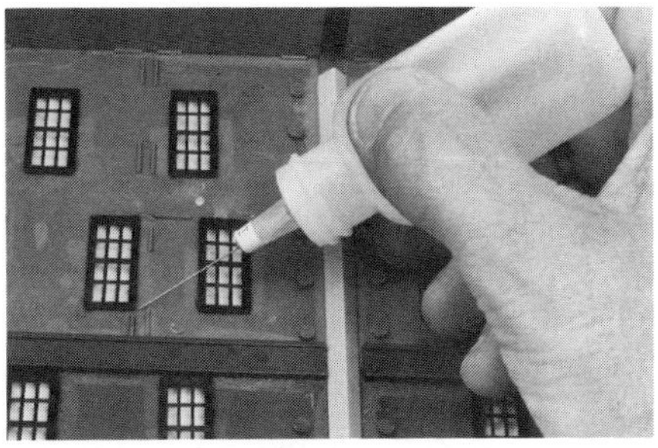

Fig. 2-8. To properly use a needlepoint applicator, work from the back, position the needlepoint to direct the cement where you want it, and control the quantity of cement by squeezing.

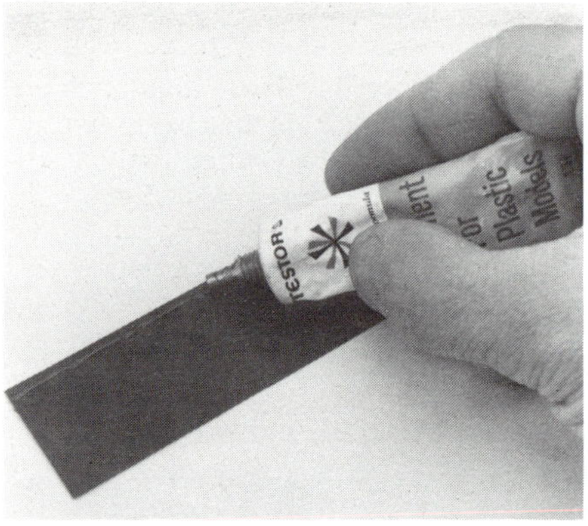

Tube cement for plastic is useful for long joints or in cases where parts cannot be made to mate closely. Practice spreading a bead of cement along the edge of some scrap plastic sheet stock before using tube cement on your model.

applicators such as those sold by A-West, Brookstone, and Labelle, figs. 2-7 and 2-8. These applicators consist of a fine hollow steel needle supplied by a plastic squeeze bottle. Their biggest advantage over a brush is that you don't have to keep going back to the cement bottle to apply cement to a long joint. Don't leave liquid cement in a needlepoint applicator overnight. The flexible plastic used in the squeeze bottle is somewhat porous, and the volatile solvents can pass through it and evaporate. Decant only what you need into the applicator and return unused cement to the glass bottle.

There *are* a few situations where tube-type plastic cements can be helpful. These heavy-bodied cements dry much more slowly than the liquids, and this feature makes them useful for long joints. The 45-degree corner joints on a structure are a good example. With a little practice, you can run a bead of tube cement about the diameter of a straight pin right down the seam. Keep the cement well away from the outer edges of the joint or it will squeeze out when you push the parts together.

Tube-type cement is also the thing to use where it's impossible to get pieces to fit well, where the joining surfaces are so small that you need a fillet of cement to add strength to the joint, or where an alignment peg is too small for the hole it is supposed to fit. Just remember that you must hold or clamp joints made with tube cement longer than the same bond made with liquid cement.

Liquid cement can be used in combination with tube cement on long joints. Sometimes you'll discover that a short

A typical plastic structure

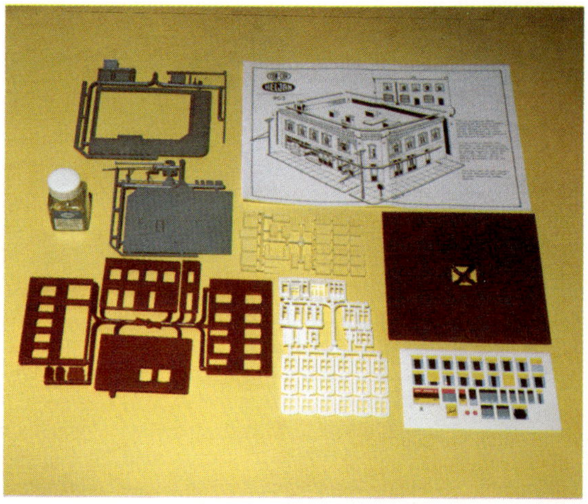

A. Con-Cor imports this Heljan Corner Bank Block in both HO and N. This N scale kit includes extra details such as a sidewalk, telephone poles, and even a sheet of plastic cobblestones for the street. The instruction sheet is an easy-to-understand exploded-view drawing.

B. Carefully cut each part from its molding sprue with a modeling knife. Double-check the instructions from time to time to be sure you're cutting away sprue and not part of the detail. Trim away flash, too.

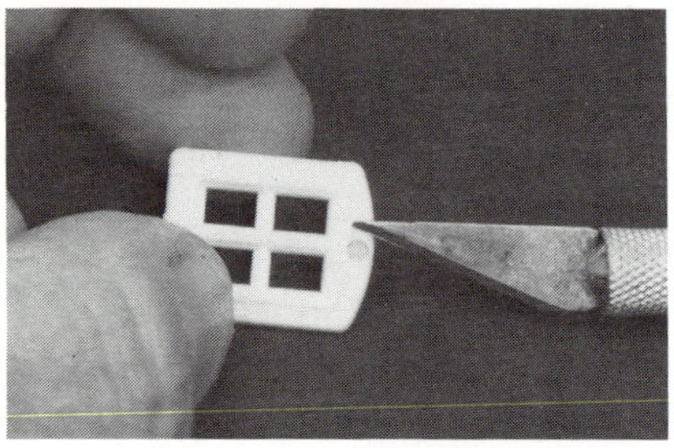

C. One minor problem area in this kit (and many other structure kits) is the little round wisps of flash left where the ejection pins pushed the window castings from the mold. If you don't file or slice away this extra plastic, the window cannot be positioned flush with the inside of the wall and it will be difficult for the cement to hold it in place. Remove the wisps now.

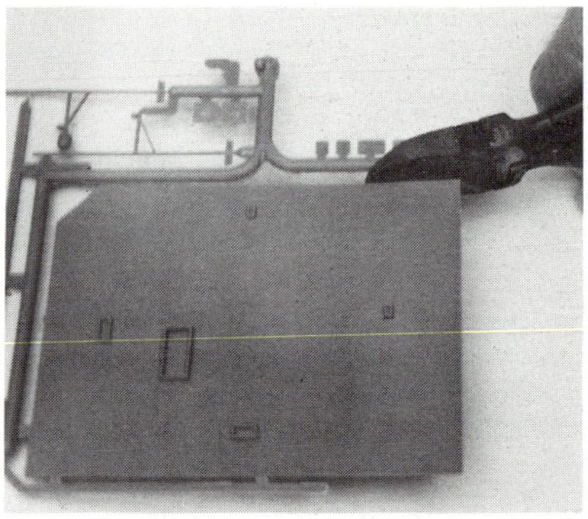

D. You can use flush-cutting diagonal nippers such as Lambert's Rail Nippers to remove parts from the sprues. After separating the parts, trim the excess plastic at the attachment point with your knife.

stretch of a cemented joint either has no cement, or that the cement dried before the parts were mated. The liquid cement can be used to complete the bond by brushing it over the inside of the seam where it will soften both the plastic and the previously applied tube cement. To blend in tube cement smears, brush liquid cement over the smear, smoothing the blemish into the surface. Use the same technique to remove the wispy strings that often result from using tube cement.

Cementing clear plastic parts. Clear plastic parts are a special case, since any place that cement etches the clear plastic will turn frosty white and can't be covered up by touchup painting. Even the fumes from solvent evaporating nearby can frost the clear windows in a structure, car, or locomotive. To guard against this, add clear parts as late as possible in your assembly sequence. *Never* use tube cements for attaching clear parts. Their slow dissolving action and long evaporation time spell trouble, and etching can occur even several days after the model is assembled. Where clear plastic parts overlap on the interior of the model, you may be able to get away with a few traces of liquid cement, applied at one or two corners of the part and spread by capillary action.

Some clear window material—particularly molded parts—has a mild roughness, a surface tooth, that allows solvent cement to creep across the face of the part by capillary action, our old friend. Test for this tooth on a window insert that won't be used. To be safe, and in all cases where the clear plastic part makes an edge-to-edge fit, use a water-soluble white glue such as Elmer's Glue-All instead of plastic cement. This type of glue will hold the parts firmly, but the bonds can be broken with gentle pressure to remove the window should you decide to repaint the model.

Leftovers. Don't be surprised if you have a few leftover parts when you finish a kit. Manufacturers include extra pieces for many reasons—so a certain sprue of windows or doors can be used in several kits, because the diemaker made extra cavities, or because the manufacturer wants to be your friend. Keep these parts and establish a scrap box to keep all your kit leftovers. You'll find these "useless" goodies come in handy for all sorts of things, especially when you start kitbashing.

E. Use a 10″ medium-cut mill file to smooth the edges of the larger parts. Test fit each wall with the adjoining parts to ensure the fit is correct. There are always areas that need filing for a proper fit.

F. Run a thin bead of tube cement down each of the corner seams and squeeze the joints together. You can usually hold the joints for a minute or so and the cement will set enough to hold the parts together. If the plastic is warped even slightly, however, you'll have to use wide masking tape strips to hold the joint overnight.

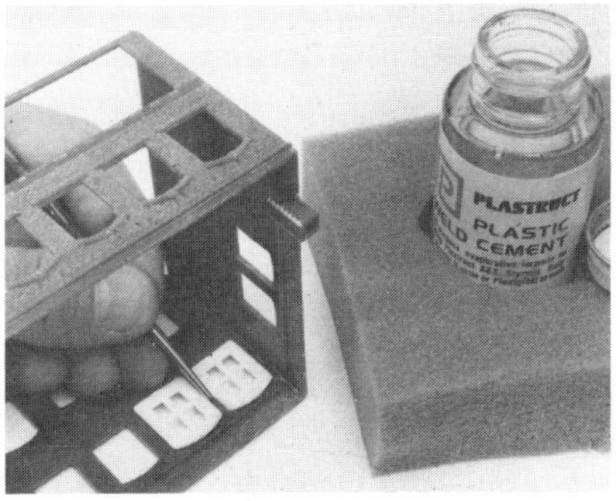

G. Paint the mortar lines with a wash of thinned Polly S reefer gray. The roof was sprayed with flat black. After painting, the windows can be positioned inside the walls and a drop of liquid cement applied to two corners – capillary action will draw the glue around the edges of the window.

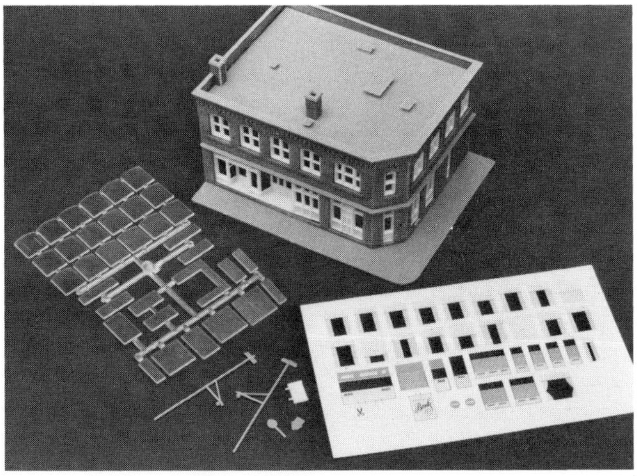

H. This kit includes molded clear window glass and printed window backings that simulate an interior. For a more realistic effect, omit the paper backings and install scrap cardboard partitions inside the building so you cannot see through from side to side.

I. Most plastic structures are furnished with a base to tie them into the scenery. Bases don't have to be used on country buildings, but the sidewalk and curb that come with this kit are excellent in that they make the building look as though it is resting in concrete.

Basic painting and weathering

All plastic models require painting to make them realistic. Here's how.

MOST plastic kits come molded in several colors, seemingly ready to assemble without the "extra" step of painting. Sometimes, a modeler neglects to paint a model because he is too lazy—or in too big a hurry—to assemble the parts to bother to paint them before assembly. Later, when the dust has settled, the task of carefully brushing around all the clear areas and touching up the details is more than he wants to tackle, so the model stays on his layout without paint—and without much realism!

The plastics used for injection molding are translucent, and the bare, unpainted material has a waxy sheen that makes it immediately identifiable as plastic, even though the surface may be a properly textured and highly detailed replica of an old wooden barn. Plastic will always look like plastic unless you paint everything but the clear "glass" window areas. The key to making plastic look like wood, metal, stone, brick or concrete is proper painting.

Painting your models is different from painting your house, your apartment walls, or a piece of furniture. The objective is not to preserve the model against the weather, not to decorate or cover up cracks, not to nourish the material and protect it against spills and wear. Our objective in model painting is to make each model realistic by putting on as few thin coats of paint as possible to color the model like its prototype without obscuring detail. The first thing we'll need to examine are the types of paints we'll be using.

The paints made for models are quite different from paints sold for other purposes. The pigments are usually ground finer, and binders and solvents are specially formulated to form thin, tough films that will not obscure detail. Don't try to use leftover paints from crafts or other non-modeling projects in your modelwork; they just won't do the job.

Model paints are available in flat and gloss finishes. Because flat finishes bring out the detail and look more realistic than gloss, we'll use flat paints for most of our models. Seen from a distance, even a freshly painted prototype locomotive or passenger car looks dull, and that is the effect we want. Flat finishes are also best for providing a holding "tooth" for weathering effects.

Painting a plastic model is no different from painting a model made of wood, cardboard, or metal, except that some paints can attack plastic. These *incompatible* paints have solvents in them that etch and melt the surface of the plastic. This is called *crazing*, fig. 3-1. Crazing ruins any surface on which it occurs, so we want to avoid it. We can avoid crazing in three ways: by using *plastic-compatible* paints, by using a preparatory coating over the plastic to block out the solvent action, or by applying the paint in such a manner—a finely controlled spray—that the solvent evaporates before the paint reaches the surface. We'll cover the last method in Chapter 9. For now, let's concentrate on paints formulated for use

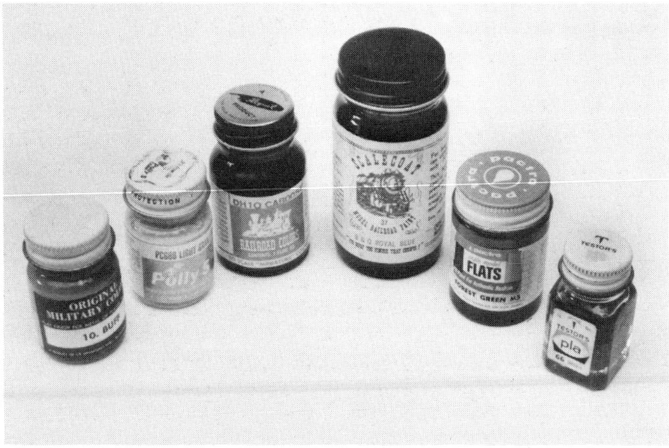

These are a few of the paints made especially for models. From left to right: Imrie-Risley Military colors, Polly S, Floquil, Scalecoat, Pactra, and Testors.

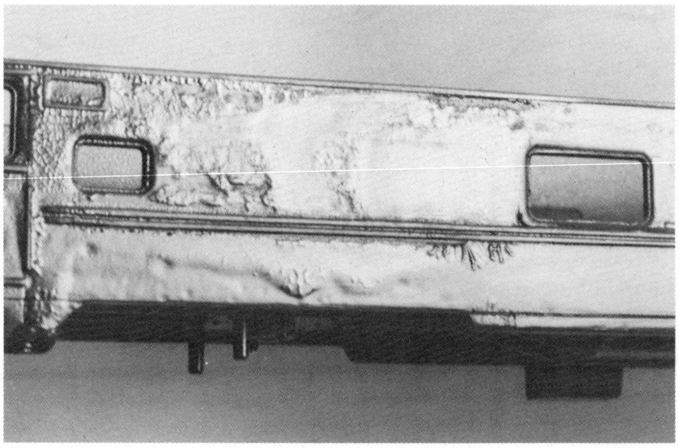

Fig. 3-1. Little can be done to save the crazed surface of this model. This melting and etching was caused by the solvent in a paint not compatible with plastic.

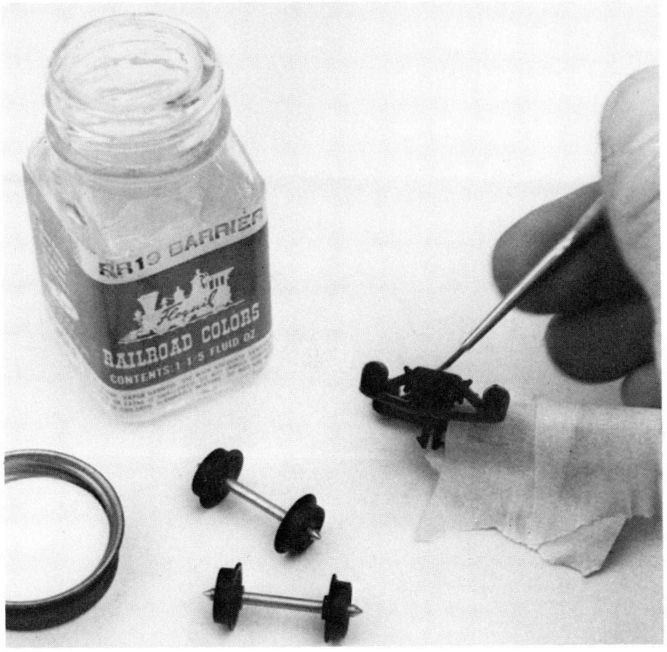

Clear finishes from left to right: Floquil flat finish, Scalecoat flat glaze, Pactra clear flat, Testors Dullcote and Glosscote, and (front) Micro Scale gloss and flat.

Incompatible paints can be used on plastic if a protective coating is used first. Here, Floquil "Barrier" is being applied so the truck can be painted with Floquil colors.

with plastics, and on barrier and shield coatings.

Plastic-compatible paints. The two types of paints suitable for use with plastics regardless of the method of application are enamels and water-soluble acrylics. Enamels are thinned with common mineral spirits (paint thinner). In the U.S., the best-known enamels for plastics are Testors Pla and Pactra 'Namel. Their lines are offered for general plastic modelwork, but their flat-finish paints are suitable for railroad models. Scalecoat II and Accu-Paint are enamels manufactured specifically for model railroad use in prototype colors such as boxcar red and reefer orange. In Great Britain, Humbrol manufactures flat enamels for military modelers that are widely distributed throughout North America.

Polly S is a water-base acrylic paint. It is available in prototype railroad and military flat colors. It has the advantage of using a non-volatile, non-hydrocarbon solvent (water) that is non-flammable and won't irritate even the most sensitive nose.

Incompatible model railroad paints. Floquil Railroad Colors, Flo-Paque, and Scalecoat I are solvent-base paints that are not compatible with common injection-molding plastics. Their thinners are closely related to liquid plastic cement. If we apply these paints to raw plastic, they will crinkle and ruin the surface detail just as brushing on a coat of liquid plastic cement would. Rather than deny ourselves the use of these products, let's find out how to work around the problem.

To "insulate" plastic from the attacking thinners used with noncompatible paints, both Floquil and Scalecoat offer protective intercoats. These are not primers, because their only function is to prevent paint solvents from attacking plastic. Floquil's product is called "Barrier," Scalecoat's is called "Shieldcoat." In use, these clear coatings are applied over raw plastic surfaces and allowed to dry thoroughly, then paints are applied just as they would be over metal, wood, or cardstock.

Clear finishes and additives. There are several types of clear finishes. Clear gloss finishes are used to coat areas to be decaled, since decals adhere better to glossy surfaces. Flat finishes are used over decals or dry transfers as dulling agents to hide the shiny decal film and give the model a realistic dull overall finish. They are also used to protect the finish and to provide a holding tooth for weathering treatments. Testors Dullcote, Pactra Clear Flat, and Floquil Flat Finish are all available in aerosol cans for ease of application. Generally, it is best to use the same brand flat or gloss finish as paint. Before using a clear finish over decals or dry transfers, check the decal or dry-transfer instructions; some lettering is susceptible to damage from clear coatings.

Paint additives. Accelerators, retarders, and other paint additives are intended for special painting conditions such as extreme temperature and humidity. Read what the paint maker says about additives and follow his advice. As formulated, model paints offer suitable drying rates for most situations, and tampering with these rates will lead to a poor finish as often as it will help to achieve a good one.

The best advice for using *any* paint—or any product, for that matter—is to read and follow the instructions. Often, you can get additional information on using paint from the manufacturer just for the asking. If you take the time to read what the maker has to say about his product, you'll find all the

Additives such as Scalecoat "Quik-Dry" are needed only in unusual situations. Under normal conditions most paints perform best without additives.

tricks that the "experts" (the guys who read the instructions thoroughly) use.

Thinning, mixing, and safety. Today's paints are complex chemical compounds, and they require common-sense treatment. When thinning, use only the solvents recommended by the manufacturer. Your buddy may have some bargain-rate brand he says works just as well as the slightly more expensive thinner sold by the paint manufacturer, but unless you can prove it's exactly the same, stick with the solvent you *know* is right. Don't *ever* mix one manufacturer's paint with some from another line. More often than not the resulting mixture will curdle like milk poured

This oddly painted Hi-Cube box car illustrates the steps in refinishing a car. From left to right: factory paint and lettering, section of stripped (bare) plastic, new paint, decal lettering, and moderate weathering.

into lemonade, or you'll end up with a jellylike mess that will never dry.

In the same vein, be careful about applying one manufacturer's paint over that of another. You can usually do so if the different types have a week to cure fully before the next coat, but there is always a chance that the second coat will cause the first to blister, or vice versa. Admittedly, all the prototype colors you need may not be available in a single line of paint, but if possible, start a project with one brand and complete it with the same.

All paint solvents—except water—are potentially hazardous. Don't get them in your eyes, mouth, or allow prolonged skin contact. Don't breathe solvent fumes for very long, and if you spray paint more than once a month, consider investing in an exhaust fan to provide adequate ventilation. Keep containers of solvent where children and pets can't reach them.

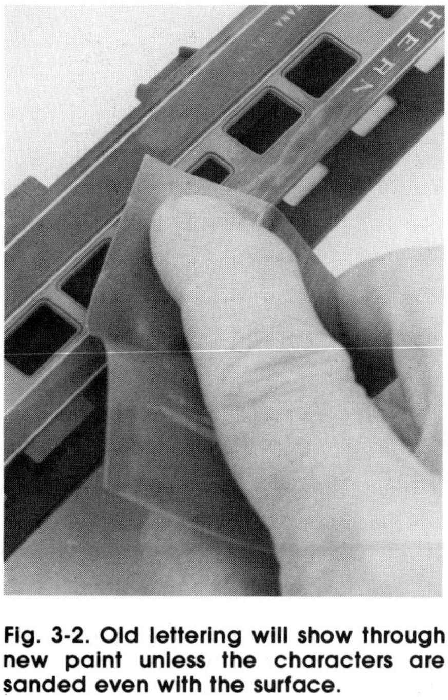

Fig. 3-2. Old lettering will show through new paint unless the characters are sanded even with the surface.

Preparing the model. This may come as a surprise, but it usually takes longer to prepare a model for painting than it does to apply the paint! Getting the model ready—really ready—is crucial to the success of any paint job. The first step in preparing the model is to decide how much of it will be assembled or disassembled before painting. A car or structure kit can be partially assembled before applying paint so that there is less chance of marring the finish with cement later on. Locomotive and car models should be disassembled to the point where it is possible to mask or remove electrical contact surfaces, gears, bearings, and other moving parts.

Sand away factory lettering on the model with water-wetted No. 600 wet-or-dry sandpaper, fig. 3-2, otherwise, the outlines of the lettering will show through. Remove all traces of the sanding grit.

Wash the model parts thoroughly in warm water and dishwashing detergent, fig. 3-3, rinse under running water, and dry. This detergent wash is necessary for two reasons. First, the manufacturer treats his molds with an oily substance to help release the parts from the molds. The mold-release film, along with the natural oils from your fingers, can prevent paint from sticking to the model. Second, styrene is a strong static electricity collector, which means any unpainted model will attract bits of lint and dust. The detergent bath washes away grease and oil and destaticizes the surface of the plastic.

If the plastic has a mirrorlike shine, you can scrub the surface with kitchen cleanser such as Ajax or Bab-O to slightly roughen the surface and provide a holding "tooth" for paint. Dry the model in still air, or with the air from a hair drier on the "cold" setting. Wiping, even with a lint-free cloth, creates a static charge on the plastic which attracts more lint and dust. Handle the model with disposable gloves or lint-free rags from the time you wash it until it is painted. No matter how many times you wash your hands, the natural oils in your fingertips are always present to be deposited on the surface and act as a barrier to proper paint adhesion.

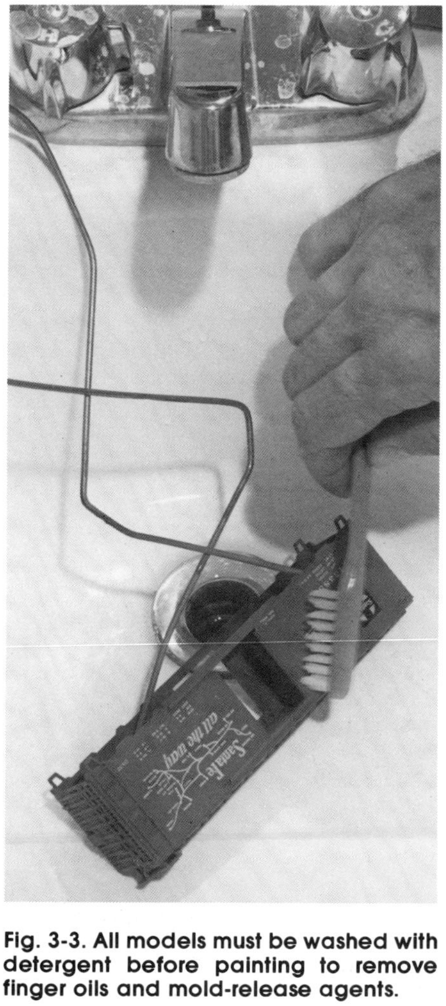

Fig. 3-3. All models must be washed with detergent before painting to remove finger oils and mold-release agents.

Particularly for spray painting, you'll need some way to hold the parts while painting so you don't have to touch the painted surfaces. A wire coat hanger bent into a series of S-bends, fig. 3-4, is a useful tool for holding car and locomotive bodies and structure subassemblies, and special holding fixtures, fig. 3-5, are available. A "third hand" scissors-action tweezers with stand can also be used. Wide masking tape stapled sticky side up to scrap corrugated cardboard, fig. 3-6, is very versatile. Whatever sort of holding fixture you use, make sure it isn't going to collapse in the middle of the job or while the paint is drying.

Primers and priming. A primer is usually required over bare plastic before the first color coat is applied. The chief function of a primer is to provide a strong bond between the raw plastic surface and the finish coatings, but primers are also formulated to level and seal the surface. A primer provides a comparatively heavy pigment coat that fills in hairline cracks, dries hard, and allows sanding. Most primers are light, neutral colors that will bring out imperfections in the model—so you can correct them before applying the finish coats—and that effectively increase the covering power of the subsequent color coats, even if they are white or yellow. Talk to the people at your hobby shop to find out what primers they have. The black primers that are used for automobile models work well under darker colors, and light gray primers used in full-size auto body work can also be used. Specially formulated metal primers, such as zinc chromate, are not needed with plastic since their metal-bonding and anti-corrosive qualities are wasted. Flat white paint makes a good primer because white paint is heavily pigmented to give it covering power. If your model has an intact, flat-finish, factory paint job, that paint coat can serve as a primer coat.

Unless you have an airbrush, an aerosol can is the best way to apply a light, even coat of primer to your model. The big thing to watch is that you apply only as much as is needed for an opaque coating—any more and you risk obscuring detail. You'll find that primers cover better in thin coats than most paints. The primer coat will show up any flaws in your model such as unsightly glue seams or weblike wisps of plastic. Now is the time to fix these problems, followed by touchup with a little more primer applied with a brush. Allow the primer to dry at least overnight so there is no chance for the finish coats of paint to blend with it.

Brush painting. With the proper techniques, you can brush paint almost any model with as much success as with an aerosol can or an airbrush. I'll admit that spray painting is almost mandatory for complex models such as cranes, trestles, and truss bridges, but with those few exceptions, brush painting will yield excellent results.

Dozen-for-a-dollar dimestore brushes won't do; you'll need to invest in some sable hair watercolor brushes. You'll need a No. 000 and a No. 1 for detail work, even if you decide to spray paint everything else. Get No. 3 and ⅜"-wide flat-tipped brushes for broad surfaces. Sable hair brushes are more expensive than other types, but the hairs are soft enough to reach over details and put the paint where you want it, and flexible enough so the hairs won't break off and embed themselves in an otherwise perfect finish.

To use a brush properly, dip only the tip of the brush hairs into the paint.

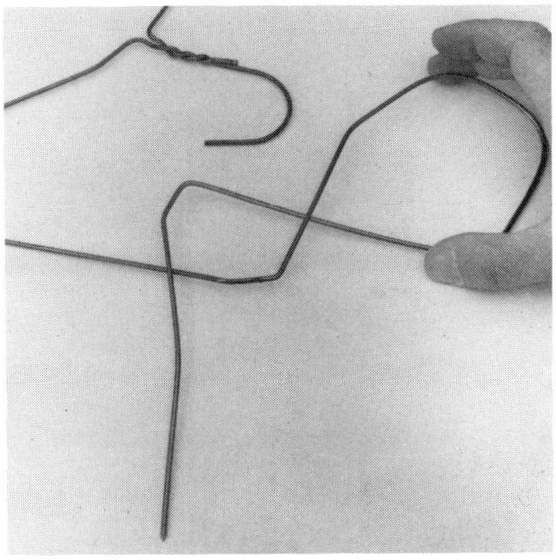

Fig. 3-4. Bend a wire coat hanger into a scissors spring to make a useful tool for holding models while painting.

Fig. 3-5. Special holders for locomotives and cars: left, a Quality Craft holder; right, a GB Engineering handle.

Don't allow paint to get into the hairs near where they enter the metal ferrule; this weakens the hairs and will eventually ruin the brush. After every use, clean the brush thoroughly, first with thinner for the paint you are using, then with plain soap and water. Store your brushes standing on their handles in a

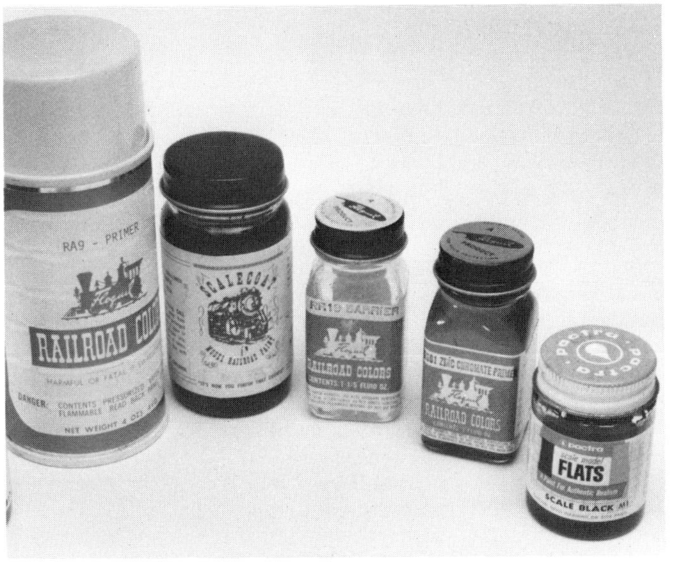

Primers give paints a better surface to stick to; protective coatings prevent crazing. Left to right: Floquil primer, Scalecoat "Shieldcoat," Floquil "Barrier," Floquil zinc chromate primer (for metal), and Pactra scale black.

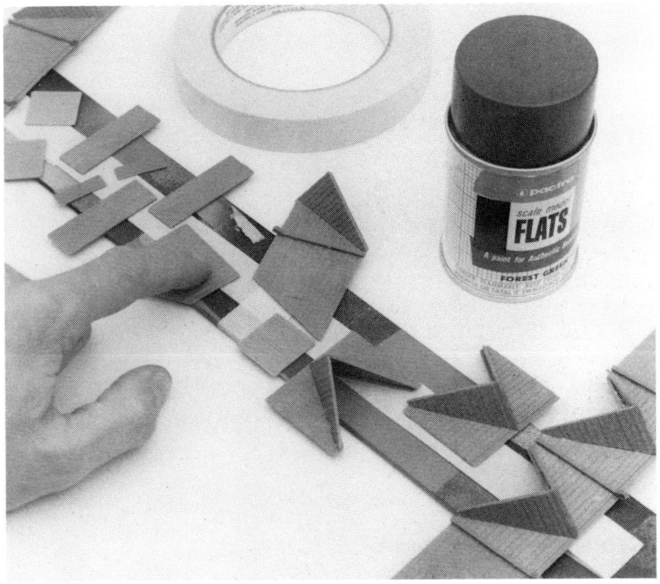

Fig 3-6. For small parts, one of the best holding fixtures is a length of wide masking tape fastened sticky side up to a flat piece of wood or cardboard.

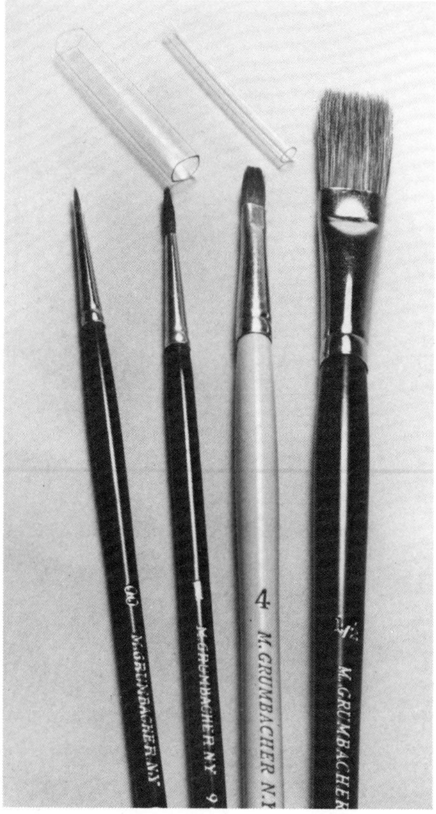

These sable brushes will handle most painting: (left to right) No. 00 round, No. 1 round, No. 4 flat, and ½″ flat.

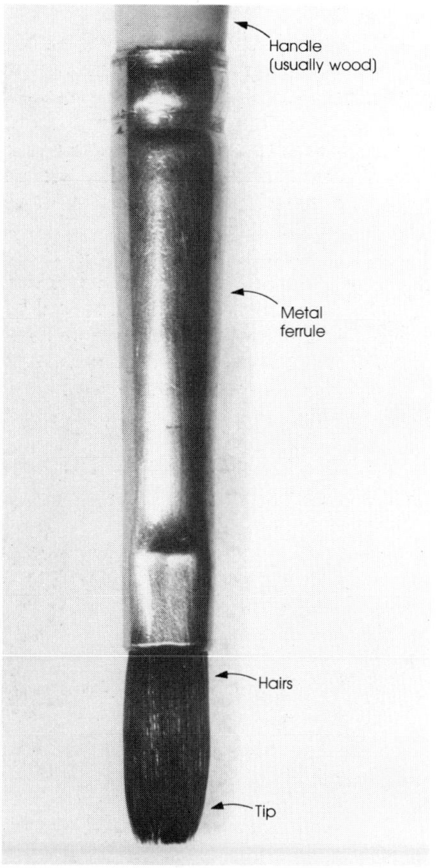

Note how the hairs form the natural shape of the tip of this high-quality sable brush. Only the bottom half of the hairs should be dipped into the paint.

jar (tips up), or lying flat in a clean drawer, *never* on their tips.

The secret of perfect brush painting is to *flow* the paint onto the model just thick enough that it will spread out and level on its own without drying too quickly and leaving brush marks. If you have trouble with brush marks, try thinning your paint with 25 to 40 per cent thinner so that the thinner rather than the brush will spread the paint over the surface. This thinned paint will require two coats for adequate coverage, but your problems with brush marks will be gone forever. Experiment, try different thinner-to-paint ratios, and make notes on what works best for you with each brand of paint.

Whether you are brush painting or spray painting, several thin coats are always better than a single heavy one. Whenever you start a paint job, allow enough time so you can finish the entire model at one sitting. If a second coat is necessary, apply it after the first coat has dried for at least an hour. Don't handle the model between coats, because the second coat needs to get a good grip on the first.

After painting, place the model where dust will not fall on it while the paint dries. Putting the model under an inverted cardboard box with props under the corners to allow slow air circulation is ideal.

Spray-can painting. No other method can match spray painting in speed and ease of application. Aerosol cans have brought low-cost spray painting to millions of projects, but they are a mixed blessing in modelwork. The good news is that spray cans furnish spray painting for the modeler who doesn't want to invest in airbrushing equipment. The bad part is that aerosol spray cans offer no control at all over the colors we spray—you can't mix your own paint—and too little control over the volume of paint and the pattern of the spray. Part of the problem stems from shortcomings in aerosol-can design, but most spray-painting failures result from lack of knowledge about the proper way to use this painting method.

Aerosol sprays have only one spray pressure and spray pattern. At least one paint maker has developed a spray nozzle that permits selecting a "fine" or "thick" pattern, but even at the fine setting the spray is difficult to control. It doesn't matter how softly you press on the spray button, the amount of paint and the pressure remains about the same until the paint and propellant in the can are exhausted. The only controls you have when spray painting with aerosol cans are how fast you move the spray pattern across the model, and how far away from the model you hold the can. There is no way to thin the paint, and no way to reduce the propellant pressure.

Successful painting with spray cans depends almost entirely on how well you "know" the brand and color you're using. Spray pattern, pressure, and paint consistency vary considerably from brand to brand, even among different colors of the same brand. Since one small can of spray paint is more than enough to paint almost any model railroad car or locomotive, plan on "wasting" about a fourth of the can practicing on an old model or a flat surface such as a kit box. You'll find that some spray paints work best when held 6 inches from the model, while others are best "dusted" on from nearly 2 feet away.

Paint consistency is important in determining how you will use a particular spray can. A few quick passes of the spray pattern are sufficient for coverage with some paints, while others—the thinner ones—cover best if the spray pattern is passed slowly over the model, allowing the paint to build up a little depth before the solvent evaporates. The only way you'll find out how a particular can of paint will perform is to test it. Spray a steady pattern on a blank piece of cardboard, holding the can at varying distances to determine the spray pattern. Not all paints spray straight out of the nozzle; some have a broad, fan-shaped pattern, while others spray in a large circle.

Shake each can every time you use it at least 100 times. If your workshop area is colder than 70 degrees, the can and the model should be warmed to about 80 degrees. You can warm the model by heating your oven on "low" for about five minutes, turning the heat off (a gas oven can have 150-degree-plus flash temperatures when the burner starts up), and setting your model inside for one or two minutes. You can also place the model in a sunny window or near a small—100 watts or less—incandescent light bulb. Don't let it stay there long—if it gets warm, it will aid paint application; if it gets *hot*, it will melt! If you use the oven method, be sure all cement joints have dried at least two days so there are no fumes.

Warm the spray can by holding it—and shaking as you do—under warm running water for a few minutes. Here again, warm is good, hot is bad—don't overdo it. You'll find that the can will become cold with prolonged spraying. When this happens, set the can aside for an hour or give it another warm-water bath to bring the contents up to temperature and the propellant up to working pressure.

If the spray can is going to sputter and splatter, it will usually do so as you start or stop the spray. Always start the spray pattern a few inches to one side of the model and swing the pattern across the model and off to the opposite side. Be sure the spray is completely off the model before reversing direction, and carry the spray *beyond* the model on the trip back, too.

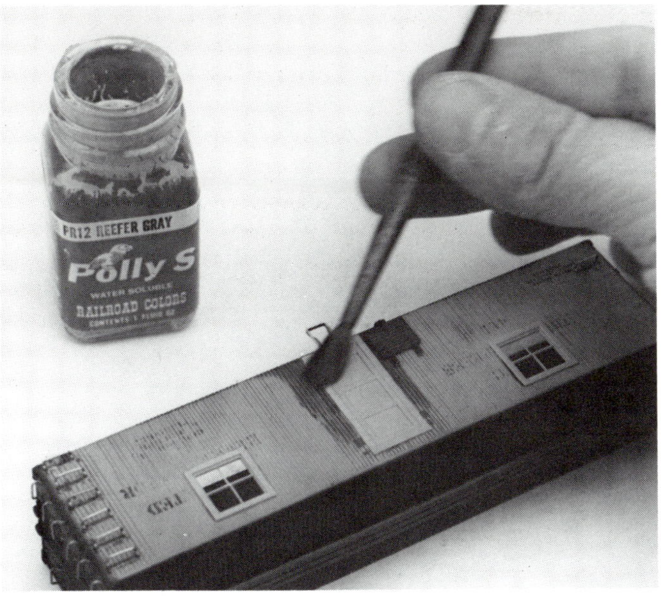

On models that have simulated boards, always brush "with the grain" to avoid paint buildup in the grooves.

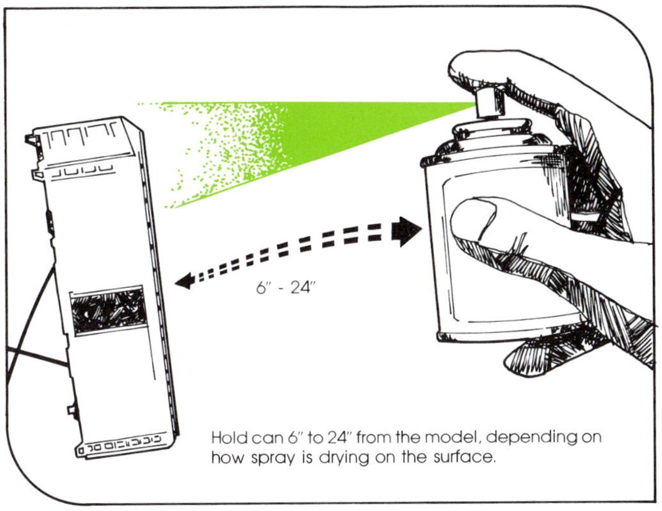

Hold can 6" to 24" from the model, depending on how spray is drying on the surface.

When you've completed spraying, turn the can upside down and direct a steady spray into an old rag or newspaper, fig. 3-7. This allows the paint to flow to the top of the can, exposing the pickup nozzle to pure propellant gas which blows through the nozzle to clean it. Remove the paint nozzle from the can and dunk it in a jar of clean thinner to further remove paint residue. When you empty a spray can, dispose of the can properly but keep the nozzle—it may save another can with a clogged nozzle in the future.

Masking and multi-color paint schemes. Multi-color paint schemes on locomotives and cars require thoughtful planning. Masking is necessary for brush painting as well as spraying. Apply the lightest color to the model first, even if that light color covers the smallest area. Follow up by masking the light areas and adding the darker colors, always progressing from light to dark.

Conventional masking tape is far too thick for model painting. When regular masking tape is removed, paint buildup along the masked edges produces a thick, unsightly paint bead or a choppy, wavy line. Thin, Scotch-brand "Magic" tape is much better for model masking. Masking fluids such as Micro-Scale "Micro-Mask" and Cary "Magic Masker" are made expressly for modelwork. These masking agents are brushable liquids that will not attack plastic or paint. They dry to a thin nonporous film which can be cleanly cut to accurate outlines and the excess peeled away from the model.

Good masking technique involves the use of both Magic tape and masking fluid. Liquid masking fluids can be used without tape to mask thin stripes, and in some cases, tape can be used without fluid if the color separation line will be covered by another part or occurs along a molded bead or panel line.

Start masking by determining where the color separation line will be located. If the separation line will be covered by a decal, the exact shape of the decal—such as the curves around the nose of many diesels—should be traced onto the mask so the line that divides the two

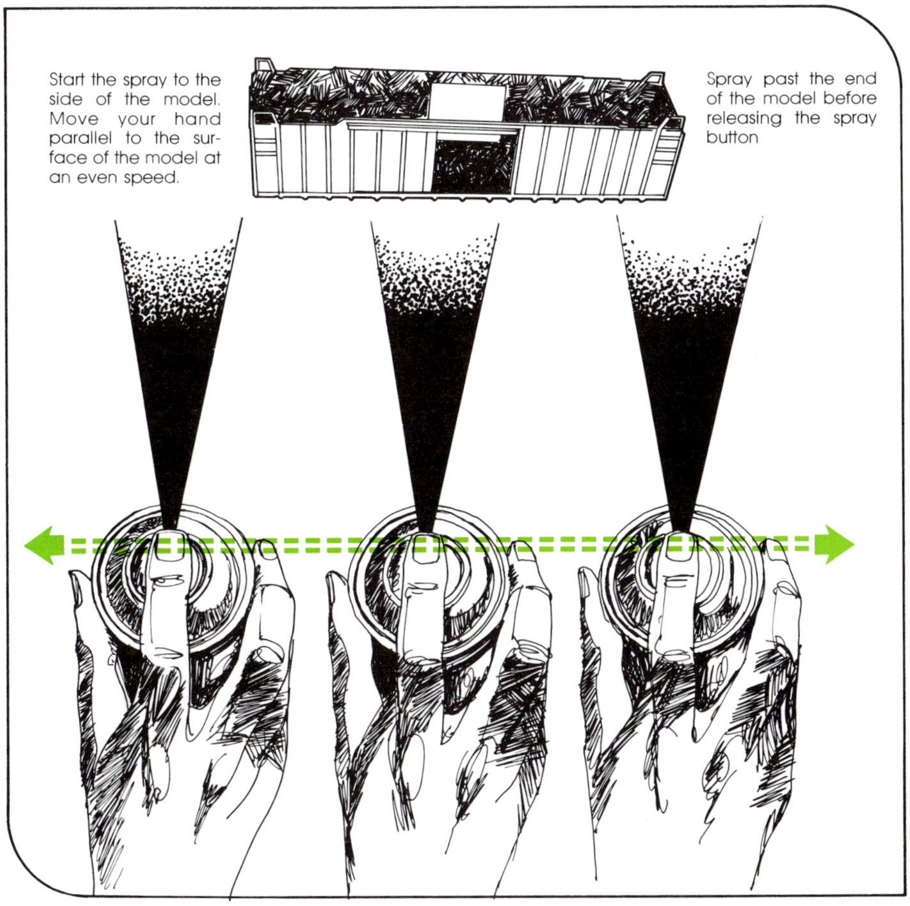

Start the spray to the side of the model. Move your hand parallel to the surface of the model at an even speed.

Spray past the end of the model before releasing the spray button

Fig. 3-7

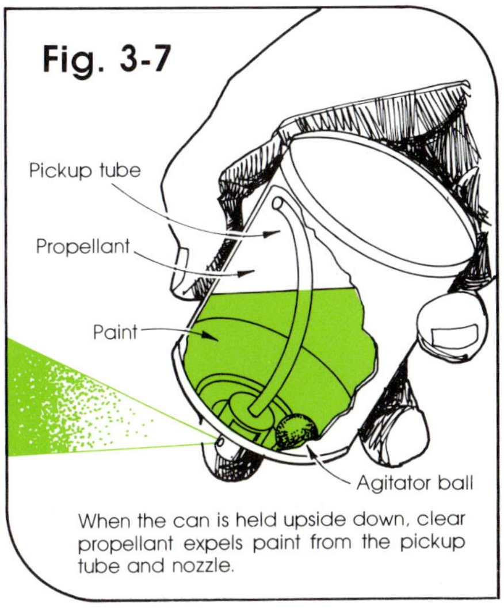

When the can is held upside down, clear propellant expels paint from the pickup tube and nozzle.

Experiment with each spray can to determine the best spraying distance and speed to move the can. Both model and paint should be warm.

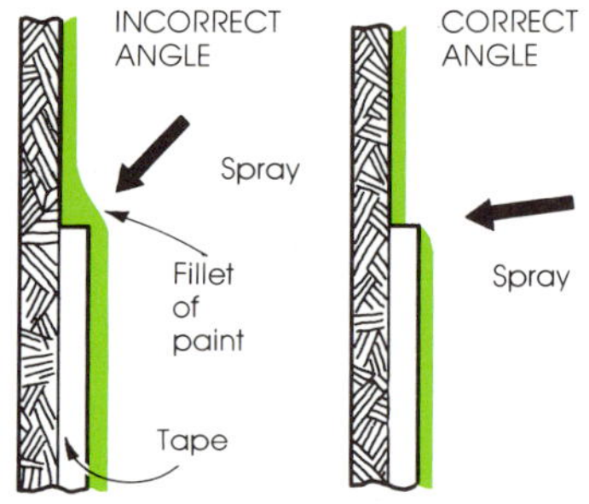

Fig. 3-8

colors will exactly match the decal contours.

Press several strips of tape down on a sheet of ordinary window glass and use a new razor blade and steel straightedge to cut a crisp, clean edge. This accomplishes two things—first, it gives you a much sharper edge than comes on the tape roll, and second, pressing the tape on the glass and peeling it up removes enough of the adhesive from the tape to make it less likely to lift paint.

Apply a strip of tape over the lighter color, about 1/16″ back from the color separation line. Brush on one or two coats of masking fluid, following the manufacturer's instructions. Overlap both the edge of the tape and the color separation line about 1/16″. Let the fluid dry, and use a hobby knife guided by a steel straightedge to cut through the film on the color separation line. Peel away the portion of the masking film that overlaps the separation line. This method produces a perfectly straight line with the thinnest possible masking agent (the fluid film) along the separation line. The Magic tape covers the larger areas of the model, while the fluid film seals the edge of the tape and masks between the edge and the separation line.

The final step in masking is to check that you have covered or wrapped every place you don't want paint to go. This means masking window openings or stuffing the model with newspaper to keep paint off interior walls.

Finally, spray or brush your paint,

Scotch Magic tape is thinner and sticks more tightly than masking tape. Use tape along the color separation line, but protect the rest of the model with clean paper.

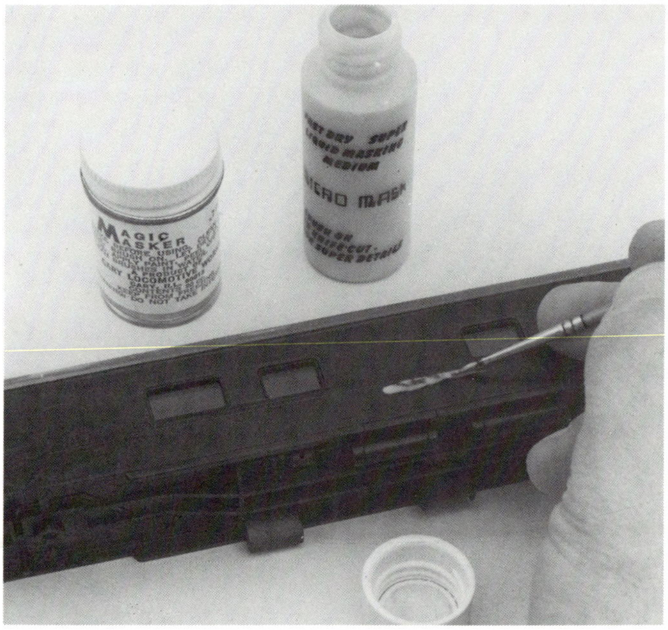

For precise color separation use fluid mask such as Micro Scale Micro Mask or Cary Locomotive Works Magic Masker.

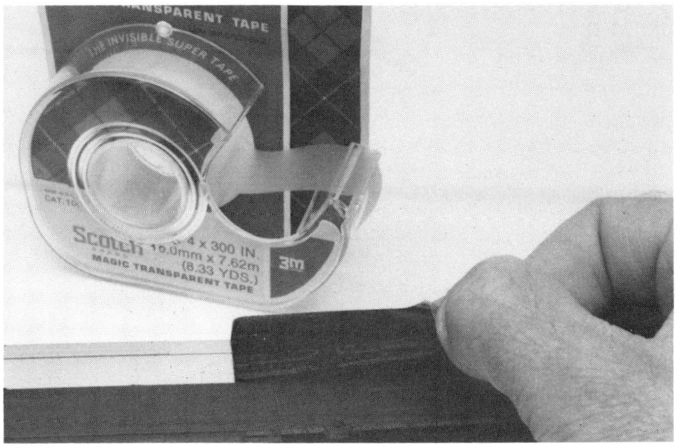

Fig. 3-9. RIGHT. Remove tape by pulling it straight back over itself. This confines the peeling action to a narrow band and minimizes the pull on the paint film.

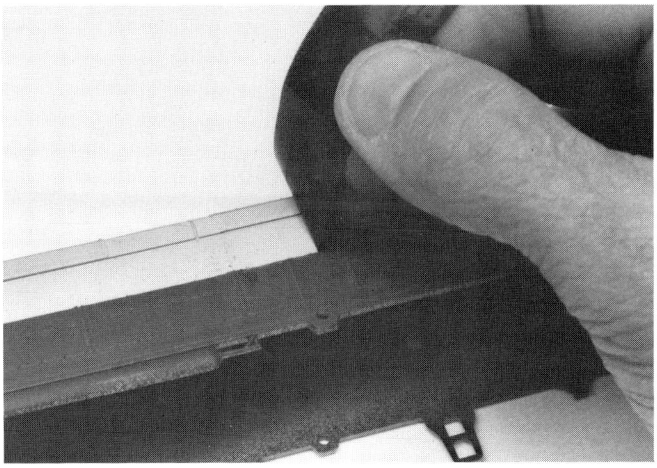

Fig. 3-10. WRONG. Lifting the tape exerts force on a broad area of paint, and can result in chipped and lifted paint.

keeping the paint layer as thin as possible next to the masked edge, fig. 3-8. If you are brushing, start your strokes on the masking and brush across and away from it to avoid buildup along the separation line. When the paint dries, slice through the paint film along the separation line. This cut ensures that the paint won't chip away along the masked line when you remove the tape and film.

Never leave masking on a model any longer than absolutely necessary. The best practice is to mask, paint immediately, and remove the masking an hour or so after the paint is applied. Leaving masking on longer allows the tape adhesive to bond to the paint underneath and increases the likelihood of leaving tape residue or pulling up paint.

To remove the masking, lift the edge of the tape at one corner and pull it straight back over itself at a very sharp angle, fig. 3-9. Pulling the tape straight up, fig. 3-10, can loosen the paint underneath or adjacent to it. The acute angle lessens the risk of pulling up paint by exerting pressure over a narrow area. Done correctly, the tape almost *rolls* away from the painted surface beneath it.

If the paint pulls away even when you remove the tape properly, there are several possible causes. The model may not have been thoroughly cleaned before painting or priming, or perhaps a primer coat was not used where one was needed. The paint underneath may not have been allowed to cure fully—2 days to a week—before masking. The best way to avoid masking problems is to follow the proper procedures *to the letter*—every time!

Weathering. Take a close look at the locomotives, cars, and structures around any railroad yard, then examine your models. Chances are that the railroad yard is a pretty grubby place, while your models look as if they just left the paint shop. The thought of applying even *simulated* dirt and grime to a highly detailed model is a bit frightening at first, but once you realize that weathering is what makes the real thing look real, you will consider aging as important as adding grab irons, paint, or decals.

There are many weathering methods. You *could* apply finely powdered dirt to your models and streak the dirt with a fine spray to duplicate the processes at work in nature, but there's a better way—match the colors and patterns of weathering with thinned paint to *simulate* dirt and wear. Real rust isn't likely to appear on your plastic models, but it's easy enough to simulate with thinned reddish-brown and dark orange paint.

There are several products intended specifically for weathering. Floquil offers weathering kits in their regular railroad colors, as does Polly S. These include "Grimy Black," (a dark gray with flecks of silver), Rust (dark orange), Dust (light beige-gray), Grime (a darker beige-gray), and Mud (yellow-beige). Floquil and Polly S also offer Earth, "Oily Black," and Dirt colors, as well as an aerosol "Instant Weathering Spray" meant for rapid, once-over dusting treatments. The Scalecoat line includes "Graphite and Oil" and "Loco Grime" colors in both Scalecoat I and II. Military flat colors

Jim C. Seacrest

Compare this prototype passenger car with the rolling stock on your layout. Note how subtle weathering brings out detail, especially around the trucks.

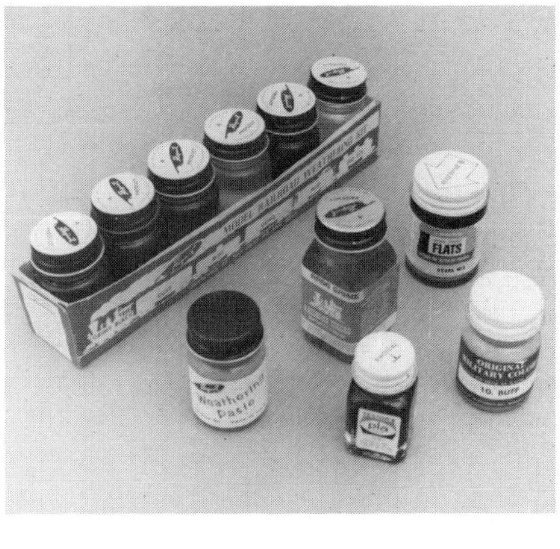

You can use special weathering colors to age and soil your models or mix your own variations using flat paint.

Floquil Weathering Paste, a thick, water-base beige paint, was brushed unevenly onto this HO box car to achieve a realistic dusty, sun-bleached effect.

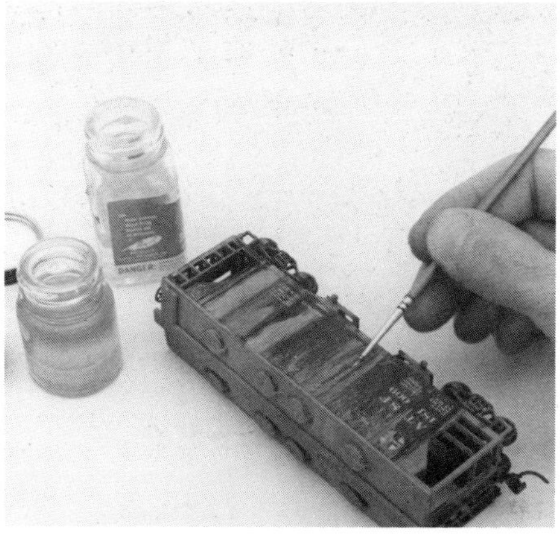

Covered hoppers are often heavily streaked with gray cement dust. These streaks can be simulated by applying light gray paint diluted 9:1 with thinner.

include many camouflage shades of dirt, dust, and mud, and most are ideal for making stains. Floquil also has a thick "Weathering Paste" that works well to simulate the streaks that occur as paint is bleached by exposure to sunlight. Accu-Paint has a weathering finish that they describe as a transparent grime color. Finally, you can use nearly any paint as a weathering agent by diluting it with thinner to make a stain or wash.

Stains and washes. Streaked paint and dirt effects can be simulated with a thin wash of color (about 80 parts thinner to one part paint) applied with a brush. Vary the shade and thickness of the streaks, making sure each "flows" as gravity would dictate. Mix several brown, tan, red, and buff washes to match the earth colors in your scenery and a few "foreign" soil colors for freight cars from distant roads. Use light gray and black to simulate dust and soot. Rust spots vary from dark brown to brilliant orange, so make up several rust washes, not just one. The safest paints to use for weathering are the plastic-compatible ones, and flat enamels thinned with mineral spirits are the easiest to manipulate.

The best weathering barely darkens or lightens the basic colors of the model. Most of your models should show evidence of light weathering; only a few examples of really dirty cars or structures are needed on the layout to set off the moderate treatment on most equipment. Keep your weathering stains weak so that you can make darker streaks by repeated applications. Always bear in mind that control and restraint are the keys to effective weathering; you should add color until you get what you want, rather than have to remove color from an overdone job to "save" the model.

Locomotive weathering patterns. It's essential that you realize how dirt looks on the prototype, where it is most likely to appear, what the different shades of dirt and grime are, and why the dirt on one freight car may be completely different from that on the next car in the train. Take color photographs of weathering patterns on locomotives, cars, and structures to refresh your memory. Don't apply a weathering effect to a model unless you can justify it by referring to the same effect on a prototype object.

A really clean prototype locomotive is shiny, but high gloss tends to hide fine detail on a model. Even your "new" equipment should receive a coat of clear flat finish and a wash of thinned gray or black around the running gear to represent a day's worth of surface dust and kicked-up ballast. Steam locomotives that are about to be "replaced" by diesels on your railroad should show streaks of rust and white boiler compound residue on their boilers, and their black paint should be sun-faded to medium gray, figs. 3-11 and 3-12. Diesels usually wear a black and dusty look from constant exposure to their own exhaust. The exhaust gases and solids are forced back over the locomotive whenever it passes beneath an overpass or through a tunnel.

Car and structure weathering. Cars are usually coated with dirt that reflects either soil types in their operating areas or their cargo. Equipment on a coal hauling railroad is streaked with black—the combined effects of coal dust and rainwater. Cars from Southwestern roads wear beige and tan—the colors of desert dust. Iron oxide red is the prevalent weathering dirt on equipment that operates in iron-mining regions. Box cars and covered hoppers are often streaked with golden wheat dust, tank

R. B. Black

Fig. 3-11. Note how the dirt and faded paint on this locomotive bring out its detail, an effect you can use on your models to enhance their realism.

Richard Steinheimer

Fig. 3-12. This locomotive is clean by most standards, but streaks of boiler compound and soot deposits are still evident.

cars show shiny black oil stains or strange green, yellow, and orange chemical drippings, and cars in cement or clay service are heavily chalked with light gray dust.

The construction of the car is also a major factor in the weathering pattern. Neglected wood cars show silver-gray patches where the paint has peeled away to expose the wood beneath; steel cars have streaks of rust where their paint has been damaged. Tiny spots of rust appear around trucks and underframes even on new rolling stock.

Most cars show light lineside dirt on their underframes and ends after their very first trip out of the paint shops. Often, extremely dirty cars have a clean spot around the car numbers so switching personnel can read the reporting marks, and in some cases, that same area may be freshly repainted while the rest of the car is faded and rusty. Seldom are two cars weathered exactly the same. Even a unit train of coal gondolas will show varying degrees of dirt and rust, simply because the cars have been shopped at different times.

Structures show the effects of rain, dust, and grime, too. The lower parts of walls are often splashed with the soil color, while the areas beneath the eaves collect sooty stains from locomotive exhaust. Nails show streaks of dark gray or reddish-brown where they have rusted through the paint and the stain has washed down the sheathing.

I've seen some strikingly realistic model structure groups where the lower portion of each building was washed with thinned red, beige, or dusty brown to match the soil color. This treatment duplicates the dusty effect of dirt blown onto structures and washed down during rain storms and showers. An occasional board—or even an entire wall—can be painted tan to represent freshly replaced siding, or one section of a weathered wall can be touched up with paint of the original color to indicate a freshly painted area.

Finally, whatever colors or methods you use to simulate the effects of age and weather, always follow these two simple rules: (A) Don't apply an effect without being able to explain what would have caused it on the prototype, and (B) Don't overdo it.

George H. Drury

This hopper carries clay. Note how the vertical streaks emphasize its rounded shape.

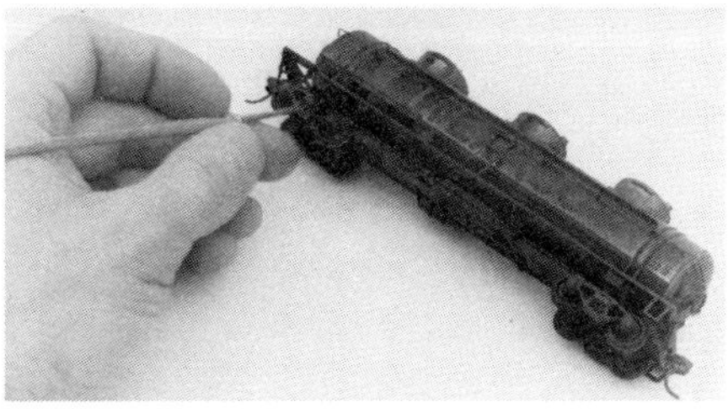

Older oil stains on this tank car were simulated with thinned flat black paint; fresh spills were made with gloss black. Orange and reddish-brown rust flecks on the trucks were added using full-strength paint.

Clean the area around the reporting marks of heavily weathered cars by brushing with thinner. If the car is really dirty, add a rectangle of paint and new decal numbers.

A wash of thinned black and brown paint helps to accentuate the mortar lines on this stone structure. All streaks should be vertical to represent rain-washed soot.

Using decals and dry transfers

Here's how to add heralds, letters, numbers, and stripes to your models.

THE SIMPLEST way to rework a car, locomotive, or structure is to paint and reletter it in a scheme that is not offered commercially. Few modelers are talented enough to letter cars and locomotives by hand. Kit and ready-built equipment is lettered by printing or silk-screen processes that are far too costly and complex for an individual modeler, and silk-screening is only practical when many—hundreds or even thousands—identical lettering schemes must be applied. Most modelers use decals and dry transfers to apply lettering, numbers, signs, railroad heralds, and stripes. With practice and patience, both materials produce lettering that is crisp, sharp, and appears hand painted.

Decals. Decals are printed or screened on a special porous paper that is coated with water-soluble adhesives. After applying a thin clear film over the adhesive layer, the decal manufacturer adds the colored ink or paint, fig. 4-1. Some decals have a second clear coating applied to seal and protect the inks.

Suppliers of decals offer hundreds of sets for all kinds of lettering schemes, and the variety increases every day. There are literally thousands of decals—for almost every railroad, for different eras of the same railroad, and even for specific locomotives and unusual cars. You can usually find just the locomotive, car, or structure markings that you want or something very close if you page through the decal manufacturers' catalogs. These catalogs belong on your reference bookshelf.

Alphabets (individual letters), numbering sets, and sheets of decal striping are also available. Dimensional data sets—the blocks of small lettering that show the size and capacities of freight cars—are offered for most car types, and you can even buy sheets of the markings found on diesel locomotive fuel tanks and inspection covers. Most decal sets include information on properly positioning the lettering, and there are also lettering diagram books on prototype cars.

Decal setting fluids. There are a host of decal-related solvents and setting fluids on the market, each intended to assist you in making the decal settle down against the surface of your model and making the clear film "disappear." Champ "Decal Set," Micro Scale "Micro Set" and "Micro Sol," and Walthers "Solvaset" are the brands you'll find at most hobby shops. All of them work by softening the clear decal film.

These setting and softening agents are not *optional*. One of them should be

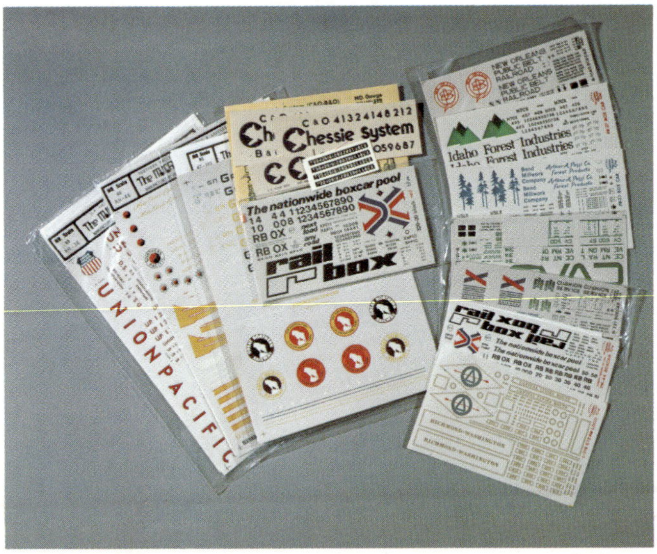

Hundreds of railroad decal sets are available and new ones are issued monthly as the decal manufacturers add new prototype color schemes to their lines.

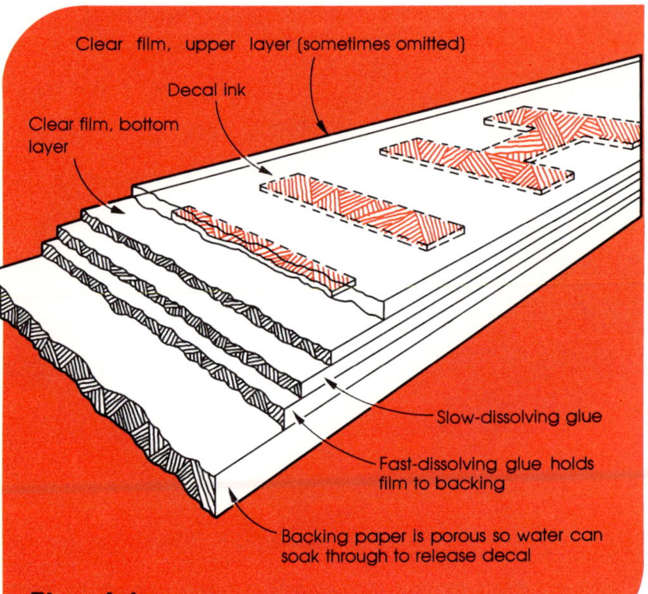

Fig. 4-1 DECAL CROSS SECTION

Decal sets include diagrams that show where to position the lettering and numbers. This undecorated HO diesel shell and Micro Scale Boston & Maine decal set will be combined to make a locomotive not offered by any manufacturer.

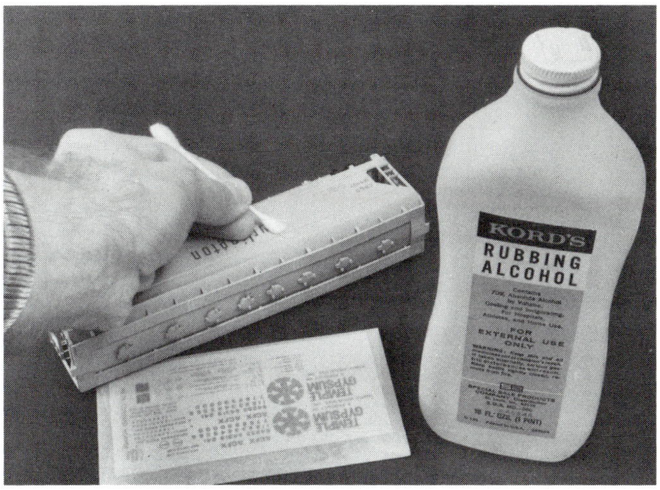

Substituting decals for parts of the lettering on a factory paint scheme is easy. Here, denatured alcohol is used to remove the Burlington markings. The appropriate decals will replace them, while the paint and dimensional data remain undisturbed.

used every time you apply decals, no matter how well the decal seems to adhere to the surface without them. They help the decal conform to irregularities, stretch over small protruding seams or details, and stick better to the surface of the model. Different brands and even different batches vary in strength of the dissolving agent. If you find that a bottle of decal setting fluid works too fast for you, thin it with water. Distilled water is best.

Decal application. A few decal brands have clear film only around groups of letters that make up the railroad name, herald, etc., but most decal makers coat the entire sheet of decal paper with a clear film layer. Railroad names, car numbers, heralds, and blocks of dimensional data must be cut apart and trimmed before soaking. If you attempted to soak the entire decal sheet, you would have a large sheet of clear film with *all* of the names, numbers, and so forth in just the positions they were on the dry paper. Trim as close as you can to the tops and bottoms of letters, but leave clear film between letters so you have a complete name (such as Pullman, or Rio Grande) with correctly spaced characters, fig. 4-2. To make car or locomotive numbers, you'll have to cut individual numbers from the sheet and position them one at a time, unless they appear on the sheet in the proper sequence.

When you start a decaling project, plan ahead so that you don't use decals from more than one set on one side of a car or locomotive. This is because slight variations in opacity (thickness) of the decal ink exist between batches of decals. It is better to use a whole decal set to letter a single side of a car than to try to piece together the side from leftovers.

The tools for working with decals

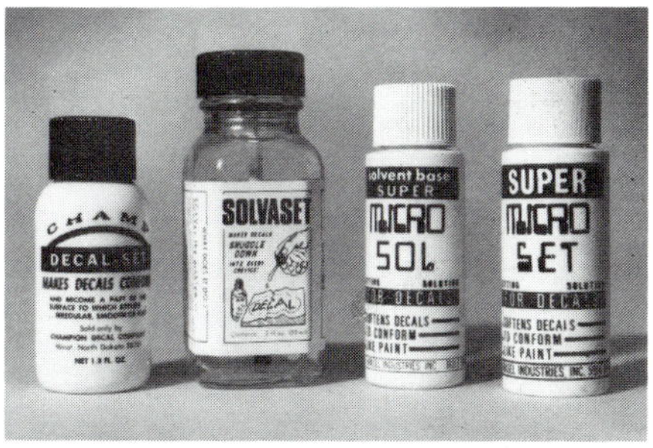

Proper decal application requires the use of a setting agent. Left to right: Champ Decal-Set, Walthers Solvaset, Micro-Scale Micro Sol and Micro Set.

are simple: a small dish or cup to hold water, paper towels, modeling knife, single-edge razor blades, needle mounted in pin vise or dowel handle, fig. 4-3, steel straightedge, tweezers, decal setting agent, and a small sable hair

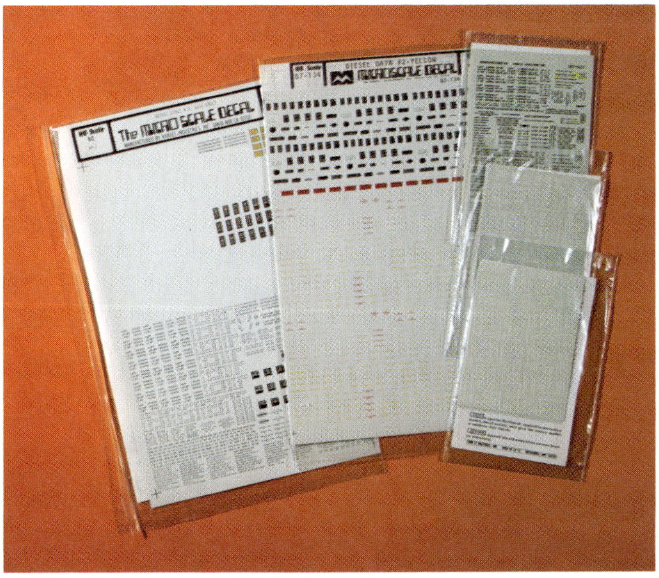

Alphabet sets (left) are offered in both decals and dry transfers. You can use them to make your own signs and railroad names. Dimensional data sets (right) provide blocks of small lettering for diesels and freight cars.

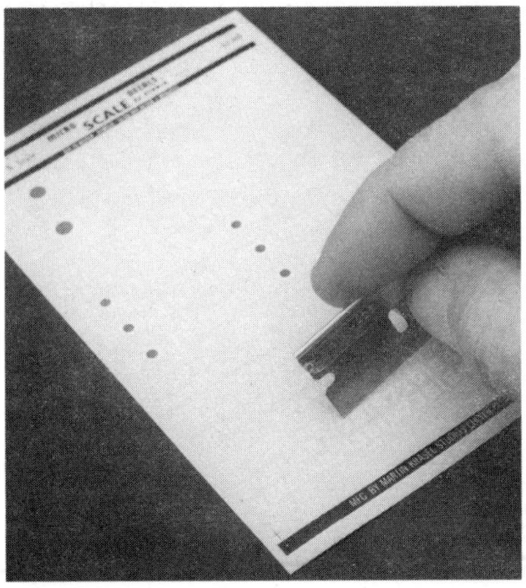

Cut individual decal sections from the decal sheet with razor blade, knife, or scissors. Cut as close as you can to the lettering or designs so there will be less decal film to hide.

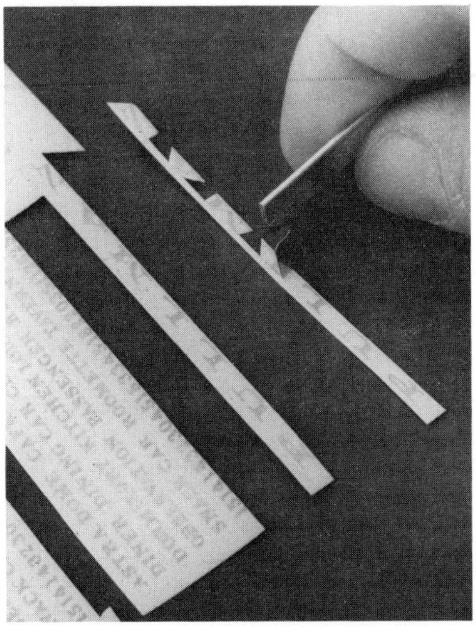

Fig. 4-2. To ensure correct letter spacing, apply long names as a single decal piece by leaving a 1/16″ strip of clear decal film attached to the top or bottom.

spotting brush (No. 1 or No. 2). Optional, but helpful if you do a lot of lettering, are hands-free magnifying devices such as an Optivisor, desk lamp with mounted magnifier, or magnifying glass mounted on a stand. Another handy item is a slab of clean foam rubber. This serves as a pillow for the model and prevents damaging the side opposite the one you are working on.

Gloss finish versus flat. Decals adhere better to a smooth, glossy surface than to a rough flat finish. Flat paints and finishes achieve their matte look by having a microscopically rough surface; light does not reflect from this surface as it does from a glossy finish. The rough surface of a flat finish makes it difficult, if not impossible, for the relatively stiff decal film to snuggle tightly against the surface, and the microscopic ridges and peaks hold parts of the film away from the surface, allowing air to remain trapped beneath the film and causing a cloudy appearance that indicates the decal is not adhering properly.

For models painted with dead-flat paints (Floquil, Flo-Paque, Pactra Flat, Testors Pla Flat), the first step in decaling is to apply a gloss finish to the areas of the model where the decals will be placed. It doesn't have to be ultra-gloss; most paint lines include an additive that will provide a semigloss finish—Floquil "Glaze," Scalecoat "Gloss Glaze," etc. This additive can be mixed into the paint without affecting holding power or drying rate. If you are using Floquil colors, try mixing 25 per cent Glaze with the colors to achieve an eggshell finish that will take decals well.

Gloss finish can be applied *over* model colors to provide a smooth surface for decaling. Micro Scale "Micro-Coat Gloss" is intended for this application, and any clear gloss finish will fill in the microscopic pores and ridges in the flat finish. Apply a thin gloss coat only to the areas that will be decaled. Let it dry thoroughly—24 hours or more—before decal application.

The area of the model to be decaled should be horizontal, so gravity is pulling the decal film against the model. Position the model on a foam rubber slab or a pad of paper towels, or hold it in a vise.

When you've cut out the parts of the decal sheet that you intend to use on one side or end of the model, drop several of them into a container of lukewarm water. If you are using white decals, use a colored container to make the pieces easier to see if they float loose from the backing paper. The reason for soaking several pieces at one time is that some can be softening while you apply others, so you can move right along with little or no waiting.

Some modelers insist that using distilled water for softening decals cuts down on the amount of residue to be removed after the decal is in place. I haven't found this to be necessary, but it might be true in areas where the water is very hard. An often-overlooked source of free distilled water is a dehumidifier, should you have one.

If the surface of the model features molded detail in the area to be decaled—rivets, scribed panel lines, simulated wood grain, etc.—pre-wet the surface with water or a dilute solution of decal-softening solvent. After you've gained experience with decaling and can work quickly, try pre-wetting with full-strength decal solvent. Don't attempt this on your first decaling job, because the penalty for a slight mistake in timing with this method is a ruined decal.

After they have soaked in the water for 10 to 20 seconds, remove the decals

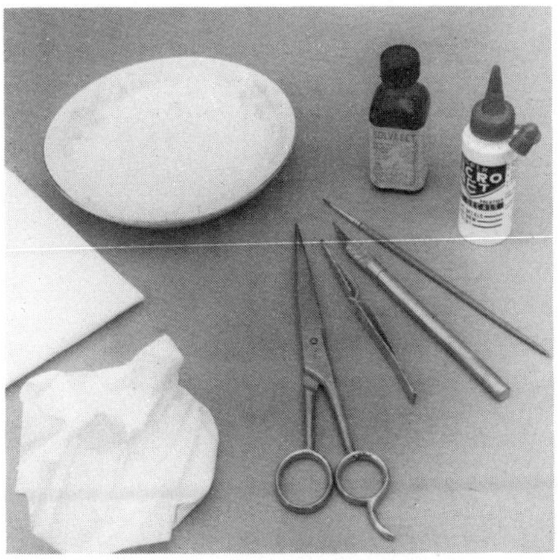

Basic decaling tools: paper towels, tissues, water, scissors, tweezers, knife, brush, setting agents.

Decals don't adhere well to flat paint. Apply gloss where they will be placed.

After dipping the decal in water for 10 to 20 seconds, place it on a clean, dry paper towel for about one minute while the adhesive that holds the film to the backing dissolves.

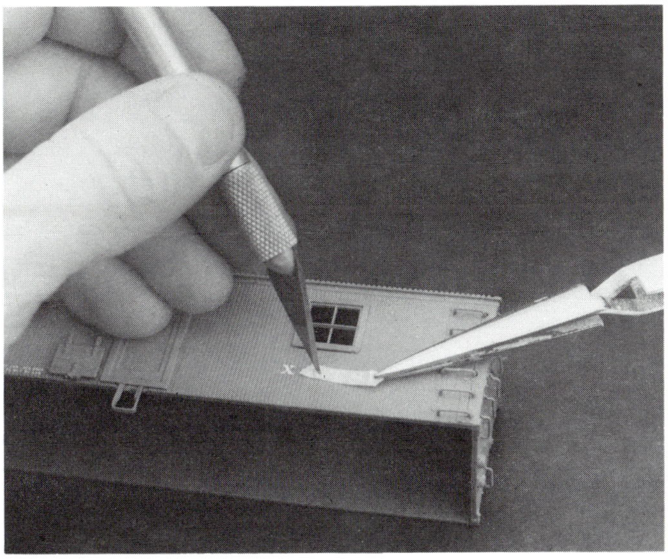

Position the decal and slide the backing out from under the film. Don't touch the decal film with your fingers.

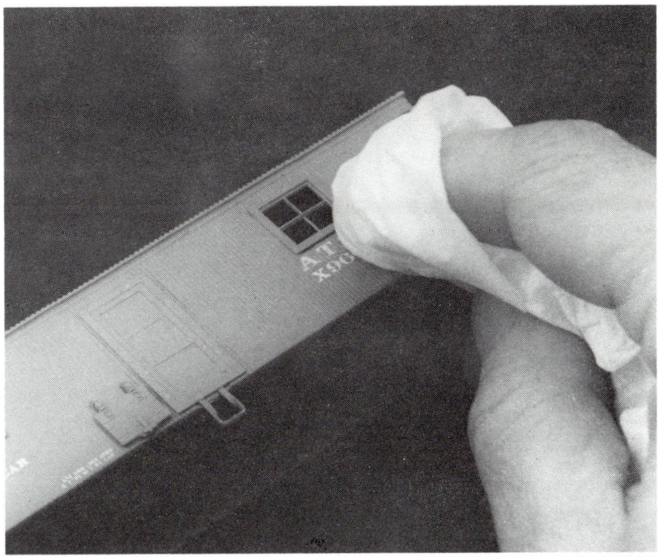

Blot up excess water with a tissue. Ensure that the decal is properly positioned and aligned.

and place them on a clean paper towel while the adhesive between the film and the backing paper dissolves. Nudge the decal film with the tip of your tweezers to determine when it is free to slide on the backing. When it is free, pick up both film and paper and position them on the model where you want the decal. Hold the decal film with your hobby knife point or needle pricker while you pull the backing paper out from underneath it with the tweezers. Never, ever, touch the decal film with your fingers, or you'll find the decal on your fingertip instead of on the model. If the decal film just floats around on the pre-wetted area, blot up excess fluid by touching the corner of a paper towel to the area near the decal. Be careful not to actually touch the decal with the towel.

When you have all decal pieces applied to one side or end of your model, go back to the first decal piece (wait about 10 minutes if you're applying only one or two pieces) and inspect for signs of air bubbles trapped beneath the film. Carefully prick each blister with a sharp needle held in a pin vise or dowel handle. Cut through the decal film with a razor blade or brand-new hobby knife where required to make the decal conform to grooves, ridges, or panel seams.

Next, apply decal setting fluid to the edges and top of the decal with a brush. Be gentle with the brush, and try to apply the fluid without touching the surface of the decal. The idea is to NOT shift the decal. Make at least two more applications of the softening fluid and allow them to work overnight. Do not apply so much setting fluid that it makes dome-like blobs that rest on top of the decal—too much fluid can cause "blowout" holes to develop in the film.

It's a rock-hard rule that you do not touch the decal with *anything* after the setting fluid has been applied. No matter how tempting it is to pop a little bubble or cut through the film along a groove, LEAVE THE DECAL ALONE WHILE IT IS WET WITH SETTING AGENT.

Inspect the decals the next day for air bubbles or blisters. Puncture them with the needle tip and apply more setting agent. Keep inspecting for air bubbles, pricking them, and applying solvent until all of them are gone. This step is important if you want top-notch results. Be fussy.

After the last application of setting agent has dried for at least 12 hours, use a cotton swab moistened with clear water to gently wash away decal adhesive residue or setting fluid stains. Be careful while working near the decal,

Fig. 4-3 NEEDLE PRICKER TOOL

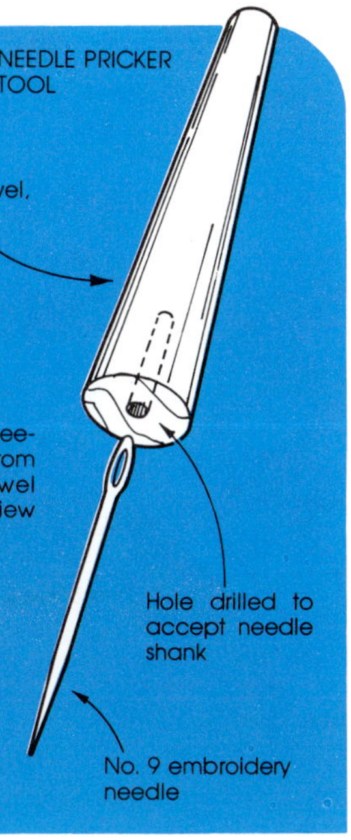

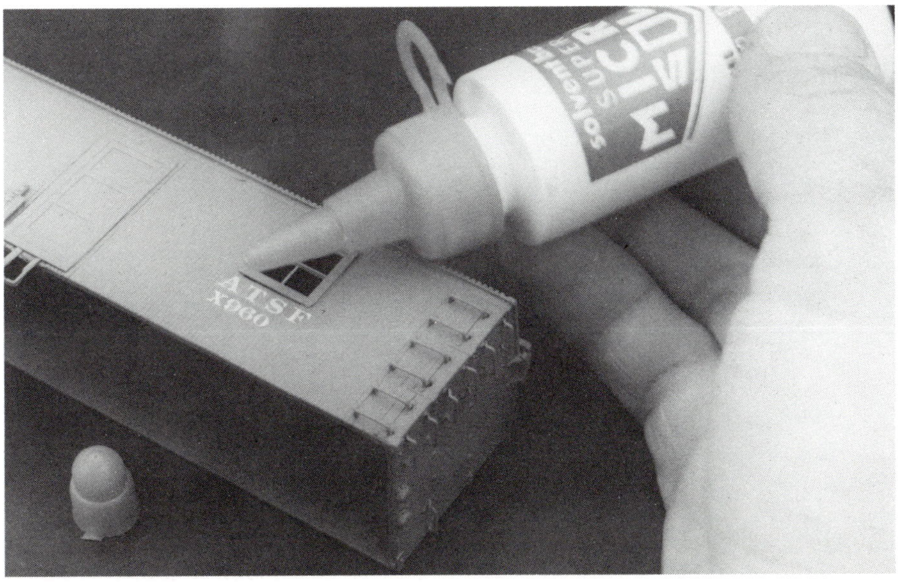

Apply decal setting fluid sparingly and allow it to penetrate beneath the decal film. NEVER touch the decal film while it is softened by setting fluid.

Decal striping is available for passenger cars and diesels. You can also use striping sets to develop your own multicolor paint schemes.

because it is easy to damage until it has been sealed with a clear protective coating. When the decals are thoroughly dry, apply a coat of clear flat finish to protect them and make the decal film blend into the overall finish of the model.

Working with decal striping. Decals are the best method for applying stripes when the striping bands are too narrow to mask and paint neatly. Special decal sets for specific prototype diesels and passenger cars are available, as are striping sets applicable to many models. Solid sheets of colored decal material are available for custom-cutting your own stripes. Application of decal striping follows the same techniques as for any decals, but there are a few extra tricks you should have up your sleeve for best results.

Just as with other decals, trim the clear film close to the edges of the striping. Use a steel ruler to guide your knife. Apply stripes as you would other decals, but hold the extreme end of the stripe in place while you slide the backing paper away along the line where you want the stripe to lie. The stripe should fall neatly into place.

When decal stripes are to cover a separation line between two colors that have been masked and painted, lightly sand the separation line with water-wetted No. 600 wet-or-dry sandpaper. This step is important to ensure that the slight ridge left by the masking won't show through the stripe. Incidentally, it's often easier to add details (such as grab irons) that straddle two colors or that pass over a striped area *after* a model has been striped with decals.

Dry Transfers. Dry transfers are a more modern method of applying lettering and heralds than decals. They are made by depositing letters or designs onto the back of a clear carrier sheet which has a tacky, waxlike coating that will release the letters when the front of the carrier is rubbed gently. The transfers contain a pressure-sensitive adhesive that sticks to any clean, dry surface, fig. 4-4. Each dry-transfer character is individual; the translucent carrier sheet does not have any film to hold the letters at the correct spacing when they transfer to the model. Application is fast and neat, and the major advantage of dry transfers over decals is that there is no clear film to hide after the lettering is in place. When characters are grouped into railroad names, you must burnish the entire name or set of letters down at one time, being careful not to shift the carrier sheet as you move from one letter to the next. When all of the letters in one area are burnished, the translucent carrier is lifted from the model, leaving the characters behind.

Compared to decals, relatively few railroad lettering sets are available in dry transfers. Dry-transfer alphabet sets are available for custom lettering and renumbering jobs. Because they are applied without soaking and setting, individual dry-transfer letters and numbers are much more convenient and quicker to work with than individual decal letters and numbers. Many modelers apply the bulk of the decoration to cars and locomotives with decals but use dry transfers for numbers. Dry transfers are also handy for changing car numbers with a minimum of fuss.

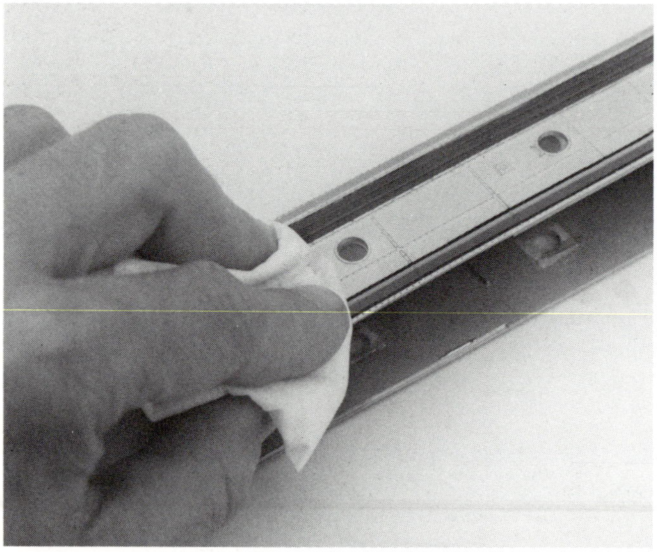

To apply decal striping, hold the stripe at one end and pull the backing from the other, allowing the film to fall into place as the paper is withdrawn.

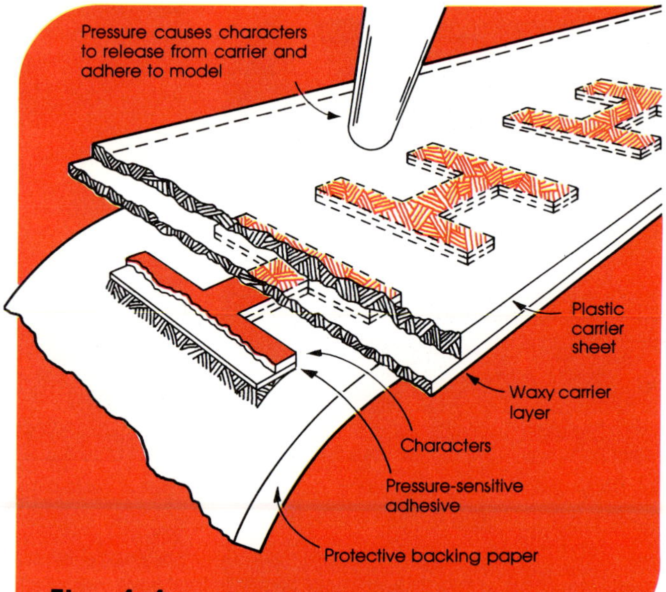

Fig. 4-4 DRY TRANSFER CROSS SECTION

The cloudy areas along the rivet rows on this car are a result of not using a decal-setting fluid. The decal is too stiff to conform without a setting agent.

The ragged blowout hole in the center of this arrow design was caused by allowing a bubble of setting fluid to evaporate from the surface of the decal.

When this decal was plucked from its backing and flopped onto the car, it folded back over itself. Always slide the paper from under the decal.

Two mistakes here: too much clear film was left around the letters, and tissue was not used to blot up excess water and setting agent. Residue around the decal can be removed by gentle scrubbing with water and a cotton swab.

This decal was ruined when it was touched with tweezers while the film was softened by setting agent.

This decal was exposed to so much heat and humidity that the film has blistered. There's no way to save it.

This decal has cracked due to exposure to heat and humidity. When no replacement is available, you can sometimes salvage such a decal by spraying with two coats of clear finish and allowing it to dry for a day before application.

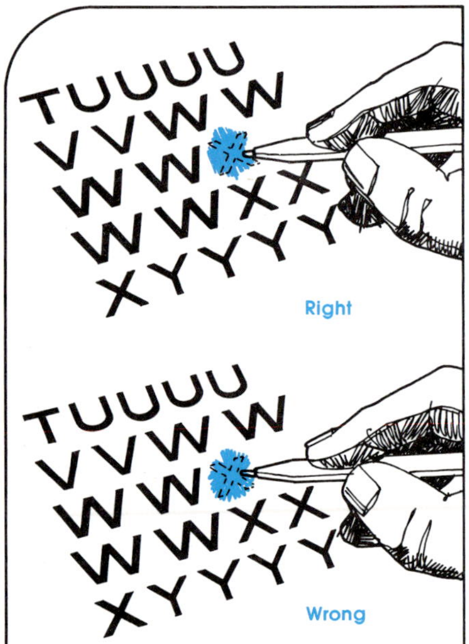

Burnish either back and forth or up and down to avoid stretching the carrier sheet and distorting the letters.

Fig. 4-5

Multicolor dry-transfer designs are usually furnished in two or more parts. One color is applied first, burnished, sealed, and the additional colors aligned and burnished on top of them.

At first glance then, dry transfers would seem to be the simplest method of lettering, but try a set or two before you decide to use them exclusively. Dry transfers adhere best to smooth surfaces such as streamlined passenger car sides, and they don't fare well on rough surfaces such as wood siding or rivets. Another relative disadvantage of dry transfers is that you cannot reposition them after they are applied to the model as you can with decals. Once the dry transfer is burnished onto the model, it must be either left as is or removed; removed, it is destroyed and cannot be reapplied.

Dry-transfer application. Dry transfers will adhere satisfactorily to a surface with a flat finish, but a slight gloss or semigloss finish is preferable. Whatever the finish, the surface must be dry and clean—free from fingerprints, dust, grease, or oil—the cleaner the better. Trimming the dry-transfer carrier a fraction of an inch above or below the characters to be transferred is a big help in keeping the characters aligned during burnishing. Position the carrier sheet with the letters or numbers precisely where you want them and burnish over the characters with a ballpoint pen tip, rounded softwood stick, or a dull No. 0 lead pencil.

Proper burnishing technique is important. Burnish the entire area to be transferred with just enough pressure to force the characters down without stretching the carrier sheet or deforming the lettering. Move the burnishing tool back and forth, either up and down or side to side but not both, which can distort the carrier sheet, fig. 4-5. Some types of dry transfers look milky through the carrier when they release, making it easy to detect when they have transferred.

If some characters that you burnished failed to stick, there are several possible causes. Too much pressure in burnishing will sometimes return characters to the carrier, while too little pressure will fail to transfer the letters at all. Paint that has not dried at least two or three days will not accept dry transfers, nor will a surface that has any trace of oil, grease, or fingerprints. Occasionally, you can improve the performance of dry transfers by holding the carrier sheet a few inches from a light bulb to warm the sheet slightly before application. This seems to increase the tackiness of the letters and promotes easier release from the carrier.

If some characters are misaligned or improperly spaced, remove them by lightly pressing Scotch Magic transparent tape over the offending parts and gently peeling them off, then try again.

When all the dry transfers in one area are satisfactorily positioned, burnish

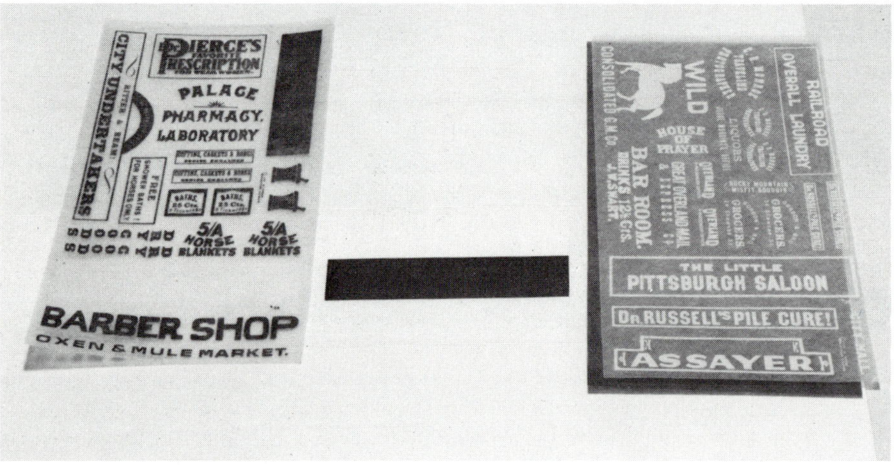

Some multicolor dry-transfer signs and heralds require burnishing down each color separately. Careful alignment of each part is important.

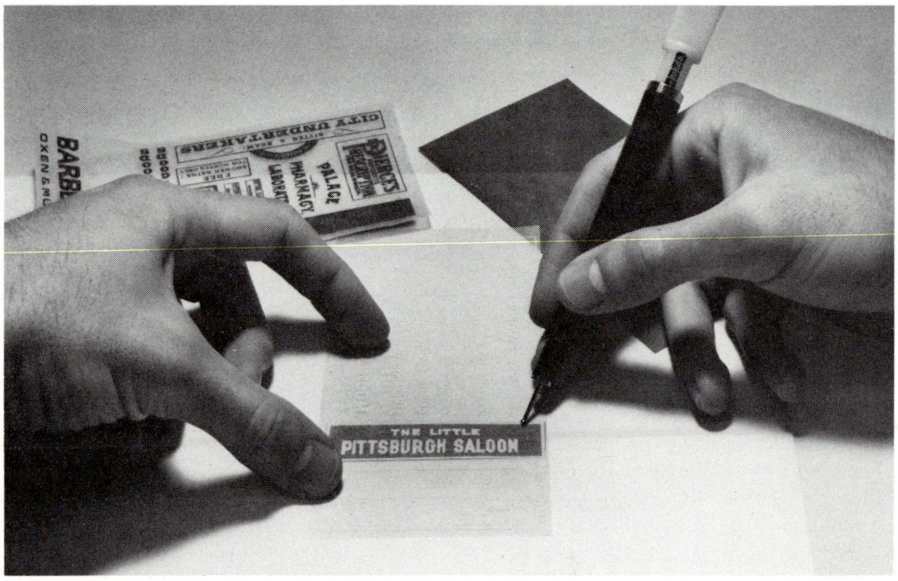

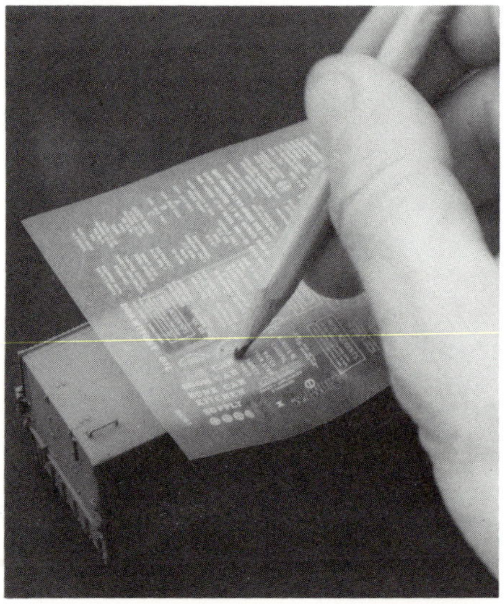

Short names can be transferred from the large carrier sheet to the model. Cut out long names and large heralds to make them easier to align.

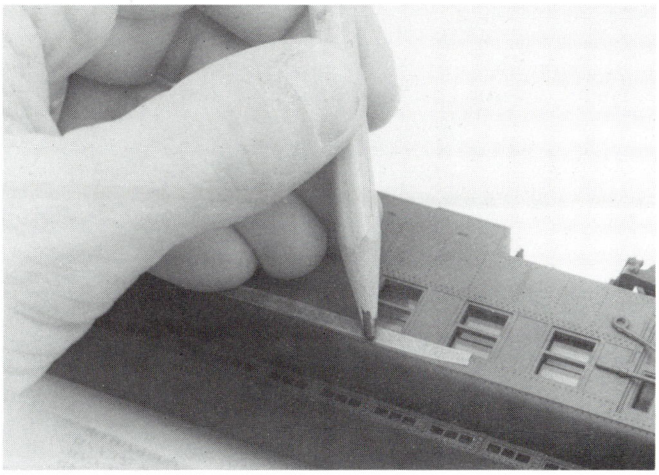

After positioning the dry-transfer lettering and carefully checking the alignment, burnish them down. Practice with some spare transfers to determine just how much burnishing pressure is required for proper adhesion.

them down again, placing the sheet of protective backing paper supplied with the transfers between the lettering and the burnishing tool. This "sets" the lettering, bonding it firmly to the surface. On simulated wood sides, use a scriber or the tip of a modeling knife to cut through the characters and fold them into the grooves between boards. Around rivets and other small raised details, place the protective paper over the transfers and dab lightly at the characters with a rubber eraser to make them stretch and conform, fig. 4-6. Finally, protect the dry transfers with a light spray coat of clear flat finish.

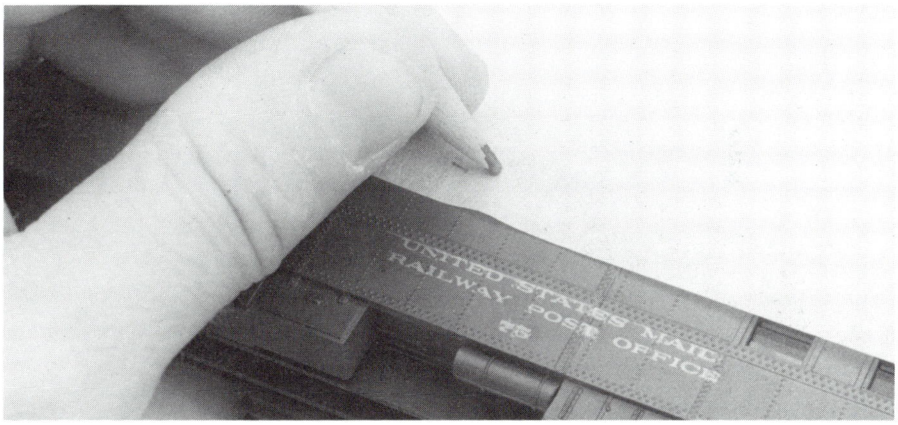

Hold the protective backing paper provided with the dry transfers over the lettering to burnish it down tightly and permanently.

There is a way to use dry transfers on irregular surfaces where you need the ability of decal film to stretch and conform. Plain decal paper—with the clear film, but without letters or numbers—is available (for small jobs, you can use the unprinted margin from decal sets). Apply the dry transfers to the decal paper, burnish them down, apply flat finish, and allow 2 or 3 days drying time. Then trim the film and apply your homemade dry-transfer decal just as you would any decal. This decal will be more delicate than a commercial one, but the important thing is that you can use setting fluid to make the lettering conform to an irregular surface.

Clear flat finishes. The final step in decal or dry-transfer application is an

Fig. 4-6 MAKING DRY TRANSFERS CONFORM

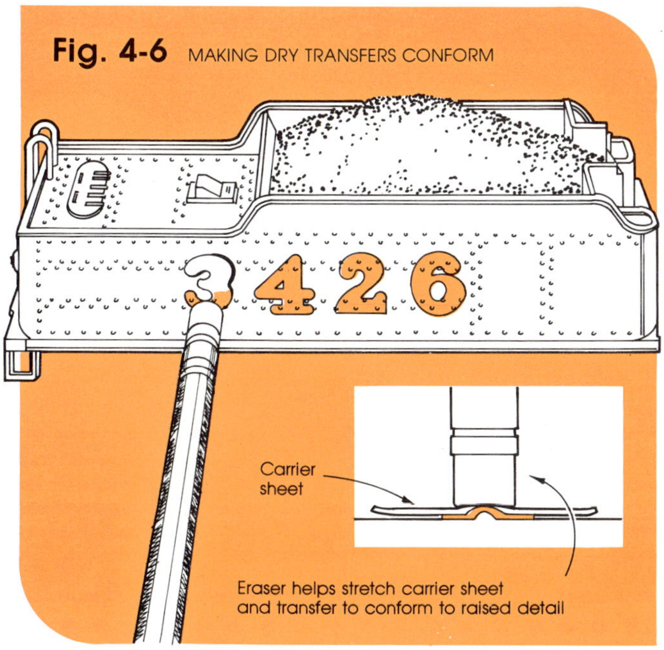

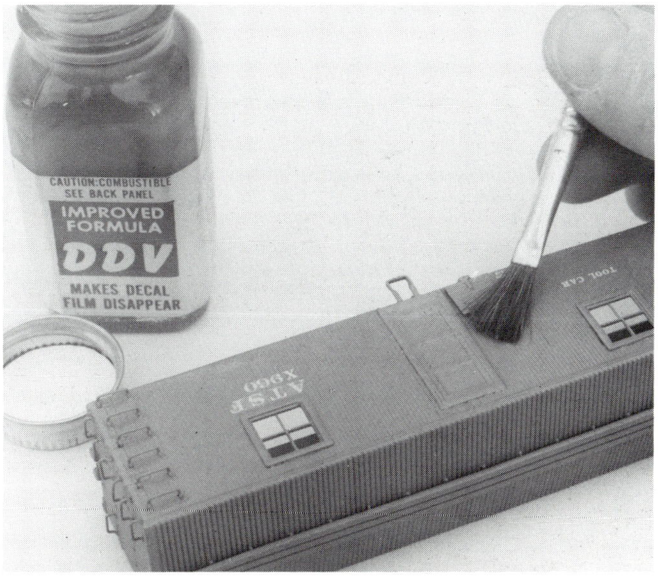

A thin coat of clear flat finish applied over decals and the areas around them helps to hide the decal film.

overcoat of clear flat finish. This gives all parts of your model the same overall tone, "homogenizing" the appearance of the paint, decal, and dry-transfer finishes. The most dramatic improvement made by flat finish is in disguising decal film. Clear finish also acts as an anti-abrasive coating to keep paint from wearing off models that are handled frequently.

Dry transfers don't need flat finish as shine-killer, but they do need the protection. If you don't protect them, they will collect dust and dirt. Their surface has just enough waxy residue from the carrier sheet to retain dirt, and it can't be wiped away or cleaned off without destroying the lettering. Some clear overcoats attack certain types of transfers, so test the clear finish on a spare transfer, and read and heed the dry-transfer manufacturer's instructions and cautions.

Spraying—either with an aerosol can or an airbrush—is the best way to apply any clear finish because you need a thin, uniform coating for the clear finish to properly do its job. Dust on the spray almost dry so there is little chance for the solvent in the finish to damage the decal film, dry-transfer lettering, or underlying paint coats. If you use a spray can, hold the can 18 to 24 inches from the model and mist on the finish with three to six passes until the surface is covered with a smooth, even layer.

Getting the most out of lettering sets. Several decal manufacturers offer custom decal service; they will make up special sets with your road name and herald. This service is not inexpensive, but neither is it so costly that you shouldn't write for the particulars, especially if you expect to letter a lot of equipment for your own road. However, you don't need custom lettering sets to have equipment lettered for your own line on your layout.

You can "scratchbuild" your own decals, using decal alphabet sets—individual letters—or decal words. Champion Decal Co. offers a large number of ready-made words that can be combined to make up your own road name—words such as "Yukon" and "Central" and "Railroad" and "Railway" etc.—there's a long list. Or, you can use standard railroad sets and rearrange the words to suit. Consider a road name like "Pacific Southern" made out of "Southern Pacific." Thousands of

Dry transfers require clear coating. Hold the can so the spray is almost dry when it reaches the model.

A modern billboard car

A. The colorful billboard-side private-owner cars of the early 20th century were outlawed, but today's railroads splash colorful heralds across their equipment. This UP "Big Herald" car is made by adding Champ decals to an undecorated Athearn HO 50-foot plug-door box car.

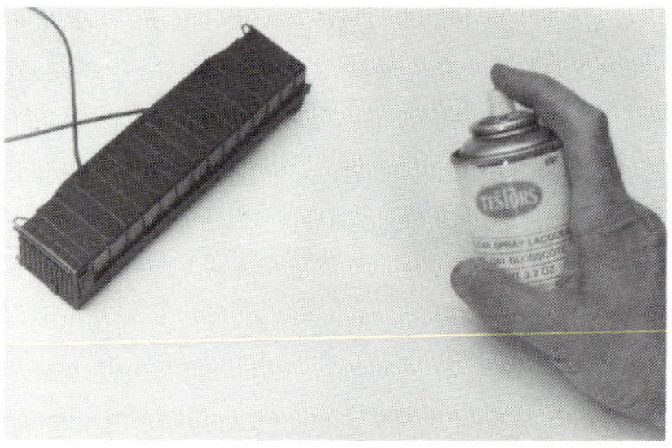

B. The first step is to paint the carbody boxcar red. If you use flat-finish paint, it must be oversprayed lightly with clear gloss to seal the microscopic roughness of the finish. It's almost impossible to get decals to adhere properly if you apply them directly over flat paint.

C. When the decal adhesive has softened enough that it can be moved on its backing paper, position the decal and backing on the car. Pre-wet the area where the decal will go with decal setting fluid. Hold the decal with your knife tip while you pull the backing out from underneath it with tweezers.

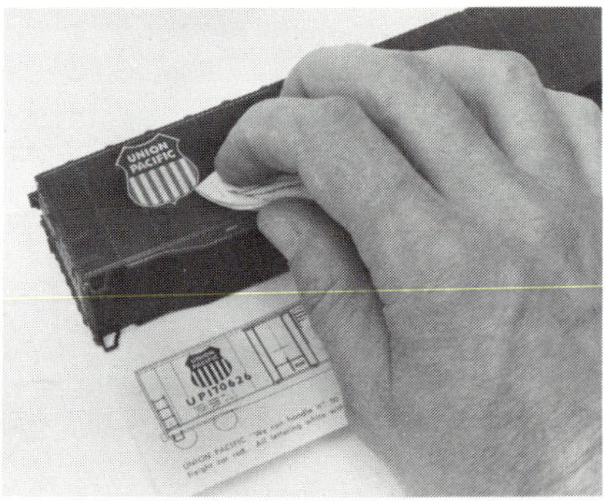

D. If there's so much water and decal setting fluid on the car that the decal floats, use a tissue or paper towel to soak up the excess, but be careful not to touch the decal.

similar rearrangements are possible.

Sometimes certain parts of an HO locomotive set will work almost perfectly for an N scale car, or O scale freight car decals can be used for signs in the smaller scales. Suppose you want to letter a certain type of covered hopper from your favorite prototype pike, but no decal set is available. Combine the dimensional data from a decal set for the hopper car (but for another road) with the herald, railroad name, and reporting marks from a *boxcar* set for your favorite road, add some dry-transfer numbers, and you have the car you want! In the same vein, passenger car decal sets can furnish the starting point for lettering a diesel.

Finally, remember that no one material is best for all lettering jobs, or even for all the lettering on a single model. Try to remain open to the idea of using a mix of decals and dry transfers, taking advantage of the special qualities of each to improve the overall quality of your models.

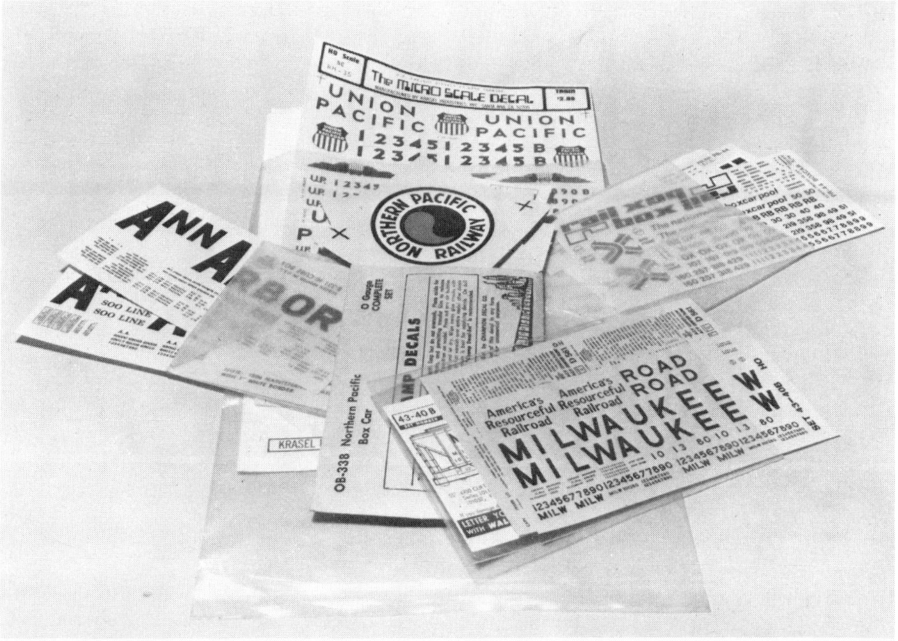

Once you've mastered decals and dry transfers every set represents a challenge.

E. When the decal is positioned according to the lettering diagram, apply enough decal setting solution to cover the decal. Leave this alone until it evaporates completely.

F. When all the decal-softening fluid has evaporated and the decal is dry, there will probably be white spots on the decal, indicating trapped air. Punch through these with a sharp hobby knife blade and gently dab the area with a facial tissue wrapped around the end of your finger to press the decal down. Then make a second application of fluid.

G. Hold the car so the reflection will show whether the decal has conformed to rivets and seam lines. It may take as many as a dozen applications of decal setting fluid, allowing each to dry before applying the next, to get certain decals to snuggle down on complex surfaces.

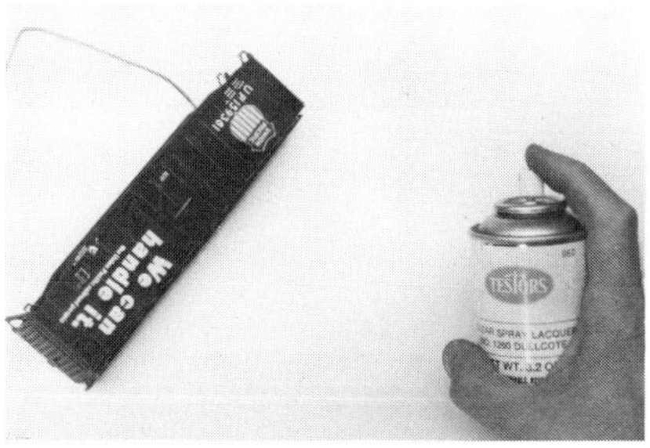

H. When the decal setting fluid applications are completed, gently scrub the car with a Q-tip dipped in warm water to remove traces of decal adhesive residue. Let the car dry overnight, then apply a thin coat of clear flat finish to kill the decal gloss and blend the edges of the decal film into the car finish.

I. The completed car is an eye stopper, and, more important, it's a car you're not likely to see on your neighbor's layout!

Basic kitbashing

Converting, crosskitting, or customizing plastic models is easy, once you understand the fundamentals.

THE EARLY CHAPTERS of this book have concentrated on techniques for assembling and finishing plastic models. Now it's time to discover how a basic model can be modified into something entirely different from what its manufacturer intended. Most of the basics of plastic kitbashing are covered in this chapter, and more specialized techniques are discussed later under the heading of Advanced Kitbashing (Chapter 10). You'll want to master basics first, then learn special techniques applicable to rolling stock, locomotives, and structures, and, finally, apply what you've learned to your own modeling projects.

Simply defined, *kitbashing* is the practice of modifying and combining kit parts to make models unlike the original kits. In practice, this definition extends to modifying ready-to-run models as well. Using pieces from existing models makes the task of building a custom version easier and quicker, so more modelers can have above-average models on their pikes without developing the skill levels of master craftsmen.

Kitbashing projects can be either simple or complex. At the simple end, you can "modernize" box cars by removing roof walks and full-height ladders to comply with post-1966 railroad safety standards—a conversion you'll find on many prototype cars. At the complex end, the sky's the limit. Sprawling industrial complexes, customized unit trains, and extensive engine servicing facilities are just a few of the larger projects made possible by the comparative ease of kitbashing.

Once you train yourself to visualize single parts instead of complete models, you'll find a window in one kit, a door and wall in another, and a platform in another that can be used to build the structure you want. Similarly, details, domes, superstructures, and mechanisms from one steam locomotive model can be used to modify another. Grills, vents, and louvers from inexpensive plastic diesel bodies can be pirated to build a one-of-a-kind model. Windows, doors, and complete sections of passenger and freight cars can be spliced together to reproduce the shape and arrangement of prototype equipment not offered in kit form. Once all the parts are properly fitted, the model can be painted, decaled, and weathered to disguise its piecemeal ancestry. When the dust has settled, you have the satisfaction of knowing that your kitbashed model is as unique as if you had built it from scratch.

The first cut is the hardest. Taking a perfectly good out-of-the-box plastic model and tearing into it with saws, files, and drills to make it "better" seems hard at first, but once you get into the swing of it, it's a rewarding process, and the possibilities are unlimited. Don't be afraid to make a few mistakes. Modelbuilding mistakes are not fatal—either to you or the model—and if you don't point them out, most slips will never be noticed, even by close observers.

There are enough different plastic model railroad items available that parts can be cannibalized from them to become pieces of almost any type of model. As you read this book and work with plastic models, learn to look at them as *collections of parts* that you can

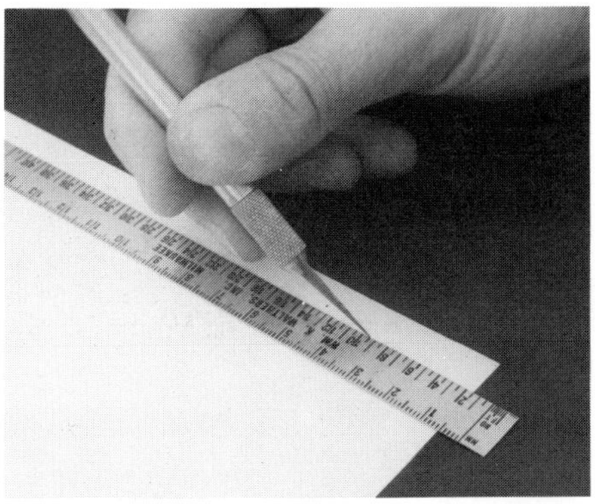

Plastic thinner than $1/32''$ can be cut with a knife, using a steel rule as a guide. Thick material should be scored and broken or cut with a saw.

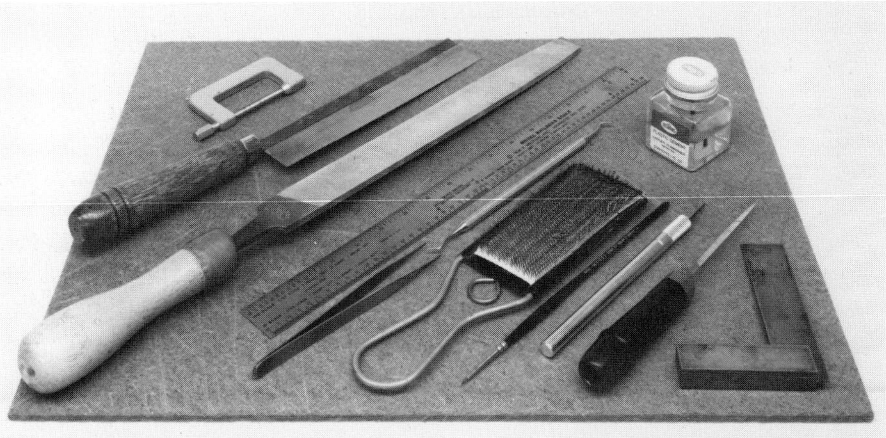

Tools for kitbashing (left to right): C-clamp, razor saw, mill file, scale ruler, tweezers, scriber (made from dental tool), file card, liquid cement, No. 000 brush, knife, needle file, and machinist's square.

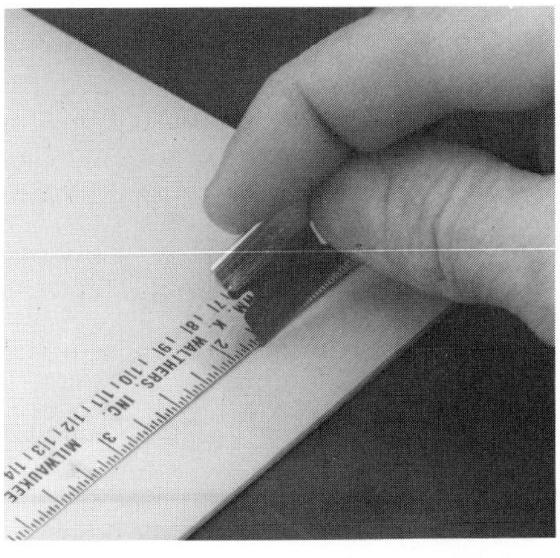

To cut heavy stock, make several light passes over the line with a single-edge razor blade, then break the material by bending it over an edge.

draw upon to build whatever locomotives, rolling stock, and structures you want. Nor does kitbashing limit your materials to parts and pieces from kits or ready-built models. Several firms sell plain sheet styrene and ABS in a variety of thicknesses ranging from .010″ to .100″. You can also purchase plastic sheets that have brick, stone, shingle, corrugated metal, and other textures molded in, precut strips of varying thicknesses and widths, tubes and rods, and structural shapes such as I, H, and T beams. There are hundreds of detail and trim parts available in all scales—windows, doors, tanks, downspouts, railings, stairs, and so on. Metal parts such as wire grab irons and locomotive details can be used on your plastic projects, too.

Plastic-working operations. The techniques you'll use to rework the parts of a plastic kit or ready-built model are the same ones you would use to scratchbuild models from raw plastic sheet, strip, and shape stock. Only a very fine line separates what modelers call scratchbuilding from detailing, conversion, crosskitting, and kitbashing. Every plastic-working operation is best practiced on scrap or the back of a part before moving on to the piece that will be part of the finished model.

Scissors are suitable for cutting very thin plastic sheet stock, but their shearing action tends to curl and distort the plastic. Plastic sheet thinner than 1/32″ can be cut with a sharp hobby knife. You must use a steel straightedge or rule to guide the knife blade. The cut will be straighter if you make it with several light passes rather than one heavy cut.

Thicker flat plastic sections can be cut using the score-and-break method. The plastic is scored on one side along the desired break line, then held in a vise or over the edge of the workbench and bent away from the score mark. A few strokes with a file will true up the edge. It's best to make the first cut with the sharp edge of the hobby knife blade, but the second stroke should be made with the *back* edge of the hobby knife. This will deepen and widen the score mark by removing a chip of material. It will also raise a small burr along the broken edge, fig. 5-1, that must be removed later with a file or sanding block.

Cutting thin styrene strip stock is easy if you use a single-edge razor blade in a guillotine-like manner. Razor blades are also handy for cutting off thin sections of parts neatly, such as slicing away the overly wide trim boards on plastic structure windows so the windows can set into the walls. Use a sharp blade, and change to a new one every time you feel it getting hard to push through the plastic.

Cutting structural shapes is easy with either a razor blade—for the thinner sections—or a razor saw—for the thicker pieces. Use scrap stripwood inserts to prevent the web and flanges of the structural shape from distorting and collapsing, fig. 5-2, and use a miter box or vise to hold the wood-and-plastic sandwich together while you cut.

Cutting operations using saws. Most "surgery" on large kit parts is done with saws. Their use is described in the Toolbox on page 40; we'll discuss here the operations you'll be performing with them.

There are several ways to make an opening for a new window or door. One method is to lay out the hole, drill several small holes within the area, and cut away the connecting bits of plastic, finishing up with files, figs. 5-3 and 5-4. A similar method is to scribe the outline of the opening, score a heavy "X" from corner to corner, and break out the triangular pieces.

Cutting a notch in a plastic wall for a new door is a three-step process. Carefully lay out the opening—a bit undersize is always recommended—and slice through the two vertical lines with the razor saw. Score the top line heavily with two or three passes of the hobby knife guided by the ruler; score on both sides, but don't try to force the blade completely through. Finally, snap the notch out, holding the wall with flat-nosed pliers. The plastic will break cleanly along the scribed line, much like glass. File the edges of the opening smooth.

To make a major cut on a carbody shell, start by determining exactly where the cut will be made. When possible, use some cast-in feature of the

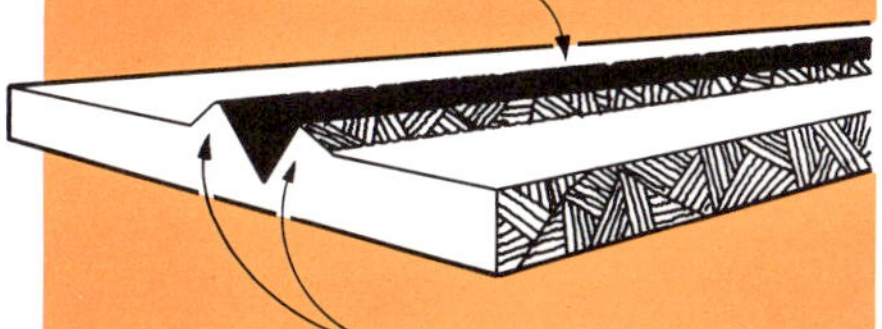

Fig. 5-1

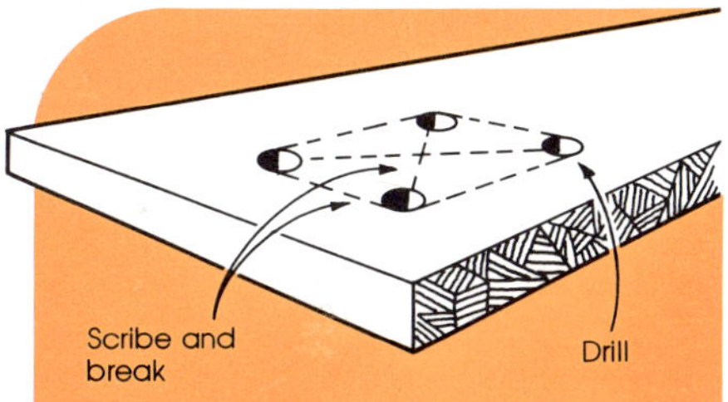

Fig. 5-3 CUTTING RECTANGULAR OPENINGS

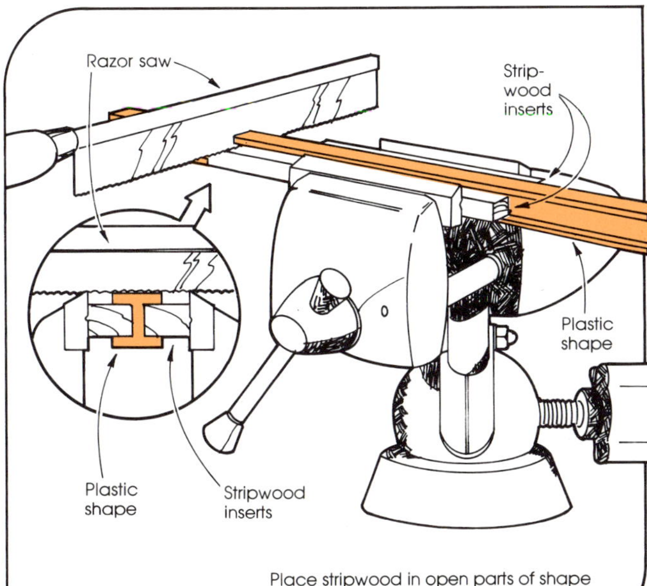

Fig. 5-2 Place stripwood in open parts of shape to prevent distortion when cutting

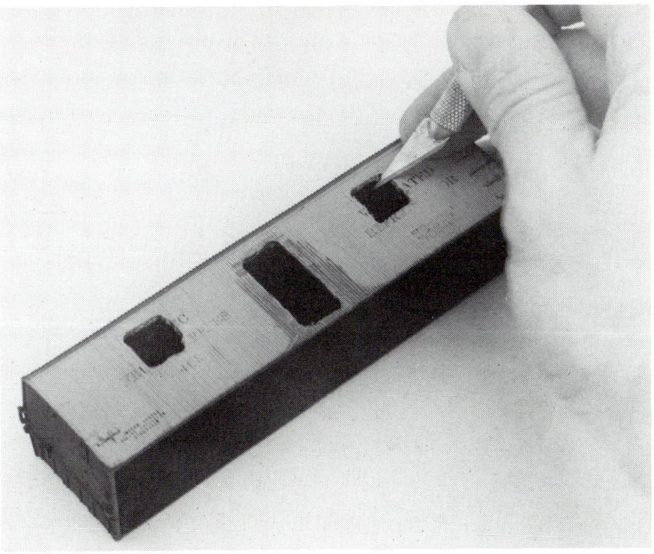

Fig. 5-4. Cut new openings for windows or doors by drilling several holes within the layout lines and shaving away material slowly until you reach the lines.

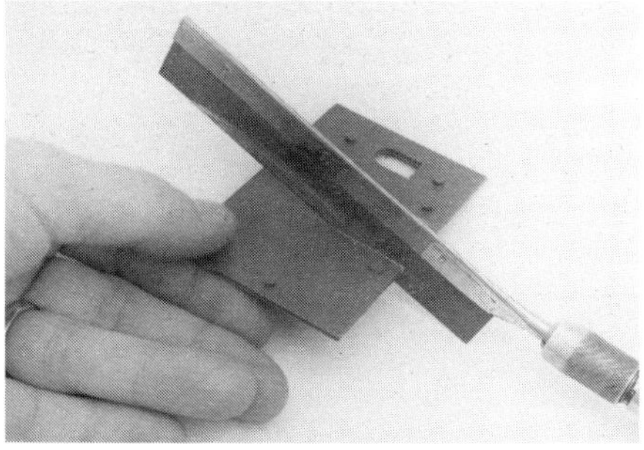
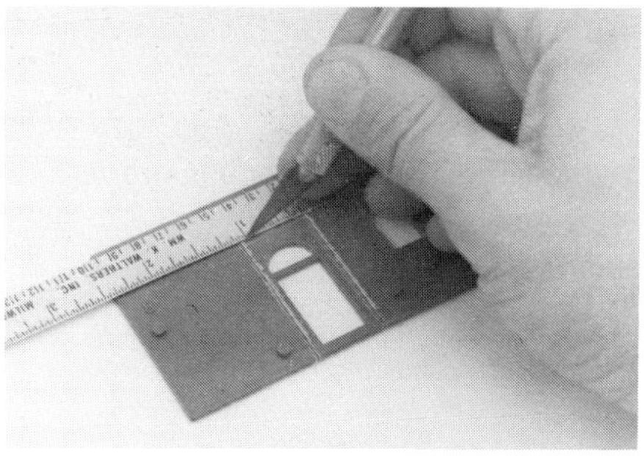

Start a notch for a new door in a plastic wall by first slicing along the vertical edges with a razor saw. Then heavily score the top edge of the opening on both sides with a knife, but don't try to force the blade completely through. Finally, snap out the section with gentle finger pressure while holding the wall with pliers.

model such as a rivet line or sheathing panel seam as a guide for sawing and sectioning. Be sure your plan of attack allows for the width of the saw kerf. To protect the portion of the shell that will be used, place masking tape over it at the location of the saw cut. Be careful in placing the masking tape because you'll be using it as a visual guide during the cutting operation. Where clear sections must be cut, cover the entire part in the vicinity of the cut with masking tape as protection against scratches, and cut right through the tape.

The tricky part of sawing molded body sections is that they lose some of their strength as you slice through the roof, floor, and sides. This can cause alignment problems. Try inserting the car or locomotive frame during part of the cut, or make a wood insert to keep the body shell from flexing. Another handy trick to ensure your saw cuts are at right angles to the top or bottom of a carbody or wall is to C-clamp a small machinist's square to the work to use as a sawing guide.

Removing unwanted detail. Detail removal can be as simple as scraping away rivets to represent more modern all-welded construction. Parts such as marker lights, sand hatches, bells, and so on can often be trimmed off and saved for reuse. Small items can be shaved or sliced away with a sharp hobby knife. Always use several thin slicing cuts instead of a single heavy one—the end results will be neater. The No. 17 and 18 knife blades, those with the cutting edge across the front of the blade at a right angle to the axis of the handle, are indispensable in this application. These blades can also be ground narrower for special jobs where the full width of the blade would remove detail that you want to save.

Some detail is best scraped away with the knife blade held perpendicular to the model surface. This is particularly effective in removing corrugations on passenger car sides to achieve smooth areas.

Removing unwanted detail is a three-step process. First, use a knife, razor blade, or other sharp instrument to *carefully* slice away the offending projections. Carefully means bit-by-bit and slowly—not slipping, not slicing away desirable detail, and not digging into the surface. Next, use No. 600 wet-or-dry sandpaper to sand away the remaining traces of the removed part. This may involve making a special sanding block just for the job, or wrapping the paper around a tool handle to fit the application.

The third step is to restore seams, joints, or detail lines that would logically continue through the removed detail. This is particularly important in the case of scribed siding when removing and replacing cast-in grabs, but it is a step you should consider whatever the surface texture. To restore complex textures, you can grind a chisel point on a length of tool steel or old screwdriver to make special tools for special jobs such as scraping corrugations to match other areas on a car side.

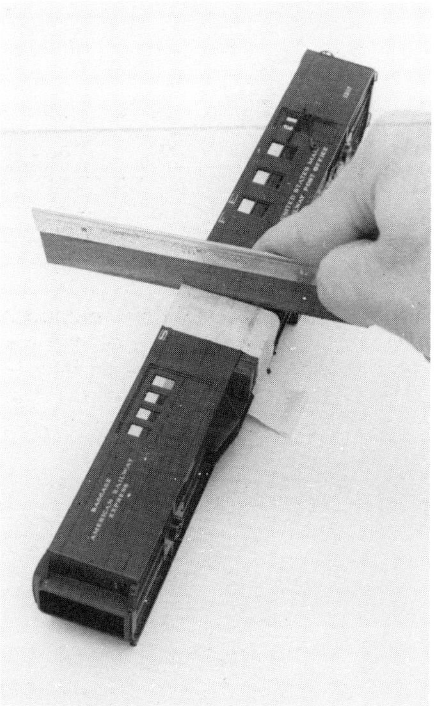

Plan important cuts using masking tape. Leave the tape in place as a cutting guide and as protection for the part.

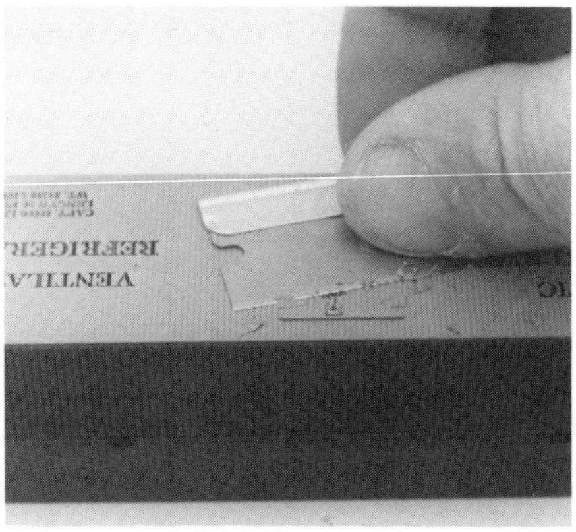
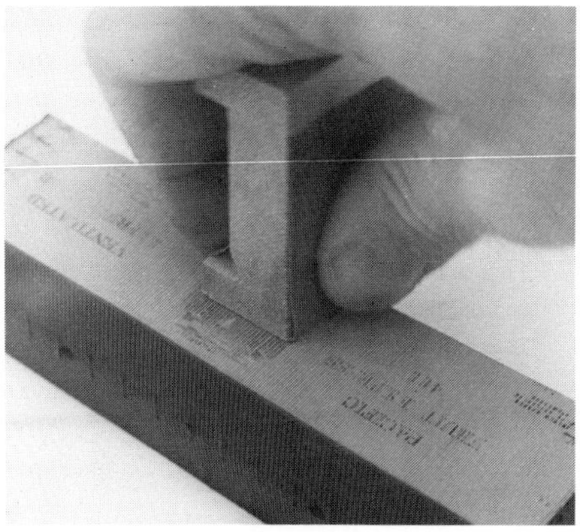

Use a sharp single-edge razor blade to slice away unwanted detail on a flat surface, then shift to No. 600 sandpaper to remove the last traces.

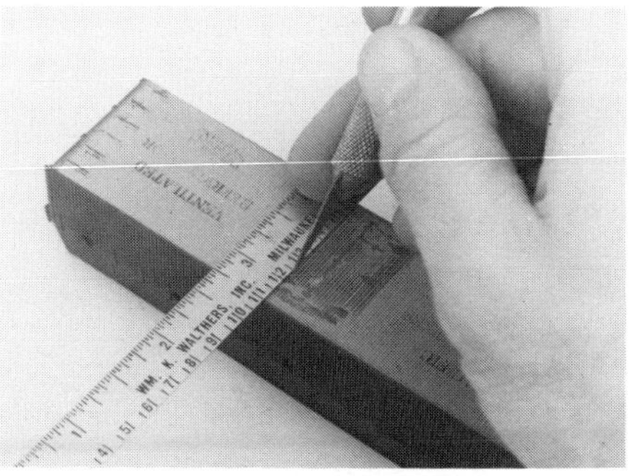

Restoring the texture beneath the removed item is the final step in removing unwanted detail. Here, siding grooves are being added where the reefer door detail has been deleted.

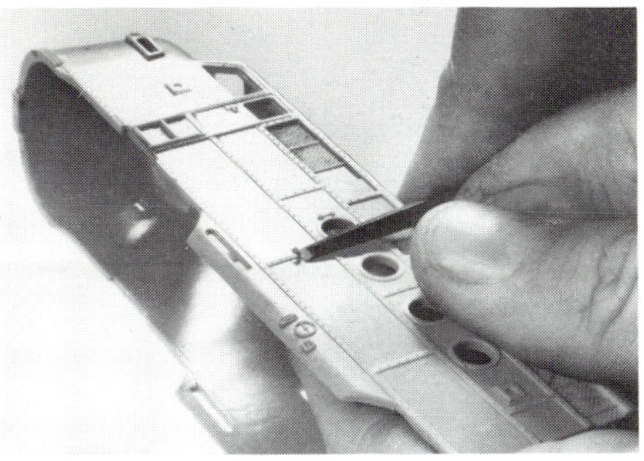

A small chisel tip ground on an old needle file is handy for neatly removing unwanted detail. See fig. 5-9.

A narrow chisel tip has been ground on this dental tool for restoring grooves. Here it's being used to clean out a line that was filled with putty.

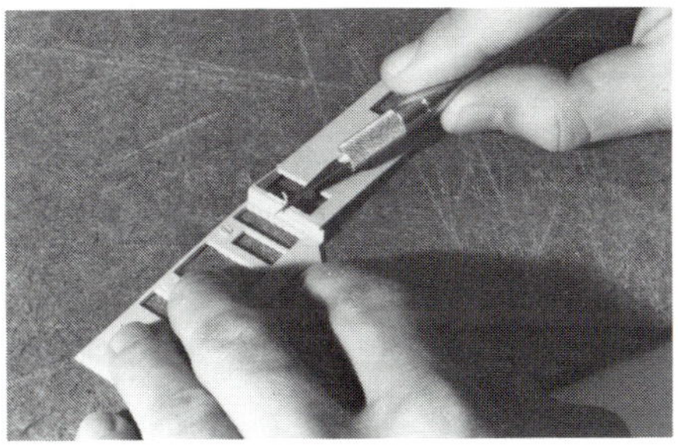

Removing cast-on alignment lugs and pins is often necessary in kitbashing projects. It can also frequently help in straightforward kit assembly.

Other things to consider while removing unwanted detail are the positioning pins and lugs on the rear surfaces of some parts. In many cases, you'll be able to do a neater job of assembly if you pare these away and use a machinist's square, a flat surface, and your eyeball for alignment.

Plugging unwanted holes. Often, you'll find holes where you don't want them—an example is a rectangular slot intended to accept a lug from a mating part in the face of a wall. To plug such a hole, whittle a piece of sprue to wedge in the hole, cement, clip off, and trim flush, fig. 5-5. Where the hole is an odd shape, consider drilling the hole to make it round, then plugging with sprue. This plug-and-trim method is much easier than filling holes with putty, since putty tends to shrink and usually requires two or more applications.

Window and door replacement and removal are essential kitbashing techniques. Often, it's easier to cut around the window or door trim and patch a larger area, especially where the trim would be hard to rework, fill, or disguise. The basic job is to open the hole to a convenient size and shape, make and install a plug, and finish the plug to look like the rest of the car or structure side. Plugs are easiest to make if the hole is square or rectangular, so open circular or rounded-corner windows with a file to give them right-angle corners.

To make a plug, hold the material behind the opening to be filled and trace the outline onto the stock with a needlepoint scriber. Then cut the plug about 1/64" oversize all around and file until it is a press fit in the hole. Align the plug surface flush with the side and cement. Fill the edge joints with putty and let dry.

Fig. 5-5 FILLING AN UNWANTED HOLE

Wrap No. 600 wet-or-dry sandpaper around a piece of hardwood to make a small sanding block. It's a good idea to keep several sizes of hardwood block on hand so you can custom-make sanding

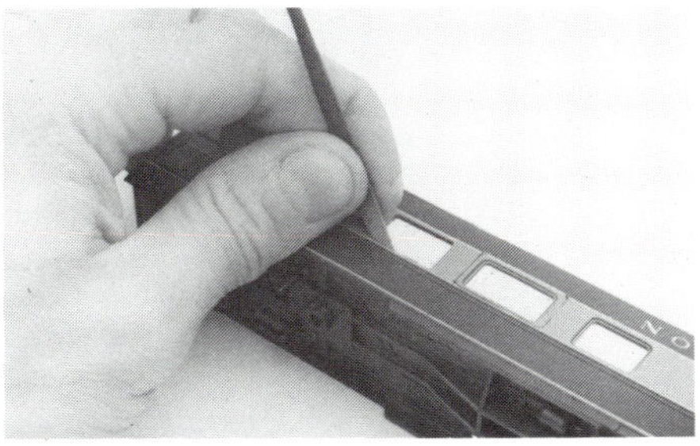

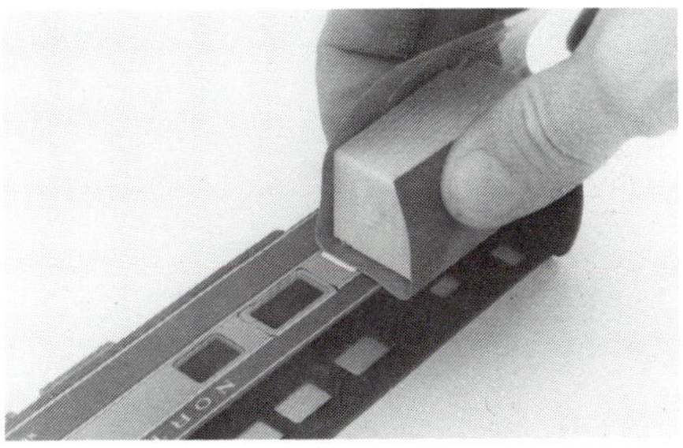

Sometimes, plugging a window or door opening involves first making it larger. These windows include a recess that is difficult to fill with putty. We'll enlarge the window hole and square off the corners to make it easier to fit a plug. After cutting out the plug and filing it to fit, cement it in place. Make sure it is flush with the surface of the model, and allow it to dry overnight before continuing. To ensure the plug doesn't stick out past the surrounding material, sand the surface before adding putty.

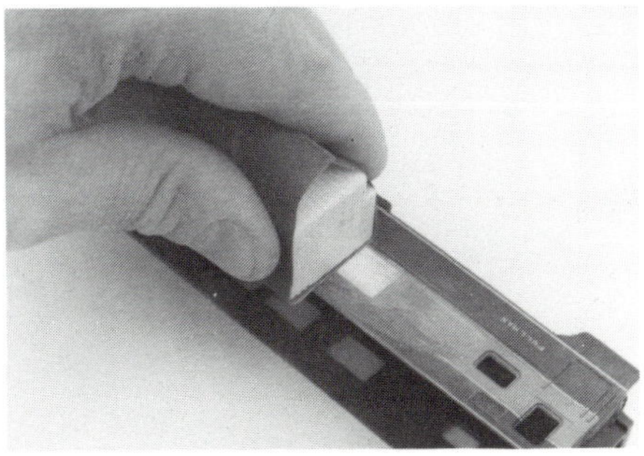

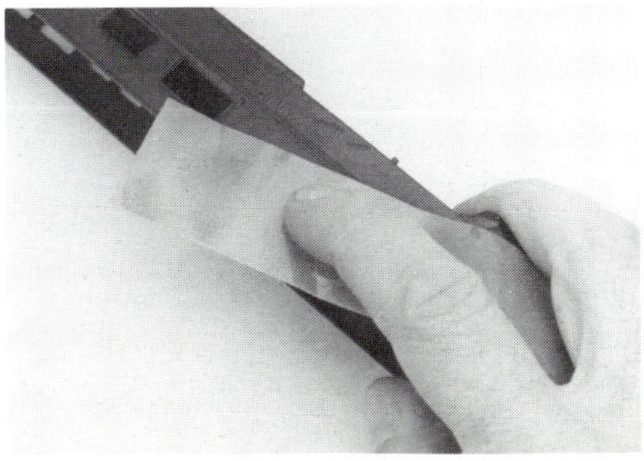

Spread putty around the edges of the plug, working it into the seam. If the plug is recessed slightly, coat the surface as well. When the putty has dried completely sand until the plug is flush. A coat of primer followed by careful wet-sanding with No. 600 wet-or-dry sandpaper made this car side appear as if the plugged window had never been there.

Saws for plastic

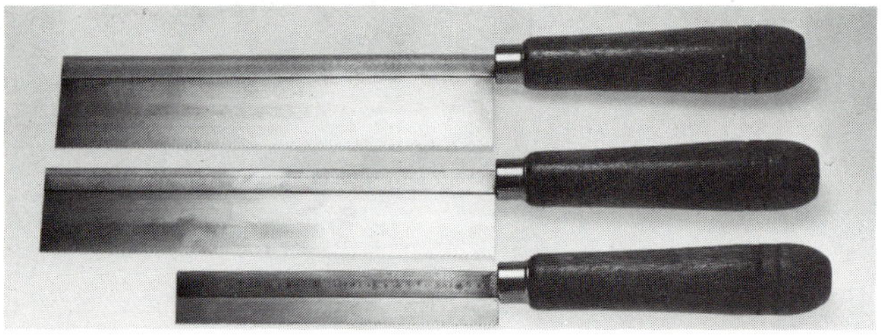

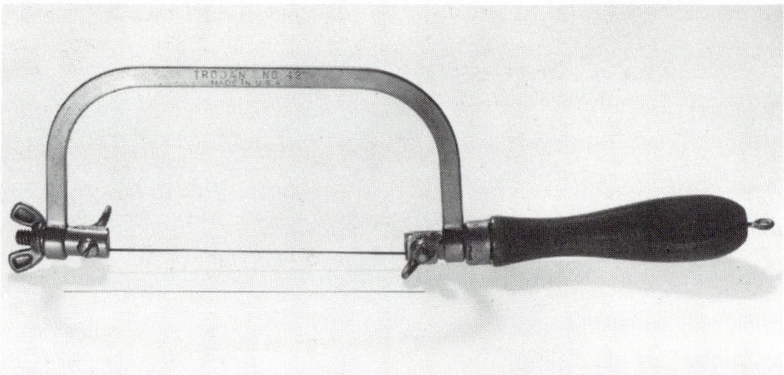

SEVERAL types of thin-bladed saws are suitable for working with plastic, and the first thing you should know is which to choose for a certain job. The **razor saw** is best for straight cutting such as sectioning locomotive or car shells or sawing structure walls. Where curves, corners, or openings are required, a **jeweler's saw** is the necessary tool. Where heavy stock such as laminated blocks must be cut, a **hacksaw** is best.

All saws cut by removing material with a series of chisel teeth. These teeth, and the blade on which they are mounted, are designed for either push or pull (draw) strokes, but not both. Saw teeth are bent slightly to either side of the axis of the blade. This bending is called setting. Setting allows the saw teeth to eject material from the cut and provides clearance for the body of the blade. The kerf is the width of the sawcut slot. You must always allow for losing the amount of material in the kerf when planning cuts.

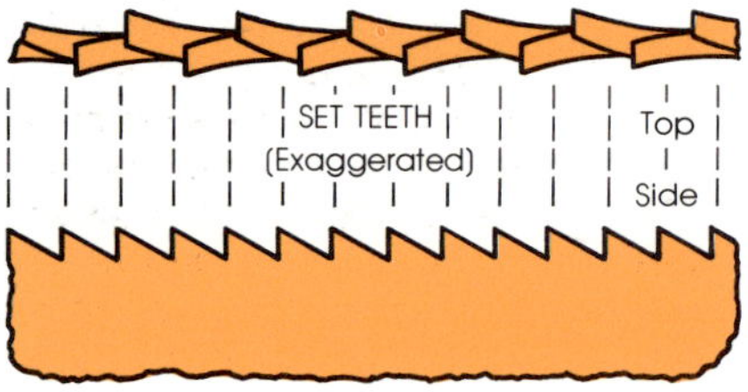

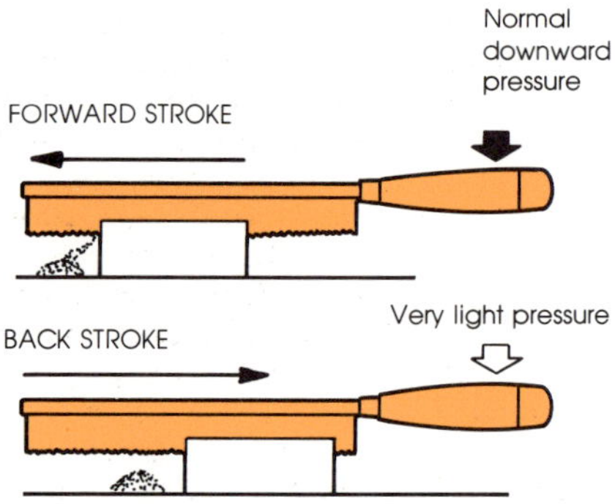

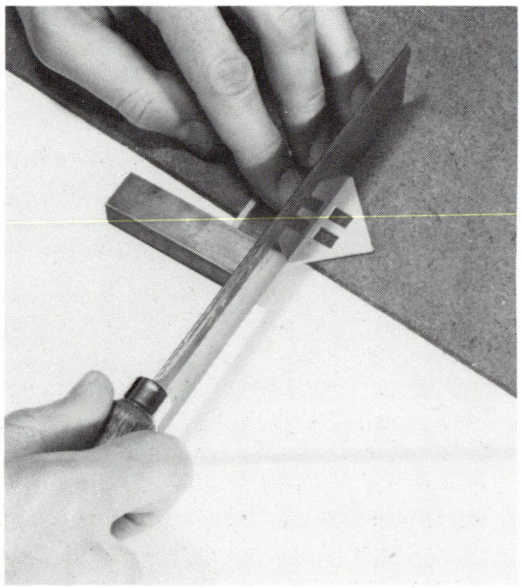

The chief problem when using any thin-bladed saw is keeping the cut straight and even. Usually, you'll cut away from your layout line and use files to remove material up to the line. For greatest blade life, try to use all the teeth of the saw. This is best accomplished by long, slow strokes. It is hard to control direction of the cut when sawing fast, and short strokes wear out the teeth in the center of the blade, rendering it useless in a short time.

RAZOR SAWS

A razor saw isn't the only kind of saw you should own, although it's the first one you should buy. A razor saw is actually a small, fine-tooth backsaw. Most are 8″ to 9″ long with about 4½″ of cutting edge. Most have 30 to 42 teeth per inch. The teeth point forward – away from the handle – and cutting action occurs on the push stroke.

Razor saw blades are very thin – about .010″ – and have a U-shaped metal channel along the back edge to stiffen them. This stiffener limits the cutting depth of the blade. Where the material to be cut allows, use the shallow blade to take advantage of its stiffness.

Smooth, accurate cuts with a razor saw require cutting with the blade parallel to the surface of the material. Hold the saw securely, placing your thumb along the axis of the blade. Use slow strokes so you can control the direction of the cut and the angle of the blade to the work. Ease the pressure on the return stroke so the teeth are not dulled. Start the cut with a single backstroke while carefully guiding the blade with the thumb of the hand that is not holding the saw. The tip of the thumb should contact the blade midway up, away from the teeth. A 3″ machinist's square can be used to guide cuts through plastic carbodies and structure walls. Position the square on the work, and hold the saw blade against it. Make a few light cuts to start an accurate slot, then remove the square to finish the cut.

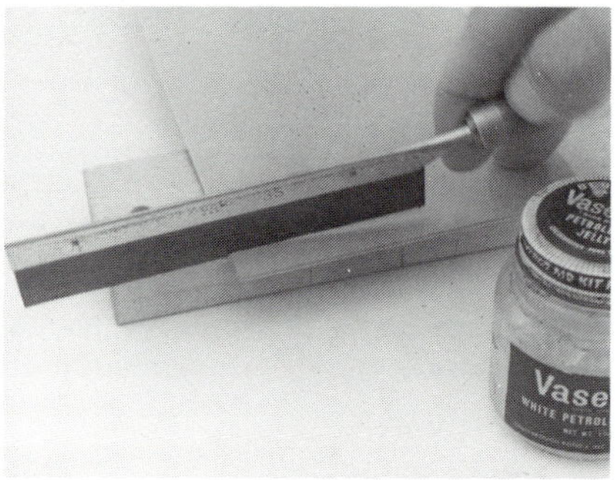

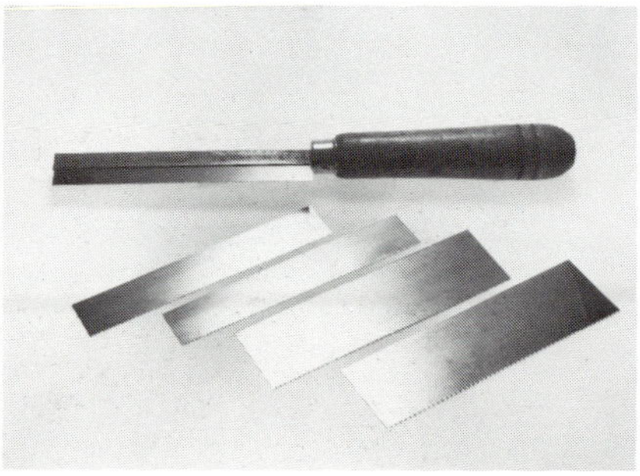

You can cut through heavy plastic sections smoothly if you lubricate your razor saw with Vaseline. Work slowly; excess heat causes plastic to soften and turn gummy. If nothing else is available, soap is a good lubricant. Wash the material thoroughly with detergent to remove all traces of lubricant before priming and painting.

The blades on Zona-brand saws are replaceable. Pry the old blade out of the backing with pliers. To install a new blade, insert one corner into the slot in the backing and set the teeth of the blade on a softwood block. Then, push down on the backing.

JEWELER'S SAWS

The jeweler's saw has a C-shaped frame with clamps to hold each end of its thin, narrow blade. It is a pull, or draw, tool. The teeth should point toward the handle. The big advantage of the jeweler's saw is that the blade can turn while sawing. This means you can make nearly right-angle cuts. Openings can be made by drilling a hole, disconnecting one end of the saw blade, inserting it through the hole, and reassembling the saw. The depth of such an interior cut is limited by the depth of the saw frame. The blade clamps can be turned in their sockets so the saw can cut sideways or backwards.

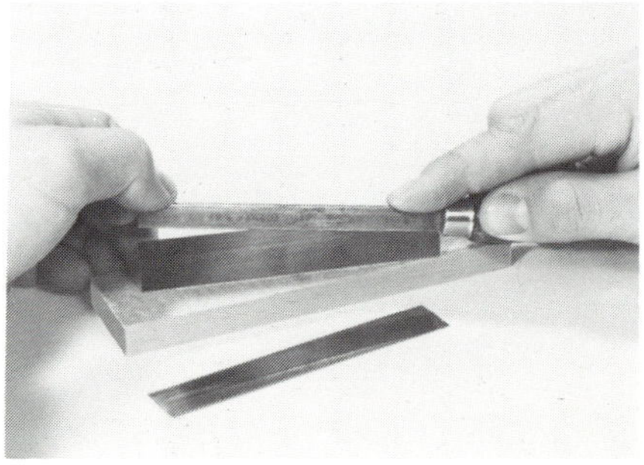

The thinner the material, the greater the number of saw teeth per inch required to make a smooth cut. The following sizes are applicable to modelwork:

Grade	Number of teeth per inch	Width	Height
8/0	81	.006"	.013"
6/0	76	.007"	.014"
4/0	68	.009"	.017"
1	51	.012"	.024"
4	36	.015"	.030"
6	32	.018"	.036"

The blade must be both straight and taut or it will break. Secure the front end of the blade in the frame, secure the rear end, and pull the frame tight to stretch the blade. Turn the frame tension screw or twist the handle to place the blade and frame under tension. There should be no twist in the blade, and the blade should be parallel to the frame. If it isn't, release the tension and start over. The blade should be tight enough to produce a musical note when plucked. Blade tension should be relaxed when the tool is not in use.

To saw, start with the handle close to the work, and draw the saw straight down, using the full length of the blade. Apply just enough pressure to make the teeth cut; the blades are brittle and easily broken. Relieve the pressure against the work on the upstroke. Work slowly, because rapid strokes heat the blade, causing the plastic to melt, gum, jam, and break the blade.

A board with a V-slot that can be clamped to the edge of your workbench or held in a vise is a helpful sawing aid. The V-slot provides clearance for the blade while supporting thin stock. This fixture can be made easily of wood; the dimensions are not critical.

HACKSAWS

Don't hesitate to use a hacksaw for cutting thick plastic. The teeth in a hacksaw point forward, and cutting is accomplished on the forward stroke. Cutting should be done on a downward angle to provide maximum cutting action on a small area. A blade with 32 teeth per inch will cut plastic smoothly if you work slowly; a blade with fewer teeth will allow faster cutting but will produce a ragged edge.

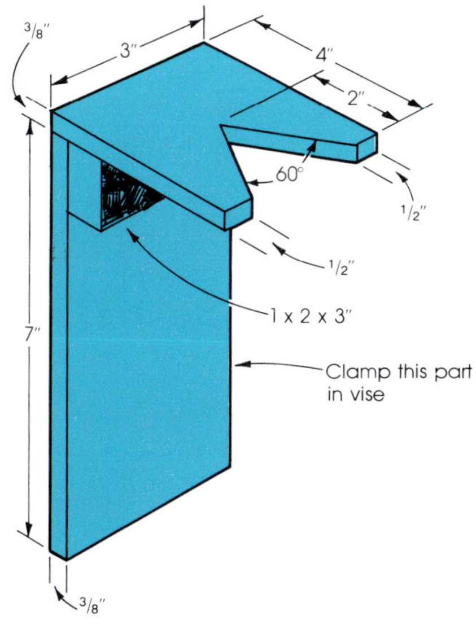

Dimensions are not critical

V-cutting board for jeweler's saw

SAFETY AND STORAGE

Always use a vise or clamp to hold the work when sawing — don't risk you fingers. If the material is free to vibrate, the sawing effort will be inefficient and the cut will be ragged and irregular. Hold and guide the saw so that a slip won't result in the blade running across your fingers.

Saws do get dull, especially if you use them for cutting rail or other metal. It's best to have at least one razor saw labeled "for plastic only" and another for all other work. A dull blade is more difficult to control because it requires more muscle to force it through the work.

Store your saws where nothing will come in contact with the teeth to distort or dull them, and where they will not rust due to moisture in the air. For top efficiency and safety in all your sawing, follow these three simple rules:

- Use sharp saw blades
- Use the right saw for the job
- Work slowly, and use long strokes to utilize the full length of the blade.

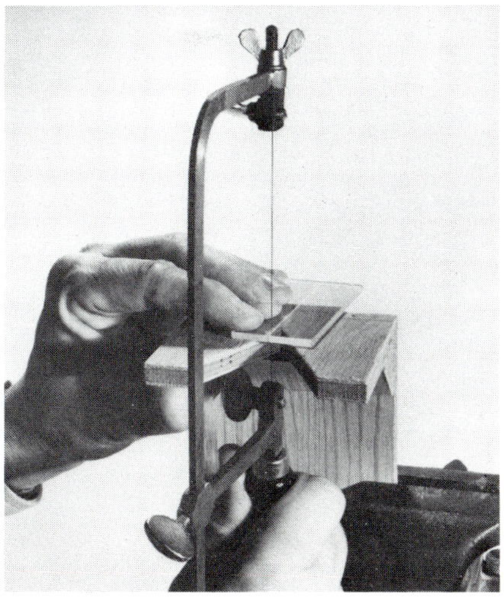

Hold hacksaw at angle to provide maximum cutting action in a small area

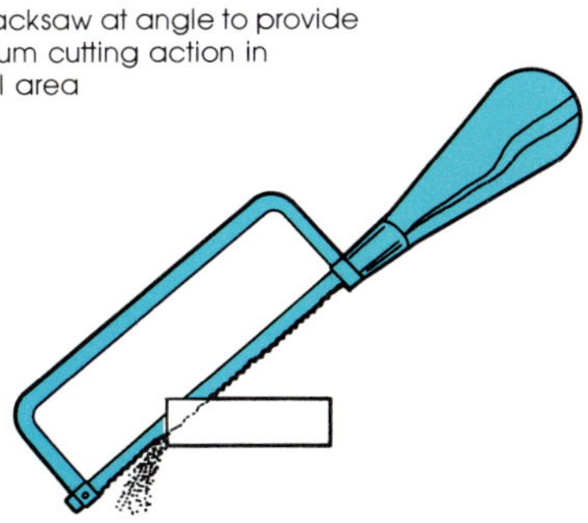

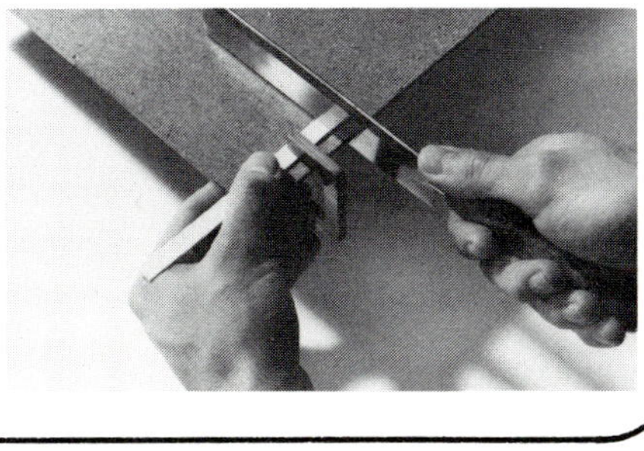

Properly handled, a ready-built structure can yield walls, roof, and a surprising number of excellent detail parts suitable for kitbashing.

blocks that are wide enough to make smooth, flat surfaces, but narrow enough that you don't accidentally sand away rib or rivet detail. Sand carefully so adjacent detail is not marred.

To finish a smooth-textured plugged hole, wash away all grit and sanding residue, wipe dry, and spray paint the plugged area. If the seam around the plug remains visible, you may have to apply additional filler putty or sand the primed surface and apply a second primer coat. Careful sanding with No. 600 wet-or-dry sandpaper and willingness on your part to keep priming and sanding until the job is right can make a plugged area appear as though the missing window were never there at all.

Disassembling built-up models. Certain models are only available in built-up or ready-to-run form, so we'll need to know some disassembly techniques. The most important step is to examine the model to find out how it was assembled. If there is a sheet of servicing instructions, a parts list, or a diagram, study it. Examine the model under a strong light to figure out how it's held together. Some models are almost entirely snapped together and will come apart with gentle prying or by spreading the body shell to allow the underframe and roof retaining lugs to unseat. Look for screws, lugs, and clips that can be depressed or squeezed together. Take your time. When working with clear parts, push on them with a dowel or Popsicle stick to avoid scratches.

Glue joints can be softened by lightly cutting along the joint with the tip of your hobby knife, then applying liquid plastic cement to "unweld" the joint. Brush the cement along the glue joint or squirt it on with a needlepoint applicator. Let the cement work its way into the joints, then try to force a hobby knife into the joint with *light* pressure. If the knife won't go, apply more cement, wait, and try again. You may need two or three applications of cement before the joint is softened enough to cut into it. When it's softened, pry the joint apart with a screwdriver—don't try to

Make several applications of liquid cement to all exposed joints. Some parts will separate easily, but often it will take over an hour for the cement to penetrate the joints.

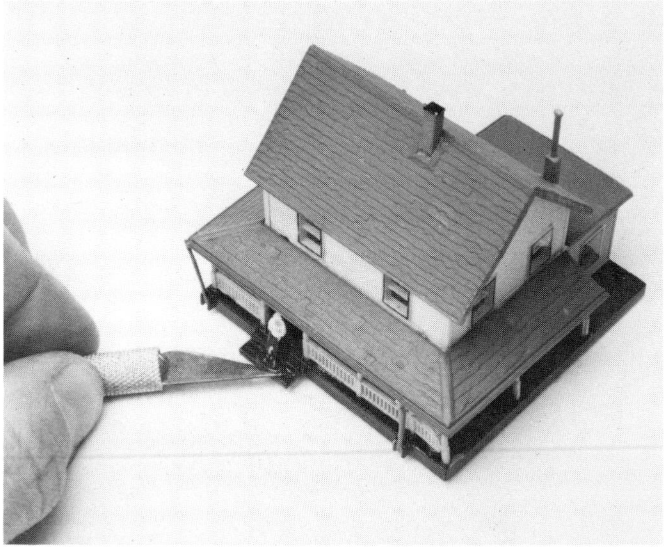

The joints are slightly more porous than solid plastic, so they will soften first. Cut and pry only in the joint areas so you don't mar surrounding surfaces.

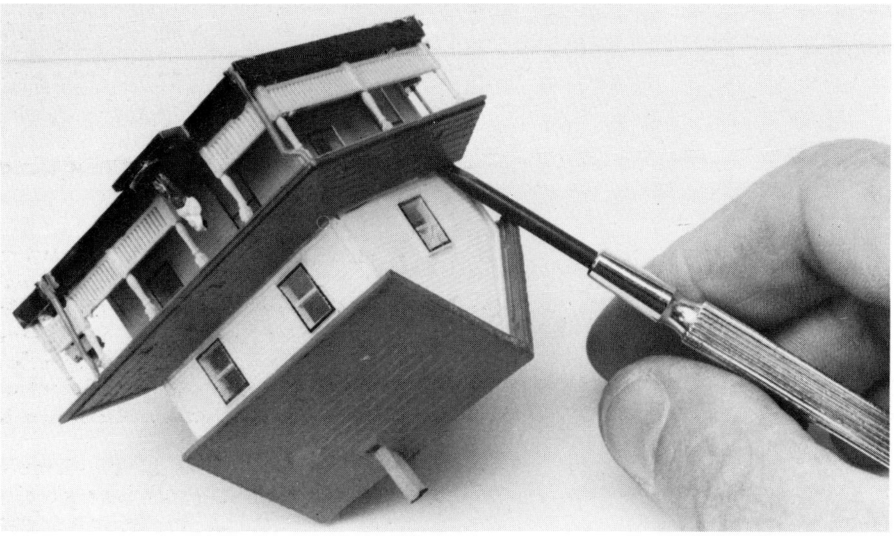

To avoid breaking a knife blade, use a screwdriver to pry larger parts free.

pry with the knife, the blade may snap. If the joint has a peg, push on the peg rather than trying to pry on the actual glue joint. When you finally have the parts apart, leave them alone for a couple of days while the cement-softened edges harden.

If you don't care about saving the surrounding areas, you can cut the parts you want from an assembled model. A razor saw, coping saw, or hot knife can be used. Keep the cuts at least $^1/_{16}''$ from the final edge of the part to leave room to smooth the edges with a file.

Scribing, shaping, and stretching. Before we talk about assembly procedures, let's consider some operations applicable to both kit parts and stock plastic materials: scribing, shaping, and sprue stretching.

To rescribe board-groove detail, or to scribe plain styrene to simulate the

Fig. 5-6. The back of your hobby knife blade makes an effective scriber if you have only a few grooves to make. Sand the surface lightly after scribing to remove burrs.

Fig. 5-7. It takes only a few minutes to grind this scribing tool from a piece of drill rod. Figure 5-8 shows how to grind the tip to the proper angles.

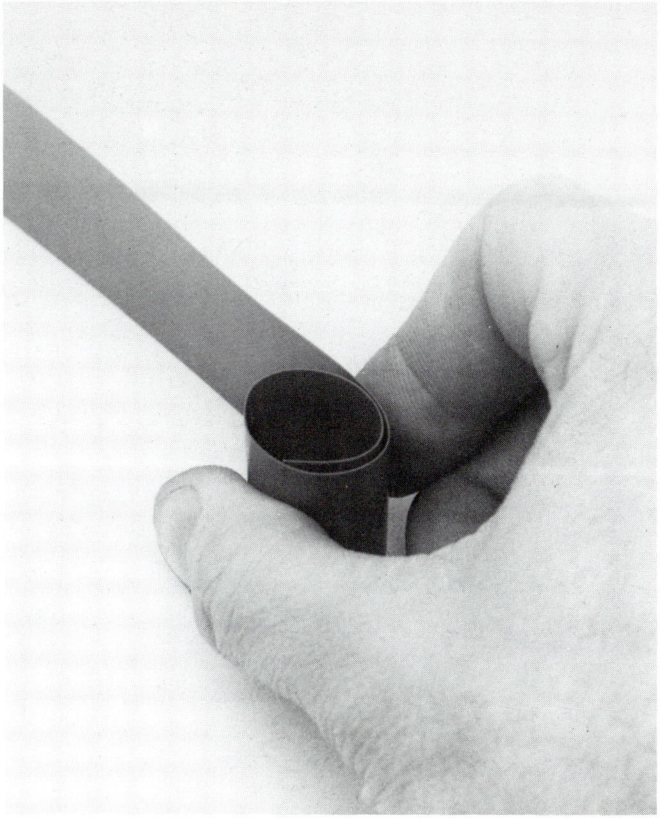

To make a curved part such as a cab roof from plastic sheet, start the bend by rolling the plastic around a knife handle. For a tighter curve, remove the handle and twist the plastic into a tight spiral roll.

grooves between board siding or the seams between welded steel plates, use the *back* of a No. 11 hobby knife to scrape material from the grooves, fig. 5-6. Figures 5-7 and 5-8 show a special scriber made from drill rod. Use a steel straightedge as a guide to ensure clean, straight lines, and work in light passes, stopping when your new scribed grooves match the existing ones. For siding that is to simulate wood, use the very tip of the knife to scribe in some wavy "grain" detail, but keep these lines light—don't overdo the effect. Sand the surface lightly with No. 600 sandpaper to remove burrs or ridges left by scribing.

Thin plastic sheet can be shaped like sheet metal. Dark gray ABS sheet is ideal for forming smooth curved surfaces such as oil tanks, cover plates, and locomotive cab roofs. ABS has the characteristic of turning to a lighter shade the moment it stresses and takes a set, so it tells you when you've bent it far enough that it won't spring back and warns you to ease up before it fractures. For a curved part, start the bend by wrapping the sheet stock around a rod of smaller diameter than the finished bend, such as a hobby knife handle. For tighter curves than can be achieved using the knife handle as a form, remove it and continue twisting the plastic into a tight spiral.

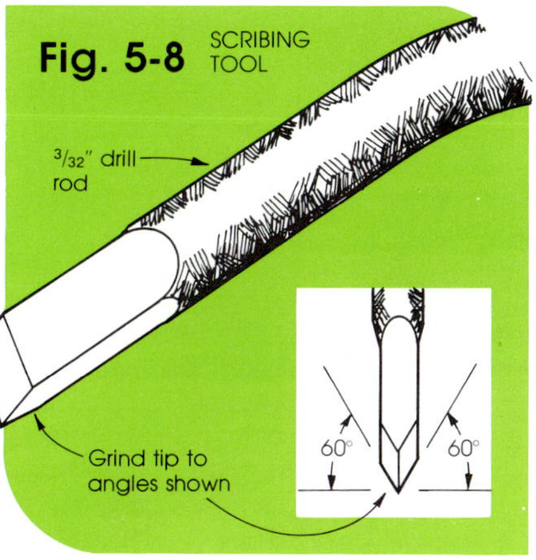

Sprue stretching is a way to make small-diameter plastic rod and "wire." Start by heating a length of sprue over a candle flame until it softens and becomes rubbery. Remove it from the flame, and pull gently at both ends to form "wire." Regulate the thickness and length of the "wire" by how fast and how far you stretch the softened plastic.

Stretched sprue is too brittle for use as free-standing items such as handrails and air-cooler piping—steel or brass wire is much more suitable for those applications—but it is great for close-in boiler piping, electrical conduits, drain pipes, and other detail that is less likely to be touched. Its big advantage, of course, is that it can be added to the model with liquid plastic cement, whereas metal parts require epoxy or ACC to hold them to plastic.

Assembly – temporary and permanent. Part of the trial-and-error nature of kitbashing is temporary assembly. When making parts to fit or when checking parts that will be painted separately and assembled later, you'll find it helpful to assemble the pieces temporarily with masking-tape tabs. You'll find that such "dry-run" assembly will often save you the expense of a replacement kit.

In most cases, kitbashing assembly follows the same general methods discussed in Chapter 2. The basic bonding techniques are the same—always strive for a neat and strong welded joint using liquid plastic cement.

Let's consider a fairly standard joining job. You've made the rough cuts, filed, and sanded the parts for a near-perfect fit. You've made a dry run through the assembly sequence and determined that all the pieces will go together as planned. Now think about how you will hold the parts while the cemented joints set. Are the pieces flat on the bottom edges, allowing simple lineup on a flat surface? Can the car floor or locomotive shell frame be inserted during assembly to provide positive alignment? Can you make a simple fixture from wood, styrene, acetate, and waxed paper or aluminum foil to hold the parts? You don't want assembly to become a juggling act with three or four cement-softened plastic parts and only your two hands to align and secure them in the proper relationship.

Remember that plastic cements, either liquid or body type, weld plastic parts together by solvent action. A joint

Stretching your own plastic pipe and "wire" is easy. Soften a sprue over a candle flame, remove from the heat, and pull gently until the strand is the required diameter. Practice until you feel comfortable with the technique.

A length of stretched sprue is an effective drip rail for this cab roof.

does not solidify until all the solvent has evaporated, and in major joints, this can take overnight or longer—in broad sheet laminations it can take weeks! Keep this in mind when joining major car, locomotive, or structure sections, and *leave the model alone* until the heavy joints dry out and set up hard. If you try to cut, sand, trim, drill, or tap in the vicinity of a joint that is not completely hardened, you'll find yourself working with a gooey, spongy, rubber-like substance—in short, a mess.

Liquid cement distributes itself along a joint by capillary action. Sometimes, you will want to defeat this action in the name of neatness. File or scribe a notch where you want capillary flow to stop. This is useful when you must make sure that solvent does not reach a prepainted surface.

For extra-tight bonds at major joints such as structure corners and carbody seams, make a second application of liquid cement a minute or two after the first. This will dissolve more of the plastic in the joint and allow you to press the parts together with a slight wiggling motion to make a tiny bead of softened plastic ooze out. This tiny bead can be trimmed flush with the surface after the joint dries completely. The "squeeze-and-ooze" joint will *seem* to be dry within minutes, but it takes 24 hours for the solvent to evaporate completely and leave the joint at full strength. To trim away the joint bead formed by the squeeze-and-ooze cementing technique, make a small chisel by grinding the end of an old needle file, a bar of tool steel, or a heavy piece of piano wire as shown in fig. 5-9.

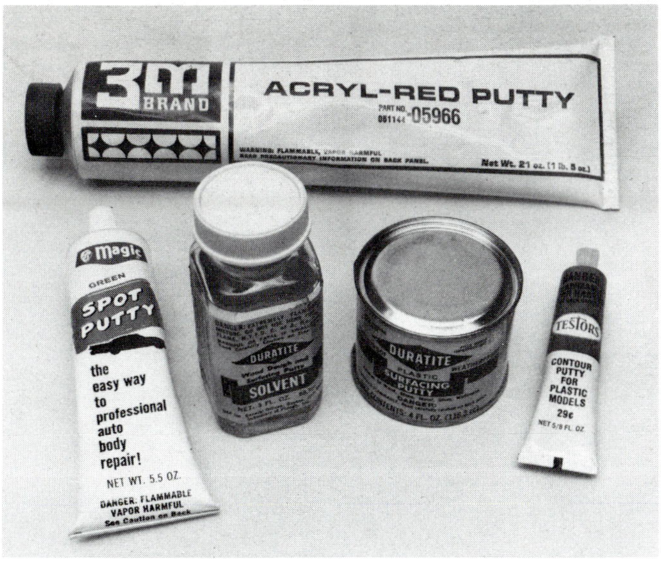

Filler putties made for auto-body work and for woodworking, as well as those offered specifically for modeling, are suitable for filling and smoothing plastics.

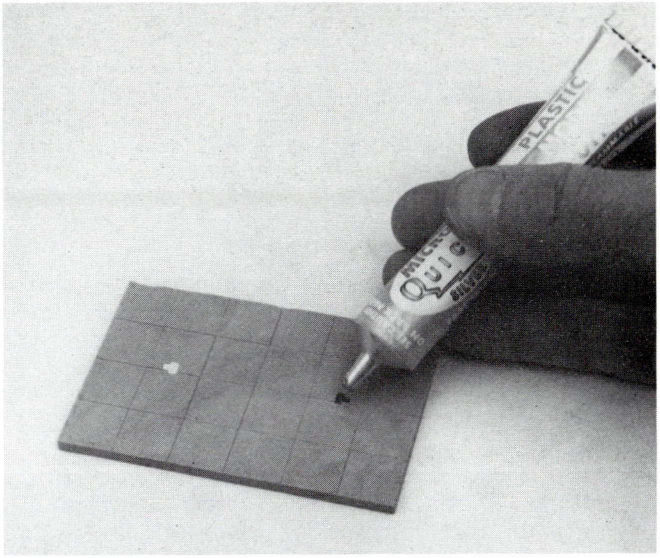

Filler putties can be applied right from the tube, as shown here, but in most cases you should use a toothpick, Popsicle stick, or other disposable implement.

Reinforcing joints. Where needed for strength, you can add reinforcing pieces either when you make the joint or afterwards. For major joints, such as those in a car or locomotive body, try to stagger the joint locations in side, roof, and floor pieces. This method has the added advantage of helping to align the parts. With many plastic cars, consider using the weight as a major strengthening member. These weights, usually intended to be held loosely in position, lend a lot of rigidity to the body when they are epoxied to the body shell or car floor, or both.

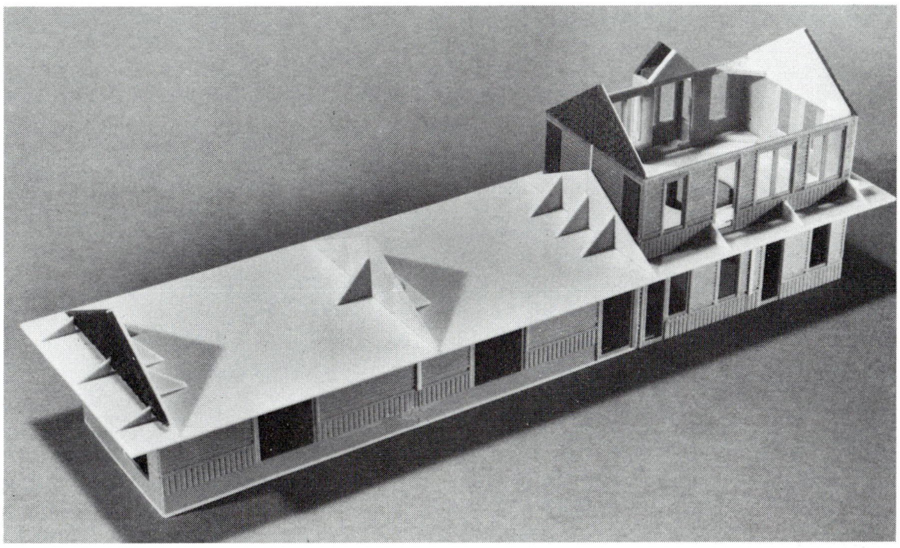

Fig. 5-11. Extensive use of gussets and reinforcing formers strengthens and aligns the wall sections of this kitbashed N scale station.

Fig. 5-9 JOINT-BEAD CHISEL

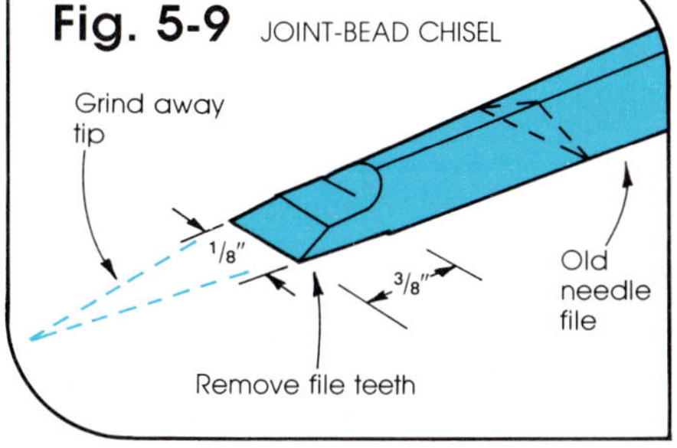

Fig. 5-10 MAKING GUSSETS

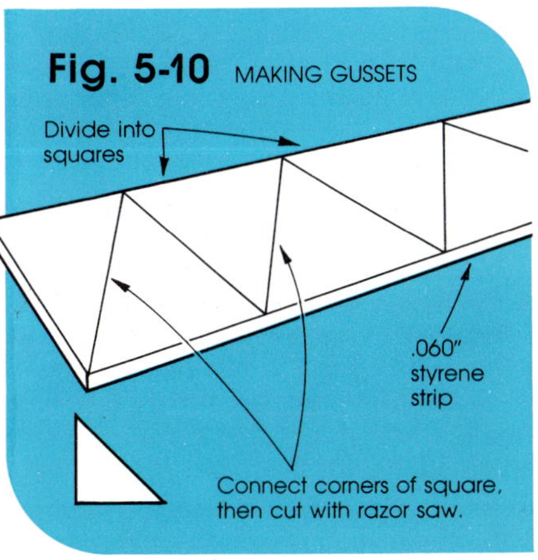

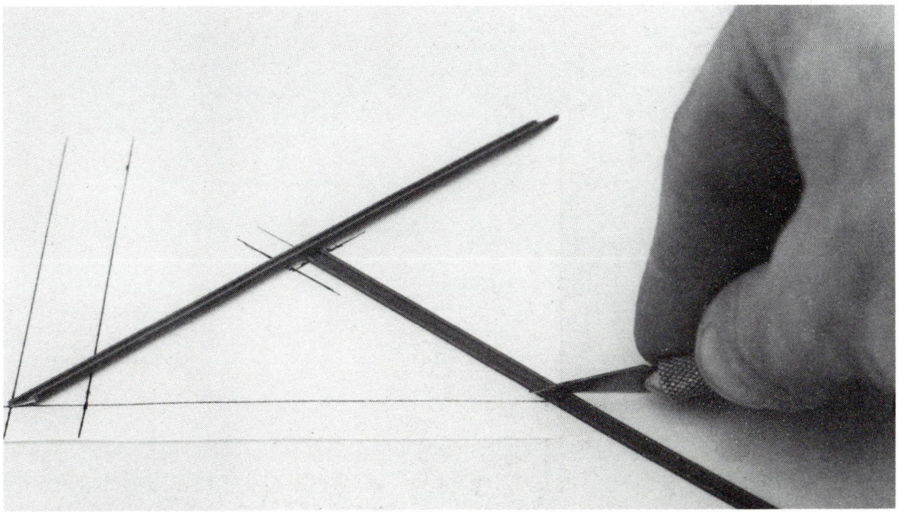

This simple pencil-line template serves as a cutting guide and alignment aid in making identical bracing assemblies from plastic structural shapes.

Where adding thickness is not a problem, run a strip of sheet stock down the back of the joint as reinforcement. This is especially good when joining large flat wall sections. Make the strip as wide as possible so it will also serve as an alignment aid. For structures that will have interior detail, use thin sheet stock. Square or triangular gussets, figs. 5-10 and 5-11, lend tremendous strength to corners. They can also serve as formers to align parts.

Filler putties. There are several brands of filler putty suitable for plastic. Auto-body filler putty such as Duco Spot Putty works well, as do Micro Scale "Micro Quick Silver" and Squadron Green Putty. You can make your own filler by dissolving scraps of plastic in liquid cement, but considering the price of the cement, the time involved to dissolve the plastic, and the fact that the commercial products have better working characteristics, it's usually not worth the effort.

Be sure to read the instructions on the filler putty package. When you apply

Work car from a reefer

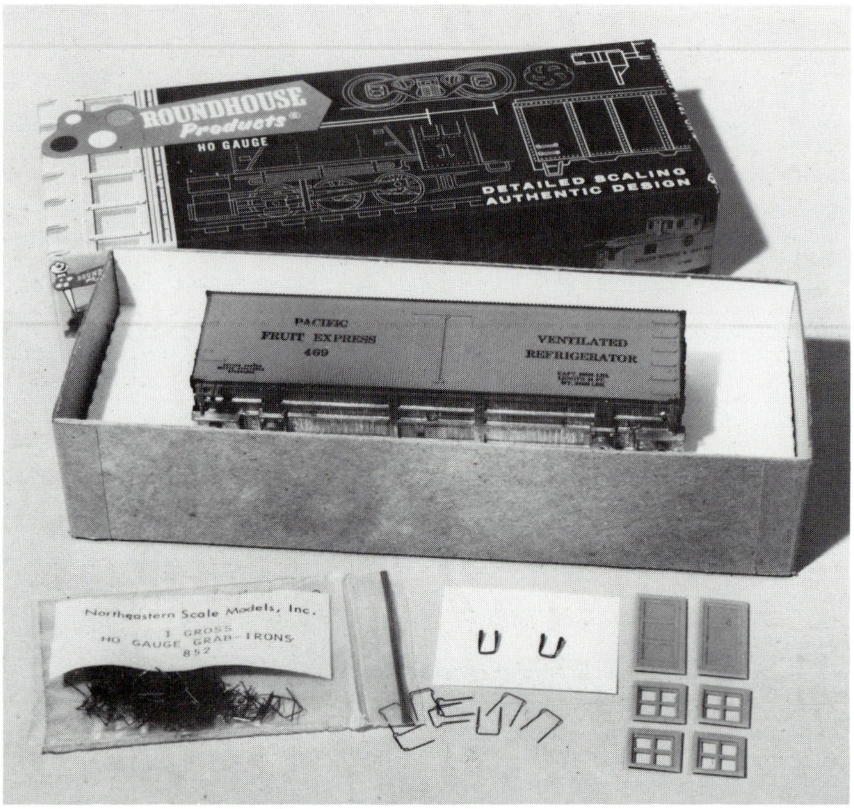

A. Because this project is based on a common freight car, it can be accomplished in any scale. The HO model starts with a Model Die Casting wood reefer, window and door castings from MDC's "Module Pack" structure series, Northeastern preformed wire grab irons, and a pair of La Belle steps.

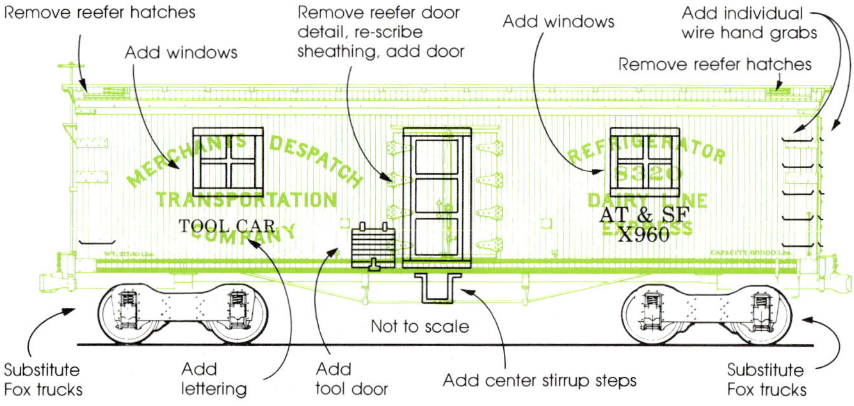

B. This drawing shows the modifications needed to convert the old-time reefer to work-train service. This car is built with the same methods that prototype railroads use to build or modify maintenance-of-way equipment.

Richard K. Smith

C. It's common prototype practice to convert an outdated box car or ice-bunker refrigerator to a kitchen, supply, or bunk car (shown here). Windows, doors, lighting, and heating are installed to make these cars rolling warehouses and living quarters.

D. After slicing away the raised reefer-door and grab-iron detail, trace the outlines of the back edges of the windows and doors onto the car side with your hobby knife. Ensure that these parts are aligned with the bottom edge of the roof and the sheathing grooves. It's not necessary to center the windows or doors.

putty, put on a little more than required, to compensate for shrinkage. Sand the surface flush with the surrounding area after the putty is thoroughly dry. Most putties require more than a single application for best results, and most require primer coats before painting.

You can do a limited amount of filleting and molding with putty, but it really isn't made for thick applications, because it shrinks. If you have a large hole to fill, use a solid plastic plug and fill the cracks and disguise the surface with a veneer of putty.

Particularly in large puttied areas, seal the surface of the putty with Floquil Barrier or Scalecoat Shieldcoat before priming. Otherwise, paint solvents can re-soften the putty, causing surface distortion.

Templates and assembly aids. The terms "jig" and "template" smack of highly technical modelbuilding practices. Not so. A template can be as simple as two crossed lines on a sheet of paper to line parts up at the correct an-

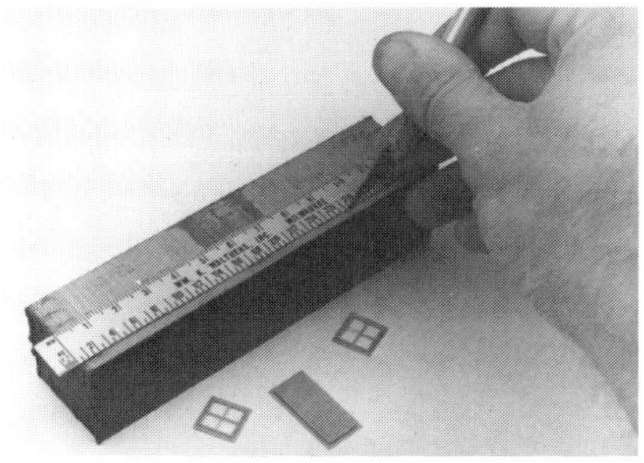

E. Use a steel ruler as a guide, and deepen the layout lines, then double-check the sizes of the openings with the window and door castings; a converted prototype is no excuse for sloppy modeling. The windows must be set squarely in the walls, and doors must be hung plumb.

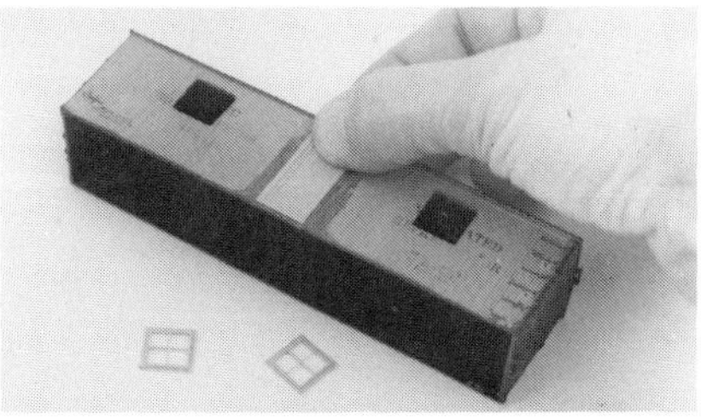

G. Position the doors and windows in their openings and apply liquid cement from the back. The doors and windows on the opposite side may be in different locations, and two windows per side is not the limit—you can use any number you like and the finished product will still be believable.

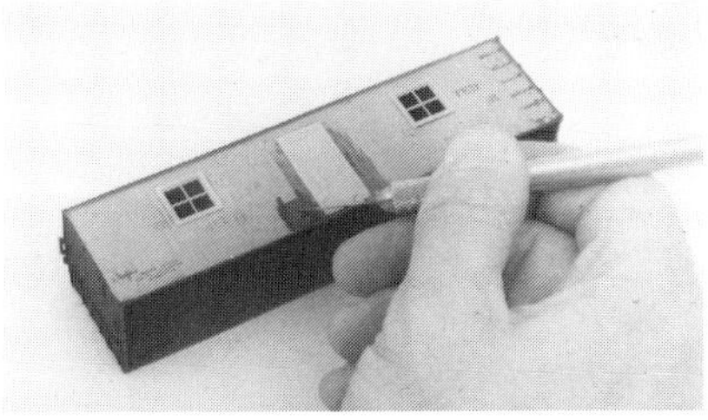

H. The small toolbox doors are made by shortening the hinges on two of the ice hatches from the reefer. You may also want to add doors to the ends of the car to facilitate passage through the work train when spotted on out-of-the-way sidings. Seldom are two work cars exactly alike.

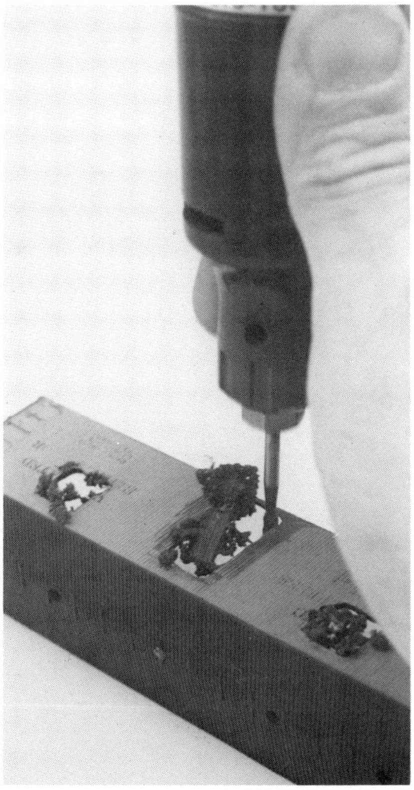

F. A motor tool makes cutting the window and door openings easy, or you can cut them with a jeweler's saw by drilling a hole in each corner and making cuts to connect them. Keep the cuts about 1/32" inside your window and door layout lines.

I. Before priming and painting, add individual wire grab irons and place a stirrup step below each door. Gray is a common color for maintenance-of-way equipment, but railroads use orange, oxide red, or an everyday boxcar red or brown. A shading of dirt and soot is the norm, regardless of color.

J. Numbers assigned to MofW equipment often start with "X," indicating that the cars cannot be interchanged with other railroads. This car was lettered with dry transfers and decals, clear-coated, and weathered.

Using files

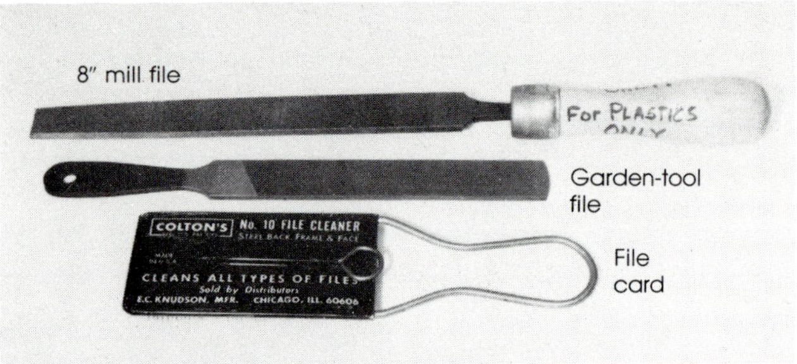

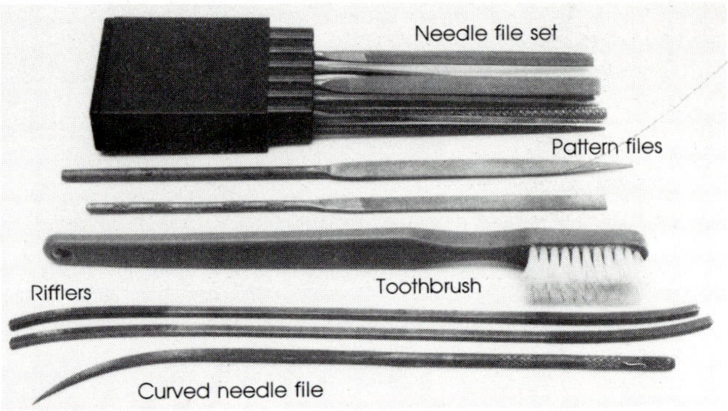

FILES are important kitbashing tools because they are used to make parts fit properly. They are made by driving a chisel into a steel blank to form individual teeth and heat-treating the completed blank to harden the points. Files are classified by length, shape (flat, triangular, round, etc.), cut (single or double), and coarseness of cut (bastard cut, second cut, etc.).

Standard-size files are graded as follows: coarse, bastard cut, second cut, and smooth, in that order. The smaller Swiss Pattern files and needle files are graded from 00 to No. 6; the larger the number, the finer the cut. Number 1 and 2 files are best for plastics. The grade number is usually stamped on the file tang.

CHOOSING THE RIGHT FILE

It is important to match the file to the job. Many modelers have only needle files. These are a poor choice for removing a lot of material or for smoothing a long edge or joint. Single-cut files provide a smoother finish for plastic. An 8" bastard-cut mill file is a good choice for kitbashing. This may seem like a big tool for modelbuilding, but it is the tool you need to true edges for good joints. You should also have a set of needle files in all the common shapes for jobs such as removing flash and filing window openings. A safe-edge file has one or more edges with no teeth. A riffler is a file that has been bent into a curve so that it can work in tight spots.

Every file with a pointed tang must have a handle to avoid painful injury should you slip while using the tool. File handles are inexpensive and easy to install. Needle files have blunt ends that require no additional handle, although a large pin vise can be used to hold them for comfort. A flat garden-tool file has a rounded tang which is handy for jobs where a handle would be in the way. Sharpness is important; as with saws, it's a good idea to have files reserved specifically for plastic work so you won't dull them by using them on metal.

USING FILES

A file cuts by peeling tiny shavings away from the work, much like a wood plane. As irregularities are removed from the surface, more and more of the file contacts it, and, as a result, the cutting action of the individual teeth is diminished and the surface is smoothed. File teeth point forward, away from the handle, and cut only on the forward stroke. Always lift the file on the backstroke to prevent breaking or wearing flats on the teeth. Use long, slow strokes with medium pressure so that as much of the file as possible is used.

Hold the work securely in a vise or support it against something to allow accurate filing and full control over the job. Otherwise, the file will vibrate, or chatter, and make an uneven cut.

Shaping with files should always be a progression from coarse to fine. Start with a coarse file and use progressively finer files as you approach the layout lines. Let's look at an edge-filing job as an example. If you start shaping the edge with a needle file, the job will be tedious because the small file will clog with plastic and require frequent cleaning. Worse, the needle file won't contact the entire edge, and your chances of achieving a long, straight joining surface will be slim. Now for the right way. Cut out the part with a saw, leaving $^1/_{32}$" to $^1/_{64}$" of extra material. Remove most of the material with an 8" or 10" bastard-cut mill file — a pretty big tool — and bring the edge to the layout line.

Round files can be used to enlarge holes. Place the point of the file in the opening, and twist counterclockwise to remove material from the edges of the hole without jamming the file. This is inferior to using a reamer, but it will work where extreme accuracy is not required.

REPLACEMENT, CLEANING, AND STORAGE

Files are a cutting tool, and they get dull and wear out. There's no sure way to tell when a file is dulled beyond use, but occasionally purchasing a new file provides a good comparison.

Files that are kept clean cut more freely, last longer, and do better work. A file card is a wood-backed wire brush with short, stiff bristles. It is intended to be used for cleaning metal filings from larger files. While the standard file card is sufficient for your larger mill files, a brass-bristled suede brush is better for cleaning pattern and needle files. An old toothbrush is also handy for removing material from the grooves between teeth.

The file card is used by stroking it across the face of a file, not up and down. When a file card or metal brush fails to dislodge material between the teeth, use a needlepoint scriber — a needle chucked in a pin vise will do the job — to gently pick out the offending material. If a chip, especially a metal chip, gets caught between the teeth of the file, it will mar any surface over which it is drawn. This is called pinning.

Occasionally, you'll find small files loaded with stubborn plastic bits that brushing will not remove. This is especially true when filing filler-puttied areas. Soak these files in lacquer thinner to loosen and dissolve the material, then brush.

Never use a file to push or pry; files are brittle and can easily snap, even when working with plastic. Store files in a manner that will protect the teeth from contact with other tools, particularly other files, and store them where they won't rust. Hang them up, make a wood rack or stand, or store them in a compartmented drawer.

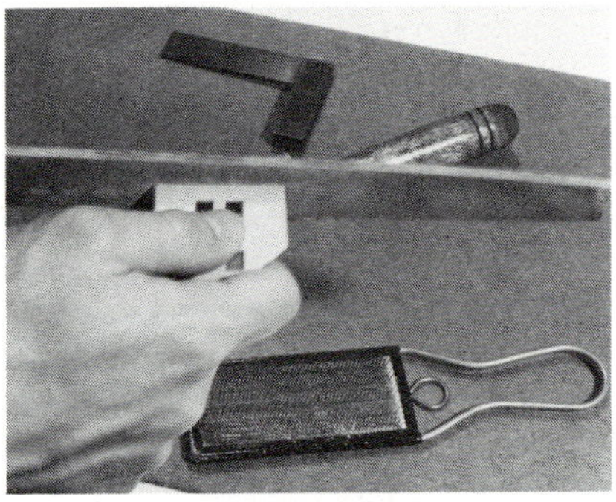

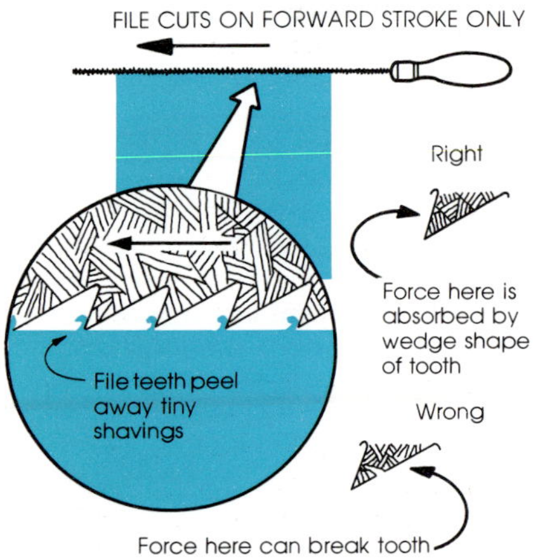

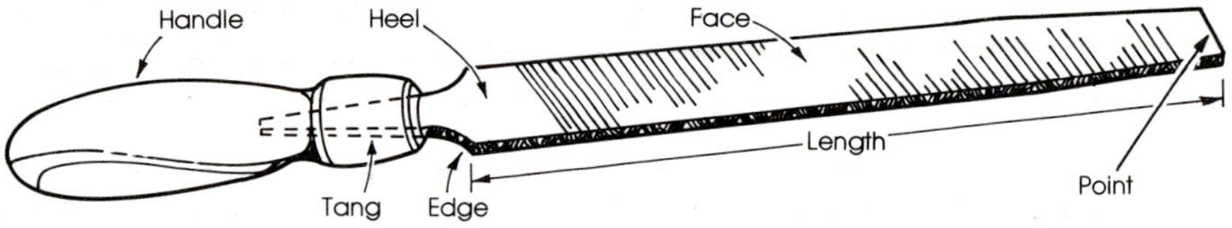

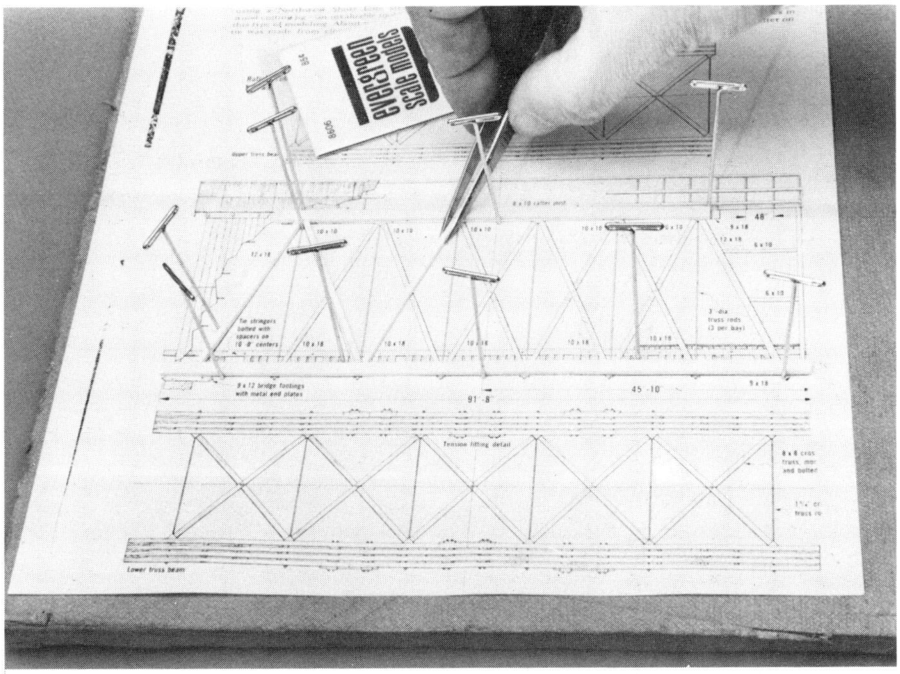

Full-size scale drawings offer another simple template. Tape the plans to a piece of fiberboard (Homasote or Celotex), cover with waxed paper, and use pins to position parts while the cement sets.

gle, and it becomes a jig as soon as you press in some straight pins to help position the parts. If you have the luxury of drawings in a magazine or book in the scale you are modeling, simply taping the drawings to your working surface constitutes a template for cutting and fitting operations.

A sheet of window glass is not a precision-ground flat surface, but it's accurate enough to make a good flat assembly surface. An assortment of weights and right-angle blocks are handy to use with the glass sheet. The blocks can be hardwood, as long as they are accurately cut, but short lengths of steel or brass bar stock are better because adhesives won't stick to them, and they can also serve as weights, fig. 5-12.

Another simple jig can be made by clamping a heavy steel straightedge to your work surface to use as an alignment aid during assembly. You can use this stationary rule in conjunction with a machinist's square to check right angles and to keep parts accurately positioned while adhesives set. A carpenter's steel framing square can be clamped to a drawing board or workbench top in the same way to serve as an assembly fixture.

When you devise jigs and assembly fixtures, choose materials that won't be affected by liquid cement: waxed paper, acetate, and aluminum foil are good choices.

Seeing kits as parts. Developing a plan of attack is important in every kitbashing project. It's hard to teach what is really a thought process, but here are some ideas. First, use scrap cardboard to make trial-and-error fitting templates and mockups to plan how you will make cuts and assemble your model. Second, enlist the aid of a copying machine. Place kit parts on the glass of the copying machine and make several paper "kits" to slice up. Experiment in two dimensions with paper copies of car, locomotive, or structure parts, or in three dimensions with the actual parts. Try temporarily assembling structures with masking tape to see how various arrangements will look.

When you are kitbashing with a specific prototype in mind, make an effort to capture the spirit of the original without trying to model every nut and bolt. Don't worry about minor inaccuracies; two or three scale inches, or even a scale foot, won't make much difference in most models, and if you succeed in making your model closer to the prototype than any commercial offering, you'll have accomplished what you set out to do. Often, the difference between a model that captures the spirit of the real thing and a model that is an exact bolt-for-bolt and inch-for-inch reproduction is a lot of work that makes little or no difference when the model is on the layout.

The only standard you must conform to in kitbashing, other than the obvious limits of size, clearance, wheel gauge, and compatibility with other equipment, is the standard of plausibility. Does your model have a prototype or, at least, a near-prototype? If not, does it represent a logical modification to a prototype that did exist, or perhaps one that was designed but never built? If you're inexperienced along these lines, the best thing to do is use prototype drawings and photographs as references—not for inch-for-inch duplication, but as guidelines to keep major part placement and overall prototype proportions realistic.

Finally, don't become so enthusiastic about kitbashing that you ignore other ways to make the models you want. There are some models that are easier to *scratchbuild*, and there are some models that can be kitbashed but require so many kits to do the job that the expense becomes disproportionate to the ease or rapidity of construction gained by kitbashing.

Fig. 5-12. A sheet of window glass makes a good flat surface and an assortment of wood or metal blocks turns it into a valuable assembly jig. The blocks can be moved around and used to hold parts while cemented joints set.

Kitbashing freight and passenger cars

Rebuild and re-detail your plastic rolling stock to duplicate the variety of prototype railroading.

ROLLING STOCK kitbashing projects range from simple detailing to extensive saw-apart-and-glue-together jobs. These projects are popular because most of them are quick, and because they yield cars that can go into service on your railroad right away. Kitbashing allows you to tailor rolling stock to the needs of your railroad, particularly if no manufacturer offers the equipment you need to carry out your theme. In this respect you'll be following prototype practice, because many real railroads often modify equipment to suit special needs.

You can shorten or lengthen most types of freight and passenger cars, modify a caboose so it is unique to your railroad, or change an all-steel car to a composite steel-and-wood design by sanding away rivets and panel lines and scribing in grooves between simulated planks. Roofs and ends can be swapped between cars to yield different styles. The modifications possible are limited only by your imagination and by plausibility. By "plausibility" I mean that you needn't duplicate a prototype board-for-board and rivet-for-rivet to make a realistic, believable model, but you must adhere to prototype practices and proportions. Car builders' cyclopedias serve as guidebooks to car building practices and to the almost incredible variety of prototype freight and passenger car designs.

Where to start. Take a hard look at the cars around your layout. Which cars do you like, and which cars don't come up to your standards? How many cars are dented, scratched, or otherwise in need of repair? When you've answered these questions, run a special train around your pike and weed out all the "cripples." Spot these cars on your rip track—they all need work, so we'll start with them.

Finding out what is available to bash is a very important part of the kitbashing process, so I direct you to manufacturers' and mail-order hobby shop catalogs. In addition to hundreds of car kits and ready-to-run cars, you'll find that thousands of parts for detailing freight and passenger cars are offered in all scales. A careful search of the catalogs is always in order before assuming that the part you need just isn't available.

For passenger cars, Walthers offers interior detail kits in HO and O, includ-

Paul Kepner added a cupola, wire grab irons, and other detail to a Model Die Casting HO Overton combine to make this free-lance caboose.

	Hand grabs	Boiler handrails	Side and end handrails
Prototype diameter	3/4" (5/8"-1")	1 3/8"	1 1/4"
O scale Exact	.015" (.013"-.020")	.029"	.026"
*Recommended	.018"	.031"	.030"
S scale Exact	.012" (.010"-.016")	.021"	.020"
Recommended	.014"	.022"	.020"
HO scale Exact	.009" (.007"-.011")	.016"	.014"
Recommended	.013"	.020"	.018"
N scale Exact	.005"(.004"-.006")	.009"	.008"
Recommended	.010"	.013"	.012"

Fig. 6-1 GRAB IRON AND RAILING SIZES

*Recommended sizes differ from exact scale dimensions for reasons of durability, visibility, and appearance of handrails compared to other detail.

Bob Gawer upgraded this Con-Cor HO Santa Fe baggage car for service on his layout. One door opening was enlarged, both door panels replaced, and numerous details revised or added to make an accurate replica of Santa Fe No. 3421.

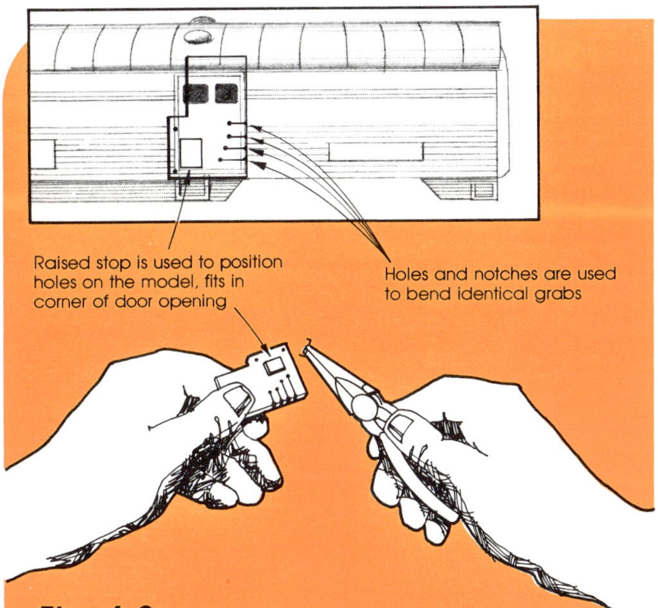

Fig. 6-2 HANDRAIL BENDING AND DRILLING JIGS

ing furnishings for every sort of car—from coaches, to diners, to business cars. Special kits for interior lighting are also available. Diaphragms dramatically improve the exterior appearance of any model passenger car that should have them, and Walthers and others have kits and ready-to-use parts for these, too.

Upgrading rolling stock models. You can make a noticeable improvement in the realism of any model that has molded-on ladders, grab irons, steps, and brake piping by trimming away the cast sections and replacing them with castings and formed-wire parts. Your hobby dealer can supply preformed wire grab irons, cast ladders and corner stirrup steps, and straightened brass wire to accomplish these modifications. You'll have to drill a few dozen holes to add individual grab irons, but styrene is easy to drill, and an average car can be upgraded in a single evening. You can touch-up paint around your added details, or better yet, repaint the car, replacing the factory lettering with out-of-the-ordinary schemes made with decals or dry transfers.

Grab-iron replacement is quite simple, but the improvement in appearance is striking, even in N scale, and even when a comparatively oversize wire part is used to replace a cast-on item (see table, fig. 6-1). The photo sequence illustrates typical grab-iron replacement. Important points to remember are to remove cast-on detail with a sharp knife and to lubricate your drills frequently with beeswax. On a freight car with molded-on ladders, it's usually easier to remove the entire ladder than to dig out the molded grabs between the ladder uprights. Practice handrail replacement on old models or leftover parts before starting on models you expect to operate on your layout.

Half-hard brass wire is the best material for bending replacement handrails, and straightened wire is best if you can get it. When you bend a part incorrectly, discard it. It is virtually impossible—and extremely frustrating—to straighten and re-bend fine wire. Brass wire hardens as it is worked, and more than one back-and-forth bend can embrittle it to the point of fracture. Simple bending jigs, fig. 6-2, are very useful.

Another simple detailing improvement is to remove the cast-on, non-operating doors on some brands of plastic box cars and replace them with individual metal or plastic castings, or

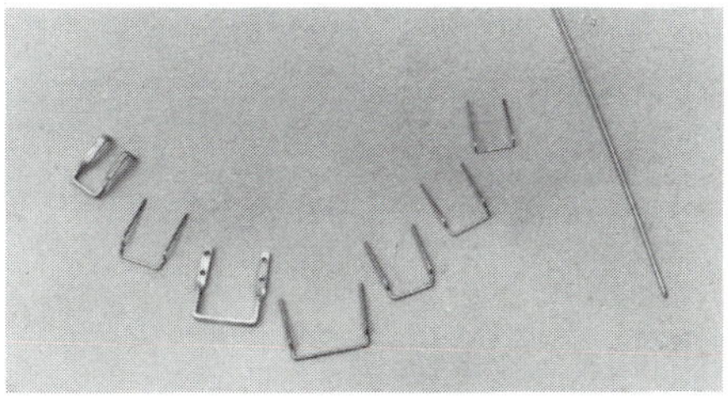

Several manufacturers offer preformed grabs and steps. Left to right: LaBelle HO step and grab, Kemtron O stirrup, Northeastern, Pacific Traction, and Detail Associates HO grabs.

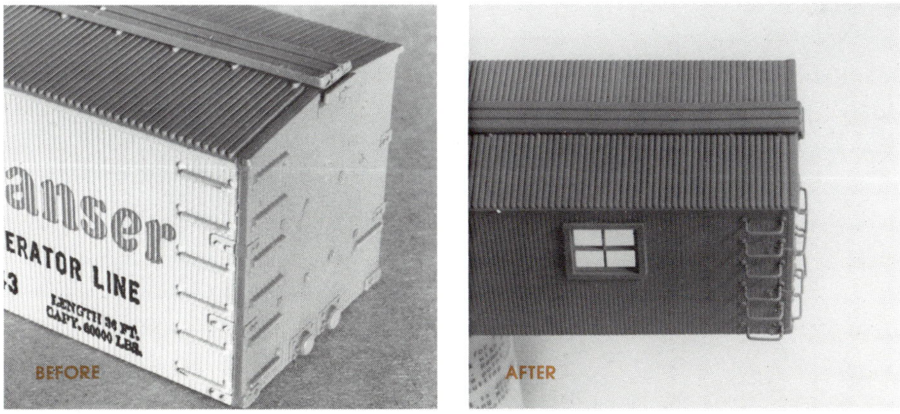

Replacing cast-on grab irons with free-standing wire parts is one of the most dramatic improvements you can make to plastic rolling stock. These carbodies came from the same mold, but the difference in realism is amazing.

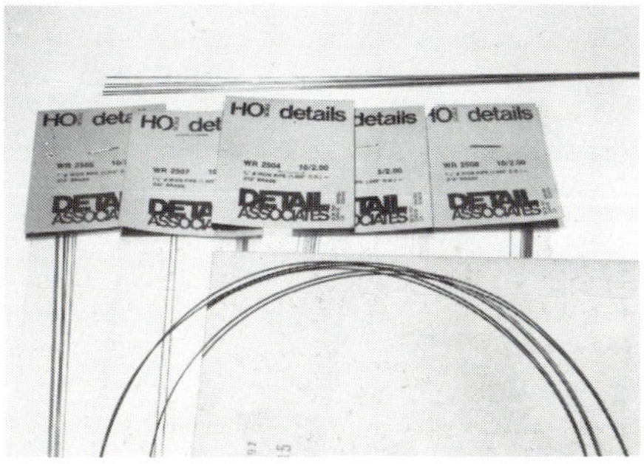

Where preformed parts won't fit you must bend your own grab irons from wire. Many wire sizes are commercially available; these are from Detail Associates, Kemtron, and Walthers.

Using small drills

MODELERS use small drills for many purposes, among them making holes for mounting handrails and other detail parts, starting larger openings, and providing clearance for attaching moving parts such as trucks. While there are other types, most of the drilling in modelbuilding is done with twist drills. The drills we use in modelwork are numbered. Higher numbers represent smaller diameter drills.

Small number drill sizes

Drill No.	Diameter in inches	Drill No.	Diameter in inches
51	.067	66	.033
52	.0635	67	.032
53	.0595	68	.031
54	.055	69	.0292
55	.052	70	.028
56	.0465	71	.026
57	.043	72	.025
58	.042	73	.024
59	.041	74	.0225
60	.040	75	.021
61	.039	76	.020
62	.038	77	.018
63	.037	78	.016
64	.036	79	.0145
65	.035	80	.0135

BUYING DRILLS

Most hobby shops stock drills individually and in sets, as do many large hardware stores. Drills are available in either carbon steel or high-speed steel. High-speed drills are more expensive, but are the better buy because they hold their cutting edge much longer and resist breaking much better than carbon steel drills. Cheap drills are never a bargain.

There is some saving in the cost of each drill in a complete set, but because such sets contain many sizes you'll probably never use, it is less expensive to purchase drills individually as you need them.

The keys to drilling in plastic are slow speed and sharp drills; as with saws, it's a good idea to have a set of drills reserved for plastic only — they will stay a lot sharper that way. The plastics we use don't dull drills much, but metal does. Small drills are difficult to sharpen, and with those smaller than No. 65 it's rarely worth the effort. When small drills become dull, replace them.

DRILLING TOOLS

Most modelers use a pin vise for drilling small holes. This is a handle with a collet chuck mounted on one end. Some pin vises have interchangeable collets to hold several size ranges of small drills. The twist drill is chucked in the collet and the pin vise is held against the work and rotated with the thumb and third finger. If you drill a lot of holes smaller than No. 70, look for an ultra-light pin vise that won't break the drill with its weight if you momentarily lose your grip.

All power tools used in drilling plastic must have speed controls. Low speeds are necessary because heat generated in drilling may melt the plastic instead of cutting it. See Chapter 10 for more information on using motor tools.

A drill press — even a light-duty one — can save enough drills is a relatively short time to justify its cost. It is one of the first power tools you should consider adding to your shop.

DRILLING PROCEDURES

The main goal in drilling is to make straight holes of the correct size without breaking the drill in doing so. All holes require a punched location mark; otherwise, the drill will wander over the surface and start where it wants to. A decal pricker (fig. 4-3) is a good punch, as is a needle chucked in a pin vise.

The pin vise, drill chuck, or motor-tool collet must hold the drill concentrically. If you can see the drill wobble as it turns, loosen the collet and readjust the drill to center it properly.

It is important to keep the drill square with the work. An accurately cut block of wood or metal or a small machinist's square can provide a good reference for keeping the drill and pin vise at a right angle to the surface being drilled.

Side and bending forces are the enemies of small drills. Either force can cause a crooked hole or a broken drill.

A sharp drill cuts easily with only light pressure, discharging chips readily. A long, curling chip is a sign that the drill is sharp and the cutting speed is correct. Never force a drill. A drill that must be forced is dull, or in the case of motorized drilling, turning at the wrong speed.

All twist drills, even brand-new ones, drill a hole that is slightly oversize. This is because the drill wobbles a little as it cuts. When you want a more accurate hole, drill first with a drill one size smaller than the required hole, then finish with the correct size. This eliminates most inaccuracy due to wobble.

PREVENTING BROKEN DRILLS

Beeswax is an excellent drilling lubricant because it won't attack plastic as will some synthetic lubricants, and it requires no cleanup. You can find beeswax at a fabric store, craft store, or in the ship model department of your hobby shop. To use it, run the drill into the cake of beeswax as if you were drilling the wax, and then make your hole. Work in stages; lubricate, drill, clear the chips, then lubricate and drill again.

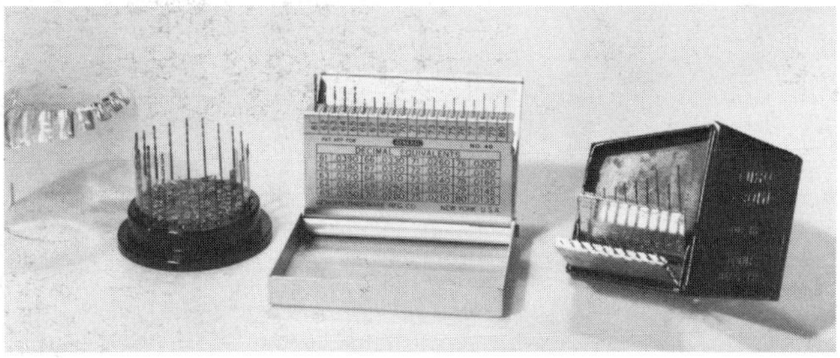

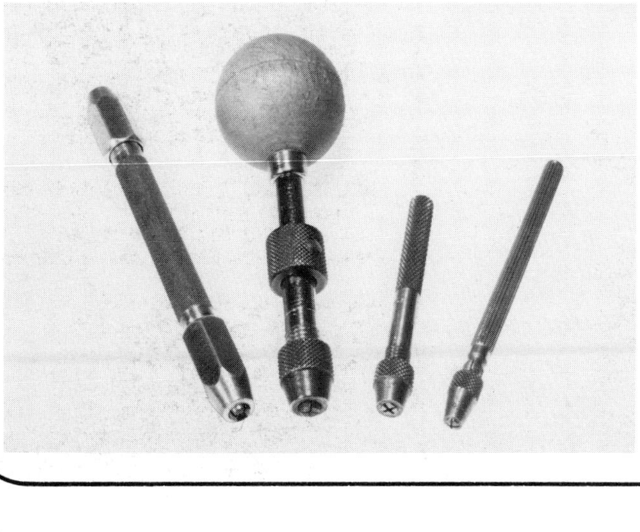

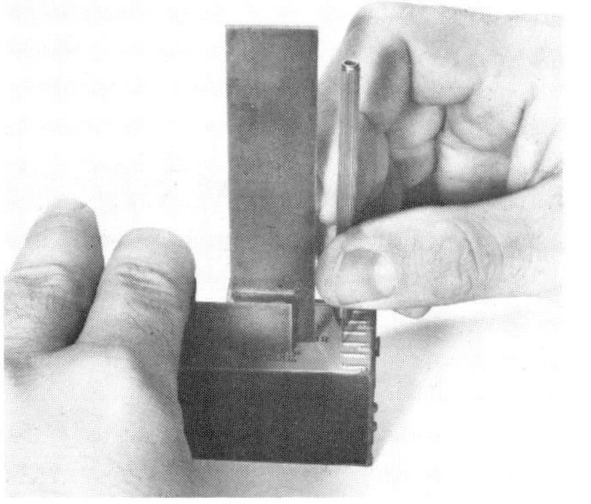

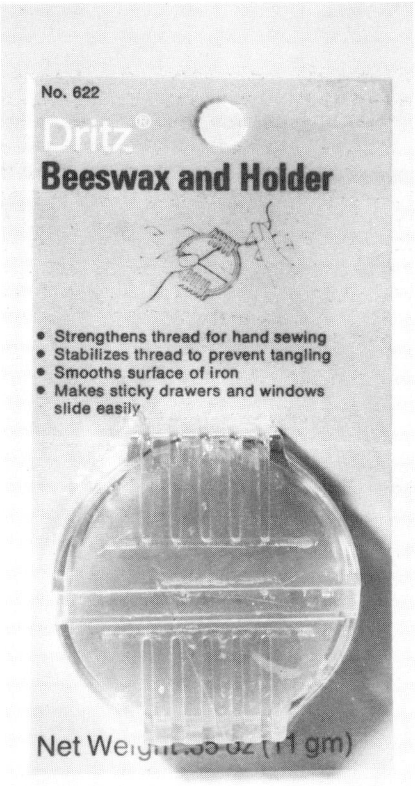

When using a pin vise, keep as little of the drill exposed as possible to reduce breakage. When drilling deep holes, remove the drill from the hole periodically to clear the chips and to lubricate the tip. When drilling thin materials, place a backing such as a scrap of lumber behind the material. This allows the drill to continue cutting after it breaks through the material and makes a cleaner hole. The backing also eliminates stresses on the drill that would otherwise occur when it breaks through the material.

Drills do become dull, and it's worth using a brand-new drill for a job where a drill broken off in the work would be a disaster. All too frequently, however, even a new drill will break off in the work. When this happens, dig out the drill, drill a larger hole at the location, and cement in a plug. Then drill another hole in the plug.

SAFETY AND STORAGE

Always remember that drills are cutting tools; they are sharp. Keep your fingers away from the point of the drill and whenever possible hold the work with something other than your hand.

When you buy your first drills, buy a case or stand with them and discipline yourself to return each drill to its proper place after each use. Store drills tip up to keep the cutting edges from banging against the case and being dulled. When you insert the drill shank in the case you can determine whether the chuck has raised a burr on the shank. Remove these burrs with a file so the drill will center properly in the chuck or collet the next time you use it. If you always return your drills to their proper places in the case you won't have to use a caliper or micrometer to keep track of their sizes.

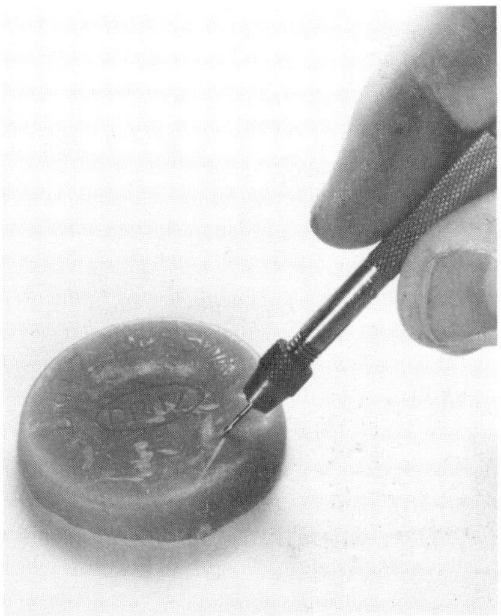

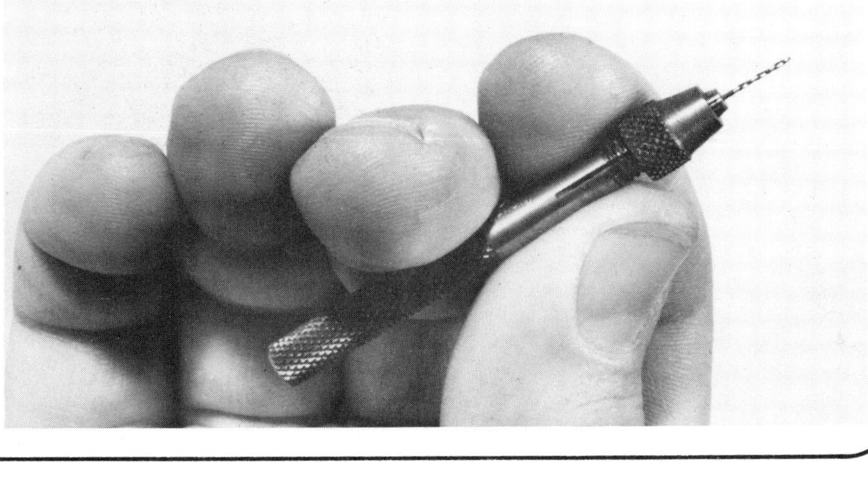

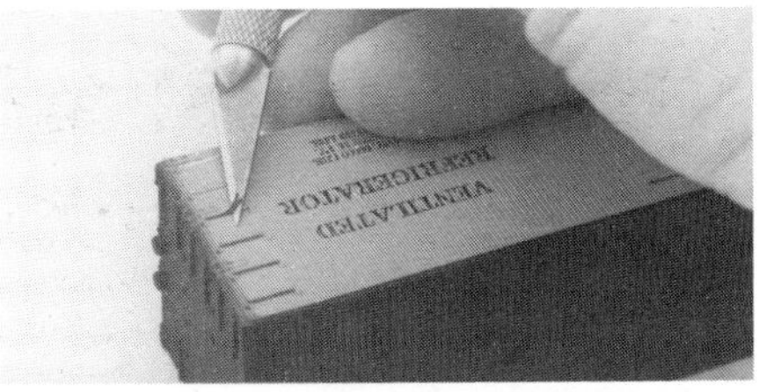

The first steps in upgrading grab-iron detail are removing the cast-on grabs and restoring the surface texture beneath.

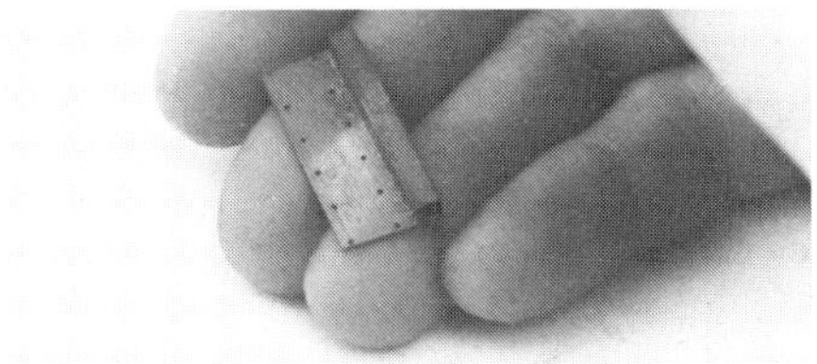

Next, drill holes for the grabs. A simple drilling jig made from two pieces of metal comes in handy, particularly if you add grabs to several cars.

On this car the bottom grabs must be shortened so they will not hit the floor. Add ACC to the back of each grab. When the cement has set, straighten.

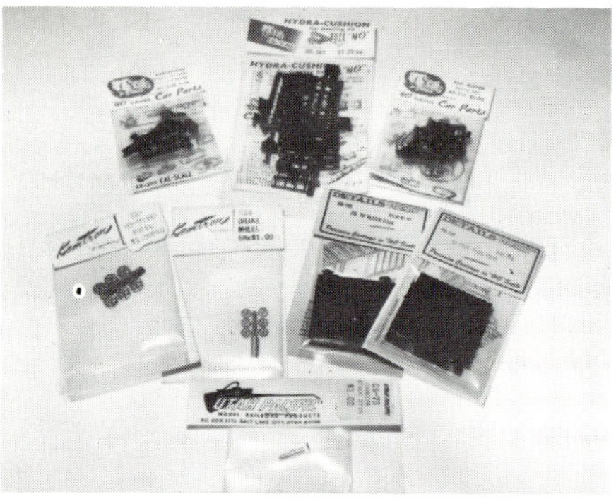

Detail parts to dress up your rolling stock are offered in plastic and cast metal.

with a set of doors cut from a separate carbody. Older style cars can be dressed up with real wood roofs, and their underbodies can be detailed with wire to simulate brake piping and linkage.

Altering panel detail and surface textures. Occasionally, plastic cars have ridges where there should be grooves. You can improve the appearance and prototype fidelity of such cars by sanding, scraping, or filing the ridges flush with the surface and scribing in recessed panel seams. Figure 6-3 shows how this is done on passenger car roofs. After the ridges are removed and sanded smooth, a bent-metal template is used as a guide for the scribing operation. The template ensures that the lines will be straight, at right angles to the roof edge, and parallel to one another. Such a template can also be used to locate vents and grab irons, so it's worth making even if you are planning to do only one car.

Passenger cars with fluted or corrugated sides present a special problem, especially where detail is cast over the corrugations. When you remove or replace that detail—car nameboards are a good example—you need to rework the surface under the removed part to match the adjacent fluted areas. Careful

Stretching a 50-foot gondola

Union Pacific

A. Railroads use extra-long gondolas to handle extra-long loads. These huge roof beams exceeded the capacity of this mill gondola.

B. Two Kadee N gondolas can be combined to make a 64-foot mill gondola. Athearn and AHM offer similar cars in HO.

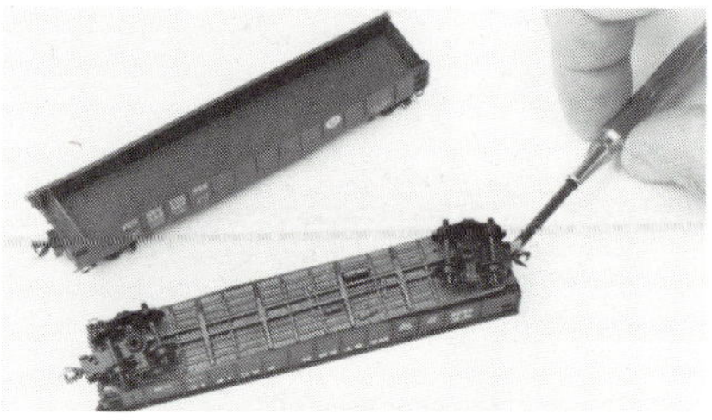

C. Remove the metal underframes of the two gondolas by gently prying upward on the metal end tabs.

D. Carefully remove the Delrin end steps from each end. The trucks can be left on the underframes.

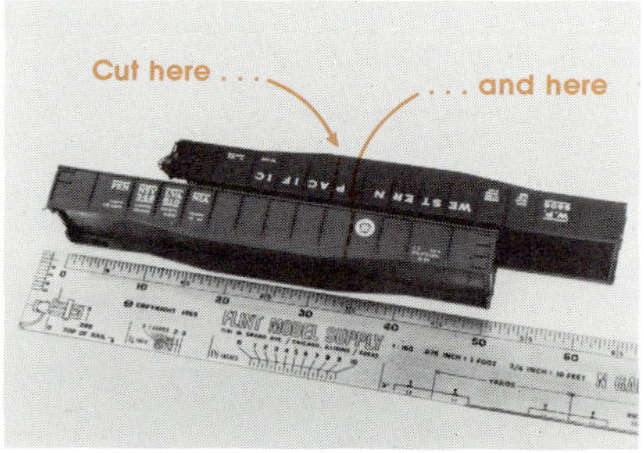

E. Carefully align the vertical ribs on both cars so your saw cuts can fall next to the vertical ribs. Cut the bodies so the rib is left on only one section of the 64-foot car.

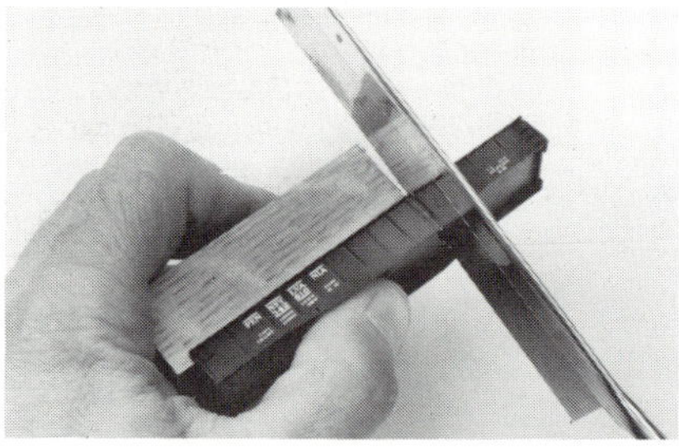

F. I chose to leave the rib on the longer (Pennsylvania) end of the car, so the first body cut is about 1/64″ away from the vertical rib. Use the rib as a guide. Only cut through the right side for now.

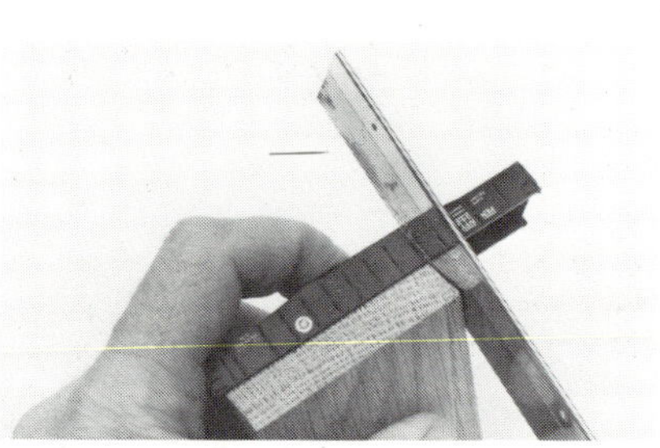

G. Now turn the body over and cut through the left side directly across from the first cut. Hold the carbody against a small block of wood so you can grip both the wood and the body while cutting; the block will help hold the carbody rigid.

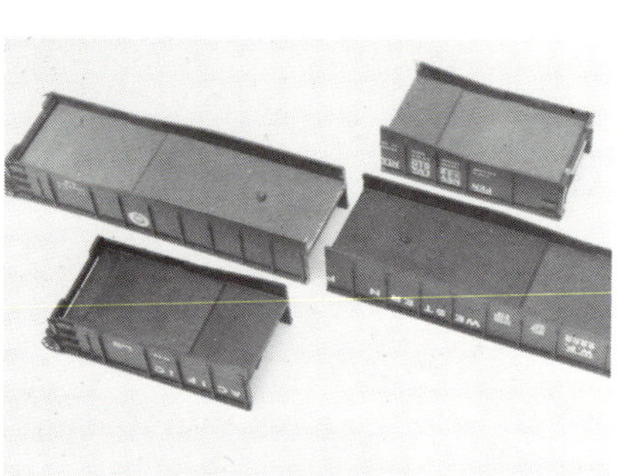

H. Make your final cuts across the car floor using the first two cuts as an aligning guide. Repeat the three-cut sequence on the second carbody, but this time cut about 1/64″ into the rib.

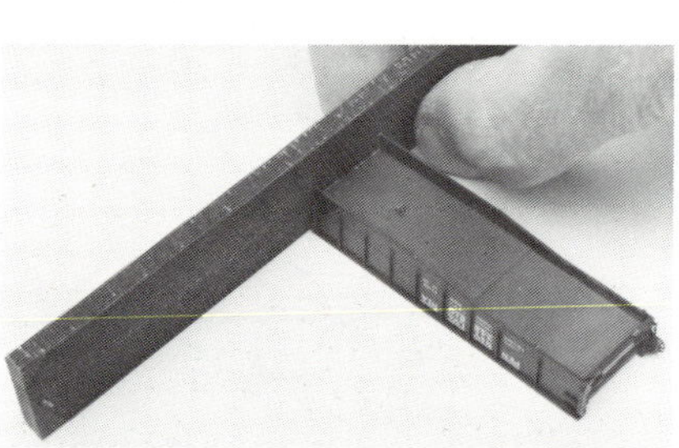

I. Use a medium-cut mill file to smooth and true the cut ends. Hold the sections together and align them by sighting along the top edges. File the joining faces until the sides are perfectly straight. This is the critical step in this project.

filing can do the job, but it's too hit-or-miss. A specially shaped scraper like the one shown in figs. 6-4 and 6-5 will do the job neatly and quickly. Grind the tip of a length of tool steel or drill rod (an old screwdriver will do) to a chisel point and cut humps in the edge to match the existing corrugations. It may take two or three tries to produce the tool, but take your time and get it right. Use the tool by drawing it over the area to be fluted. Make several light passes, and check the match between the existing corrugations and the new fluting frequently as you near the correct depth.

Lengthening and shortening cars. Abbreviated passenger cars are commonplace in model railroading because full-length cars won't negotiate the tight curves of tabletop layouts. Most prototype passenger cars are 80 to 85 feet long. In HO, both the streamlined and heavyweight Athearn passenger cars (except for the baggage and baggage-mail cars) are shorter than their prototypes and must be stretched to accurate lengths. The same is true of Athearn's Budd RDC cars and Model Die Casting's Harriman series. The foreshortened models are accurate in all details but length, so splicing carbodies can produce accurate models. Sectioning and joining are required to stretch passenger cars to full length. In lengthening, at least one of the two carbodies that you use must be cut off center and the longer body section mated to the body from the second car.

Tight curves plague modelers who want to run cars not offered in "shorty" versions. You can shorten cars to improve their performance on tight curves and make them match existing short versions by removing a section of the body shell. In shortening conversions, the area you remove must be equal to the length of at least one window, and you should try to remove

J. To remove material for the final fit, rub the cut ends of the carbodies over No. 600 sandpaper.

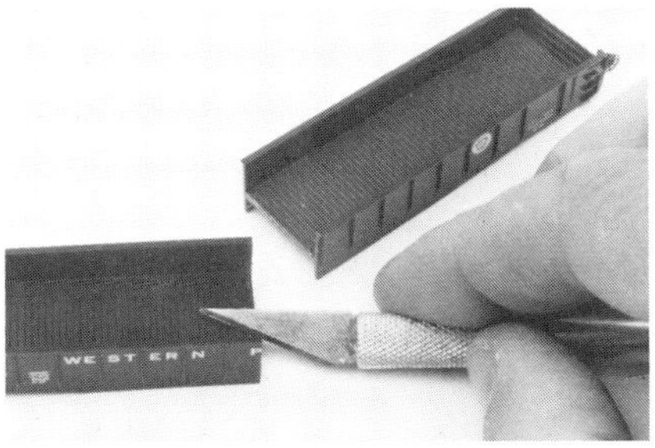

K. Carefully scrape away the cutting and sanding burrs with your hobby knife.

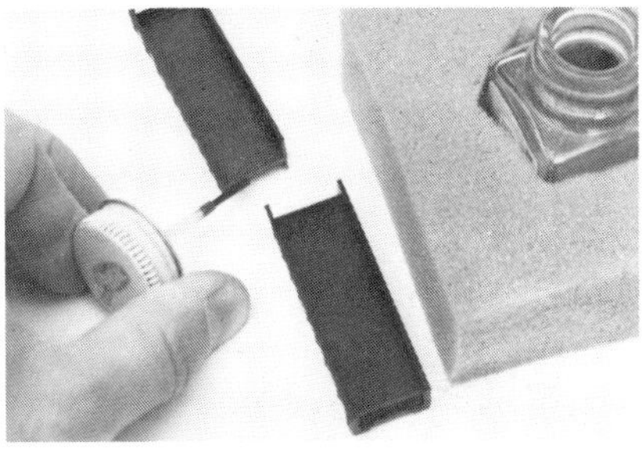

L. Make two applications of cement to the cut ends. Avoid dribbling cement on exterior surfaces.

M. Squeeze the bodies together while aligning them on a smooth block of wood. Apply more liquid cement on the inside and underside of the body. Squeeze enough that a trace of softened plastic oozes out of the seams. It's far easier to fill the seam now by squeezing the plastic than to apply filler putty later.

N. When the joint has dried for 36 hours, file the bottom and top edges of the body and slice away the bead of squeeze-and-ooze plastic. Use needle or pattern files to remove any excess squeeze-and-ooze bead from the bottom of the car where the underframe will be inserted.

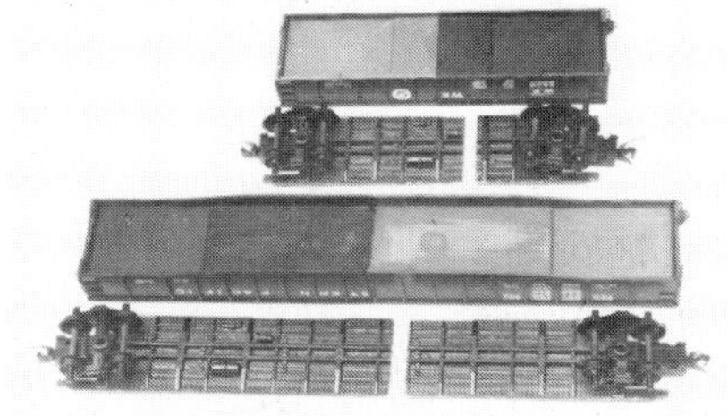

O. Wait until the joints dry on the bodies before fitting the underframes. Hold the underframes in position and mark a line across both to indicate the cuts. Position the cuts so only one set of brake detail appears on each car's underframe. I made a 37-foot gondola from the leftover parts (top). For strength, glue the underframes in with Pliobond, Goo, or 5-minute epoxy.

P. This is the 64-foot mill gondola after priming. A 67-foot version would have one more panel and one more rib, but the leftovers would be too short to be useful.

Q. Prototype railroads have operated 38-foot gondolas, so our 37-footer is plausible. Note that the fishbelly sides must be filed flush with the ends; otherwise, the conversion is identical to the work on the longer car.

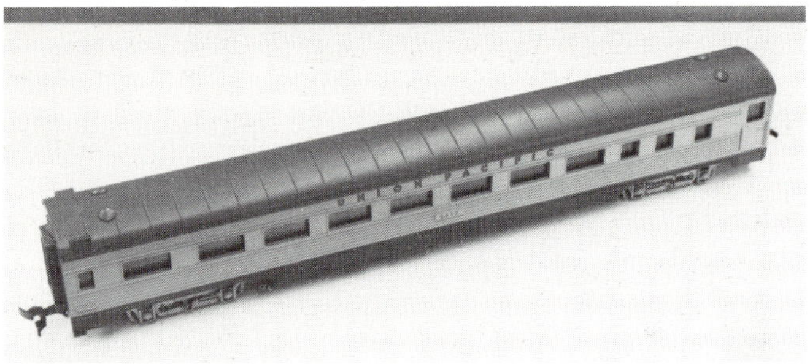

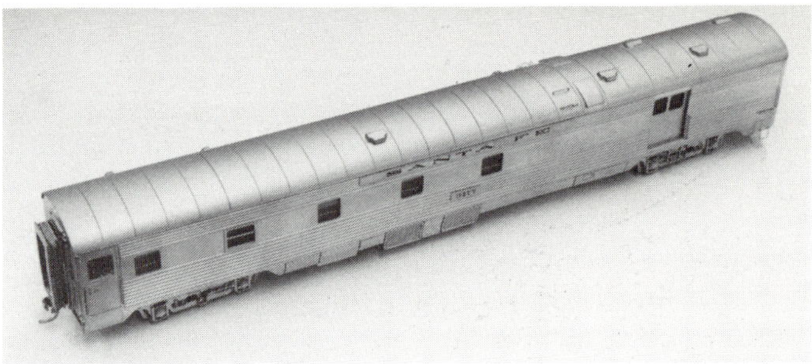

In addition to replacing the window band, reworking the roof texture, and altering the skirting, Bob Gawer scraped in corrugated areas to make Santa Fe dormitory-baggage No. 3477 (right) from a Con-Cor HO coach (left).

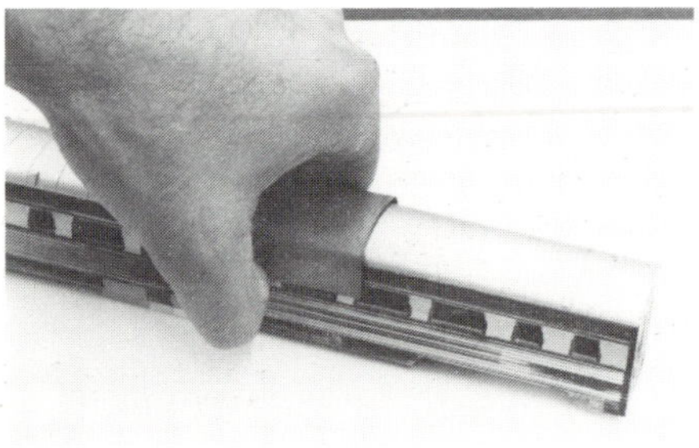

Fig. 6-3. This simple U-shaped .020″ sheet metal template matches the roof of this car and serves as a guide to scribe accurate panel lines.

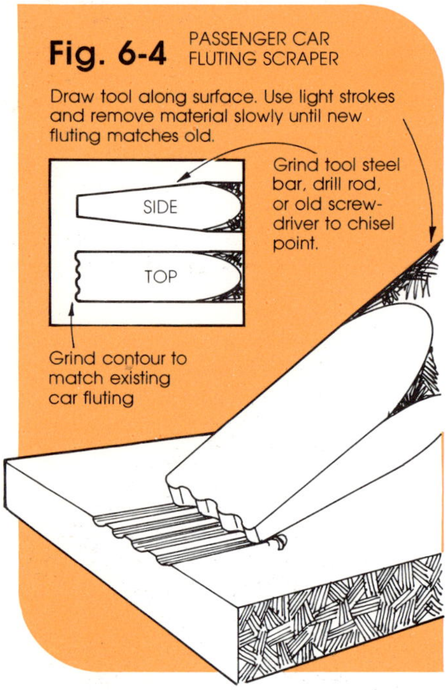

it from an area where the windows are identically spaced on both sides of the car.

Finding just the right place to slice through a carbody can be tricky. It will be easier if you try the cut first with pieces of masking tape to see how it will fall on both sides of the car, and to see whether it will create a problem with other details. Always look for symmetry, repetition of detail, seams, and other logical places to make body section cuts and joints.

Body-shell sectioning. The success of cut-and-join kitbashing, whether it is done to shorten, lengthen, or otherwise alter a carbody, depends on two factors: how well you plan the location of the cuts, and how straight you make them. You can make minor alignment corrections by filing, but mistakes in the placement of the cut, or cuts that slant or lean, will often mean that you'll have to start over.

Use masking tape to help plan your cuts. Place the tape over the model so the tape edges correspond to where you *think* you want to saw the body. Do the same on the second carbody, and before

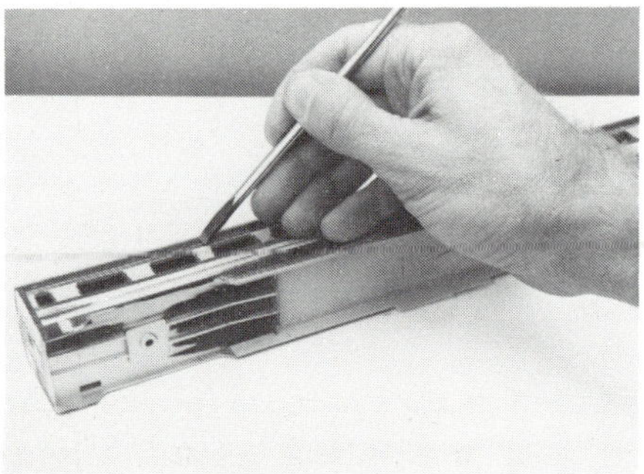

Fig. 6-5. The fluting scraper is being used here to make the smooth letterboards on this Con-Cor car match the corrugated sides. The trick is to remove material slowly, checking the depth often.

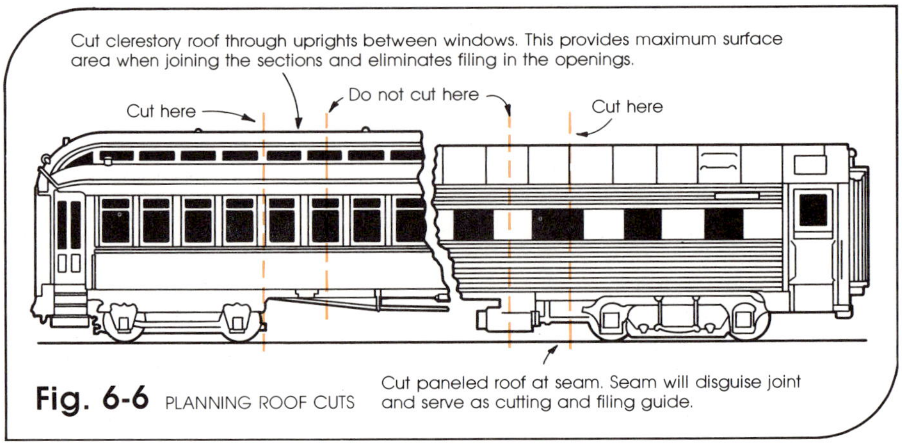

This HO Con-Cor observation car is being rebuilt as part of Santa Fe's El Capitan. The incorrect raised roof ribs on the stock model (left) have been sanded flush, and correct grooved panel seams scribed in their place.

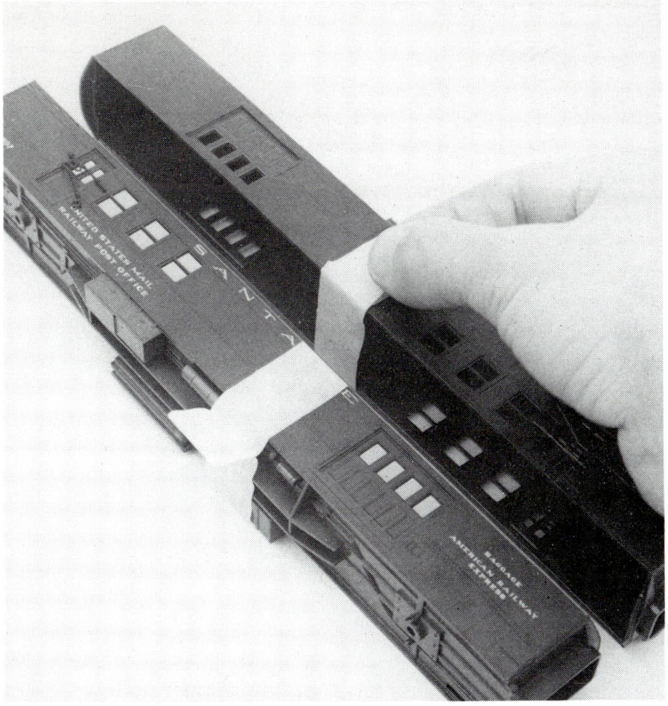

Plan body-shell cuts with masking tape – it's easier to shift the tape around than to buy a replacement body! Try several locations until you find the best one.

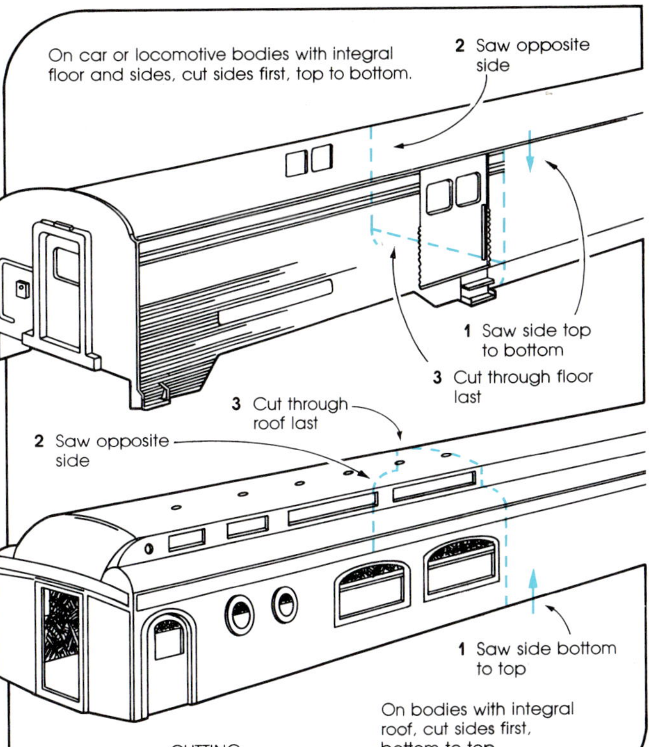

Fig. 6-7 CUTTING BODY SHELLS

you cut, hold one body on top of the other to check that the length and window arrangement will be what you want. Be especially careful on cars with windows; in many cases the windows on one side are in different locations than those on the opposite side. On some cars you may not be able to find an area where you won't cut through a window. Be aware, too, that window spacing can vary from side to side and from car to car in one manufacturer's series. This doesn't usually happen, but occasionally you'll find slight discrepancies in panel height, window spacing, or window size between one supposedly identical car and its mate. The solution here is either to fill in the opening (see the photo sequence in Chapter 5), or to graft in another window frame section from a part of the carbody that won't be used.

Once you've decided where to cut, look for minor details that require shifting the cut a fraction of an inch. On cars with clerestory roofs, for example, try to cut through the pillars rather than the windows so you don't have to file and fill joints in the close quarters of the clerestory window area, fig. 6-6. Finally, when possible, try to cut beside vertical panel joints that will help disguise the joint line on the finished model. As you check minor alignment quirks, shift the masking tape to correct for them, and again check that the resulting sections will yield the car you want.

Start each saw cut 1/64″ back from the final joint line to allow sufficient material to correct for minor inaccuracies in cutting. Some modelers use a machinist's square to guide the razor saw while cutting; you may find this a valuable aid. An alternative is to eyeball the cut, aligning the saw blade with the molded-in details such as rows of rivets and vertical body panels. Either way, hold the saw blade at a shallow angle to the car side. Cut from top to bottom on cars with floor-side castings or from bottom to top on cars where the roof is integral with the sides, fig. 6-7. Then remove the saw from the cut and cut through the opposite side. When cutting, the masking tape should protect the portion of the car body you intend to keep. Finally, saw through the roof or floor, using the slots cut in the sides to align the blade. The saw must be held at a right angle to the car side, and the cut must be straight. Attach a sheet of No. 400 wet-or-dry sandpaper to a sheet of glass or some other flat, hard surface with rubber cement, and gently rub the ends of the carbodies on the paper to smooth and square them. Don't try to sand all the way to the finished line in one operation; smooth the ends first and test them for fit. Check that the bodies fit tightly, and that sides, roof, and floor align properly. Remove material slowly, checking frequently until the length of the car is correct. In some cases it's best to keep the section to be trued stationary and make up a sanding block with a "safe" edge to slide back and forth past the surface of the model, fig. 6-8.

When the carbody sections fit perfectly, cement them together with a liquid plastic cement applied with a brush or needlepoint applicator to the inside of the joint. A simple fixture such as that shown in fig. 6-9 is often very helpful in maintaining proper alignment. These major body joints must be bonded thoroughly, so use a little more cement than you would in kit assembly. Press the sections together tightly while the joint is wet, and squeeze them so that a bead of softened plastic oozes out of the joint. Allow the joint to dry for 24 to 48 hours and trim the bead from the seam. If necessary, fill the seam with putty and

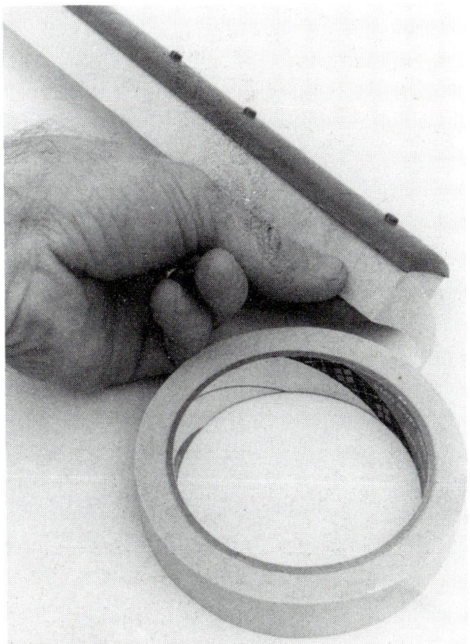

Sectioning this AHM HO passenger car roof requires special precautions to prevent marring the molded inserts. Covering the clear areas with masking tape prevents scratches.

sand flush. Joints in the roof, number boards, and horizontal ribs often require putty filling and sanding, followed by application of primer and finish sanding. In many cases you'll have to apply two or more coats of primer to the seam area before all traces of the splice become invisible.

Sometimes, because of the construction of the basic model, a cut-and-splice body will be unacceptably weak. There are several ways to reinforce weak joints and overly flexible bodies. On cars which have stamped or cast metal weights, the body can be glued to the weight with a 5-minute epoxy, and the weight will serve as a stiffener. Or, you can use a tongue of .035″ or thicker ABS or styrene sheet as the reinforcing member. Before installing such a reinforcement check that it will not interfere with other parts of the model.

Altering window arrangements. There are several ways to alter the window arrangement on a plastic passenger car. Replacement of entire side-and-roof or side-and-floor sections, as we have already discussed, is one method. When there are only a few windows to be repositioned, you can plug unwanted windows (Chapter 5), and splice in new windows from a second carbody. When extensive rearrangement is necessary,

Two RPO cars you can't buy

A. Neither of these HO heavyweight head-end cars is for sale in any hobby shop, but both are easily kitbashed from stock AHM cars.

Kenneth G. Johnsen

B. Here's a "near-prototype" for our first conversion: a Southern Pacific RPO on a post-WW II "Daylight" train. This project captures the spirit of the car without duplicating every nut and bolt.

C. The quickest way to provide an all-mail car for your heavyweight train is to replace the roof on this AHM 1930 RPO with one from a 1920 coach.

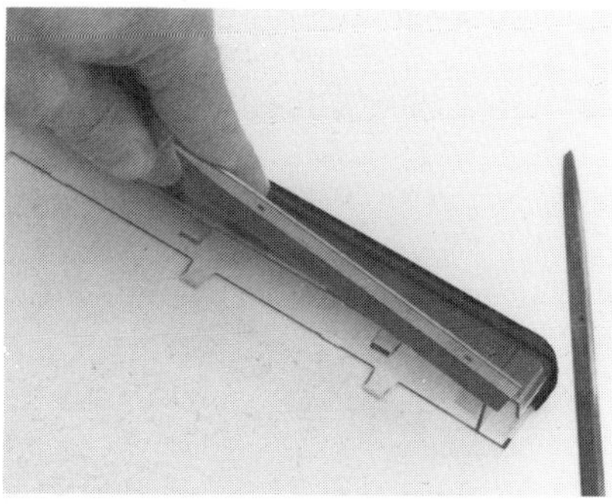

D. Trim the clear mounting tabs from the AHM coach roof and file the ends to fit the streamlined RPO body.

E. Finish by removing the raised coach drip rails from the roof corners with a few strokes of a needle file. The entire job takes less than an hour!

George H. Drury

F. This Grand Trunk Railway Post Office is the inspiration for our second conversion, an all-RPO car which is made by combining the post-office ends from two AHM heavyweight baggage-mail cars.

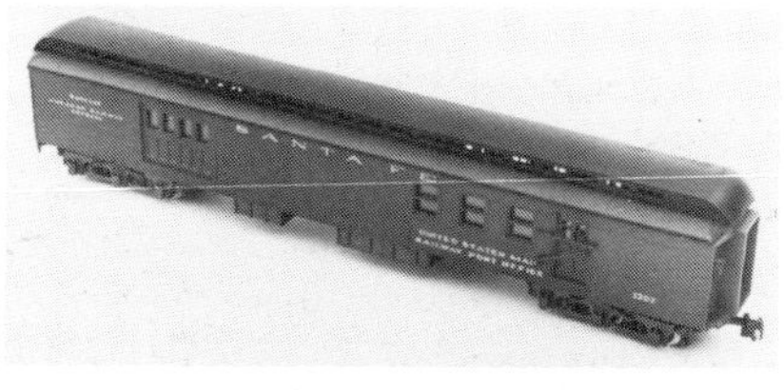

G. You'll need two AHM 1920 baggage-mail cars for this project. If you're very careful with your razor-saw cuts, the two leftover baggage ends can be combined into a 70-foot all-baggage car.

H. Disassemble both cars by lifting gently on the roof while squeezing the lock tabs where they protrude through the floor. Pop the trucks loose, by pushing on the kingpin lugs from inside the car.

you can cut the entire window band from the car and replace it with a window band from a car that has the correct window size and spacing.

Splicing in windows from a second carbody is very similar to plugging windows. You'll need to use this technique on cars that have windows with intricate frame beading or moldings. In many cases you'll be able to transplant entire rows of windows; for certain prototypes you'll only need to patch in one or two. You can often find second-hand cars or carbodies at model railroad swap meets or flea markets, and many manufacturers offer body shells separately, so your "donor" car need not cost more than a few dollars.

The photo sequence shows how a wide window was sliced out of one car and grafted into another. The important point to remember is that the spliced window must be flush and in line with the others in the car side—any twist or slant will give away the splice. Work slowly and carefully and don't hesitate to discard a window and cut a new one from the donor carbody if you ruin your first attempt.

Replacing an entire window band is a little more work. For cars without molded or beaded window frames, a strip of .010" or .015" styrene can be cut

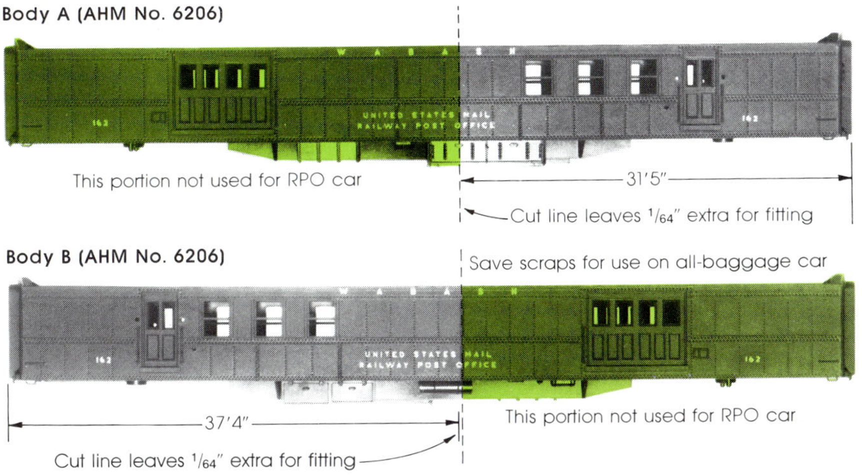

I. Use masking tape to position the saw cuts on the car bodies. The cuts are not at the exact centers of the cars – place them so the vertical rivet strip near the center of the car is cut away on one body but preserved on the other.

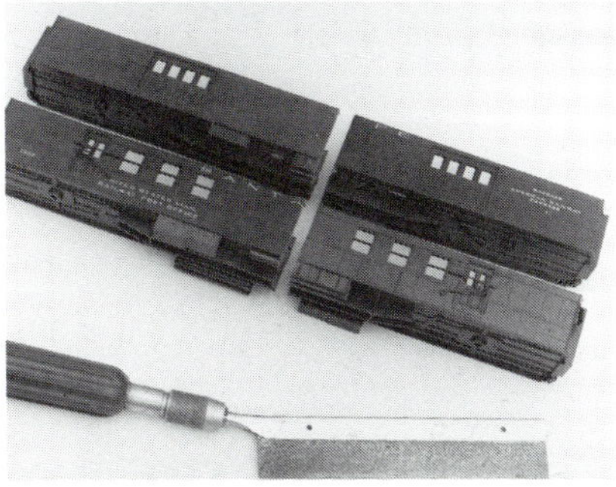

J. Cut through the sides and floor; sides first, top to bottom, then floor. Note that part of a battery box is sliced away.

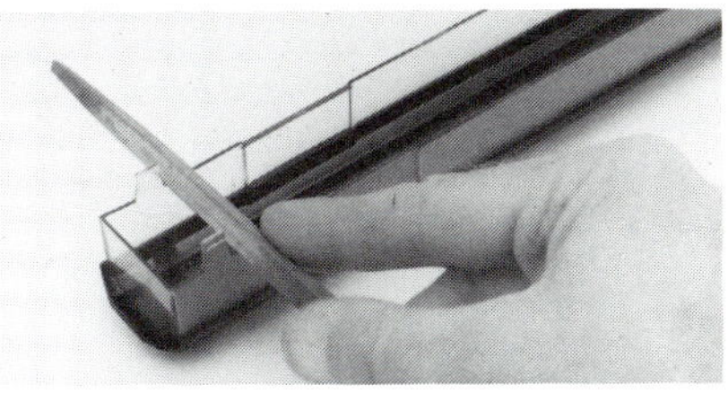

K. Modify the roof. Cut off the center lugs and remove 1/16" from the inner edges on the wide-door end lugs.

L. Check the body halves by temporarily positioning them on the roof casting. If you left a small amount of extra material on each section, the body should come out about 1/32" too long. Sand this away slowly, and when you're satisfied with the fit, cement the parts together.

M. Push the car sections together and wiggle them until a small plastic bead is squeezed from the seam. This bead should fill the seam – body filler putty and sandpaper need only be used to finish the letterboards at the top of each side.

N. Prime the body to determine whether or not the joint will show along the letterboards. If necessary, use a second application of filler putty to hide all traces of the seam.

O. Walthers and Champ make gold decals suitable for this car. Be sure to use enough decal setting agent to make the lettering conform to the rivet detail. Spray the car side with clear flat before inserting the roof.

Jim C. Seacrest

P. Looking for yet another heavyweight head-end car to kitbash? Well, you've got some leftover parts, and here's a car for inspiration!

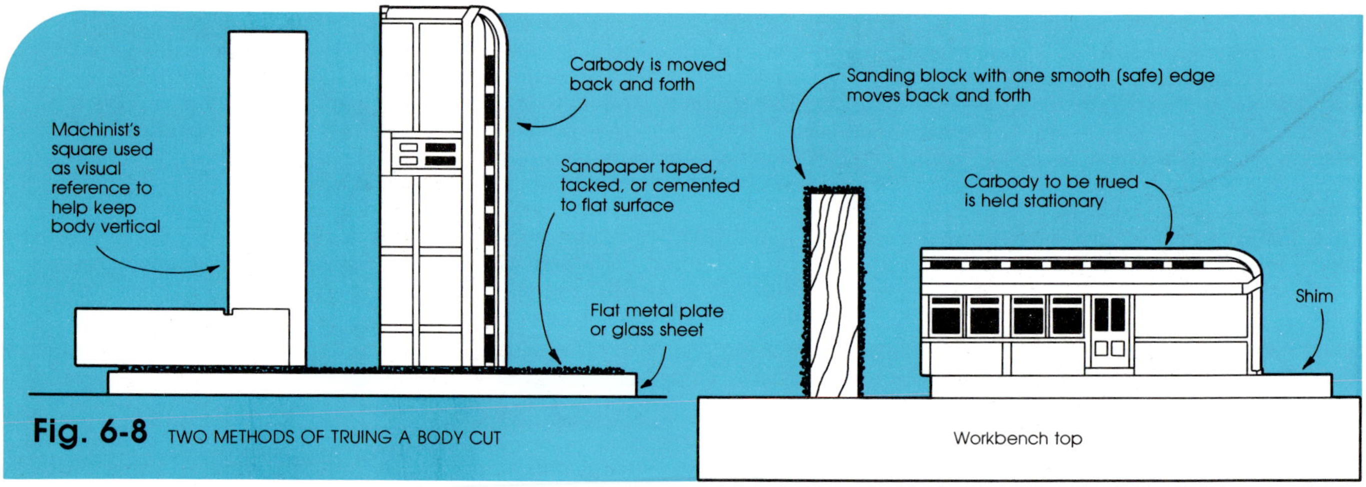

Fig. 6-8 TWO METHODS OF TRUING A BODY CUT

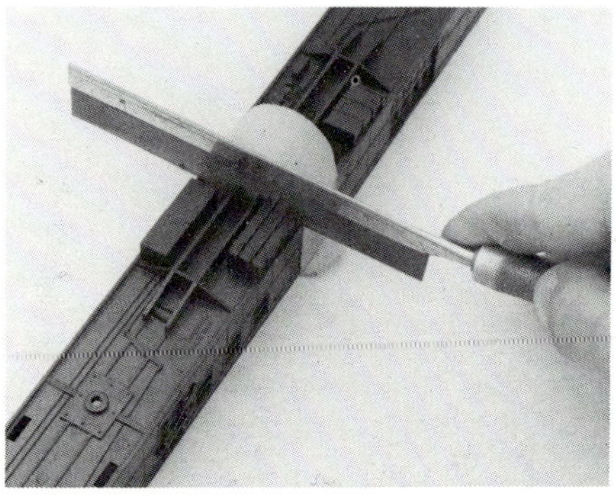

Saw through the floor or roof last when making body-shell cuts. Use the side cuts to position the saw.

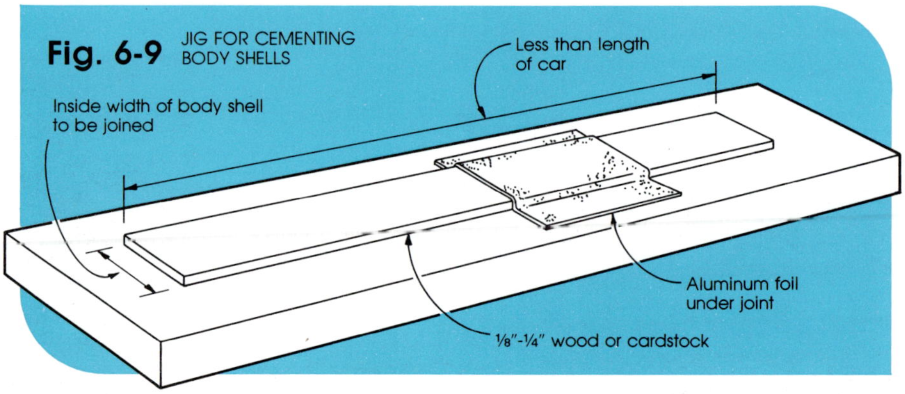

Fig. 6-9 JIG FOR CEMENTING BODY SHELLS

Smooth and true the cut ends of a sectioned body shell by rubbing it on a sheet of fine sandpaper cemented to a flat surface. Check frequently to ensure all edges are perpendicular.

To transplant a window from one carbody to another, start by making a vertical slice on each side of the window frame. Leave 1/16" of material on each side for trimming and fitting.

to fit, and the window openings carefully cut and filed to the appropriate shape. With care, you can add a strip like this to the car without filler putty. Another answer—where the windows do have a trim bead—is to cut the entire window band from a donor car and add it to the model.

Possible passenger car modifications go far beyond rearranging window sizes and locations. You can make a streamlined diner from a streamlined coach, or

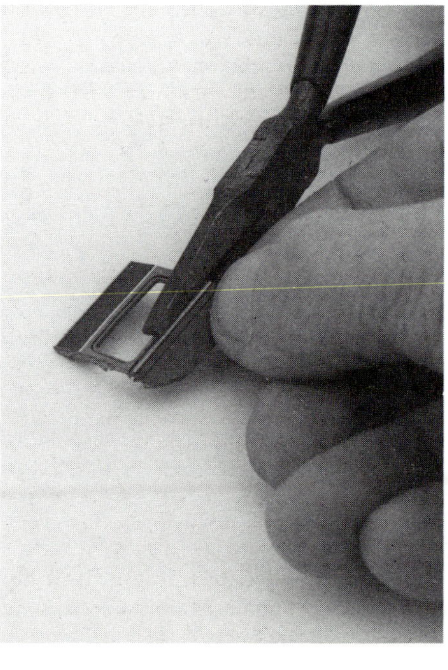

Break the window frame from the car side with flat-nose pliers and break off excess material along the horizontal cut. Saw off all but 1/16" of material above the window frame beaded molding.

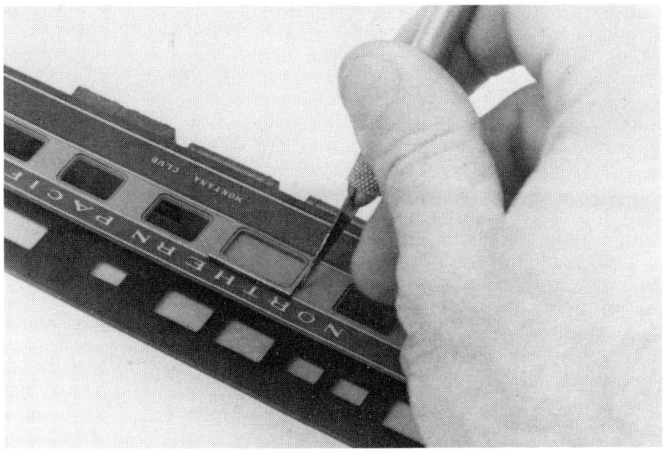

Trace the outline of the window insert onto the car side and cut the opening 1/64" undersize on all edges.

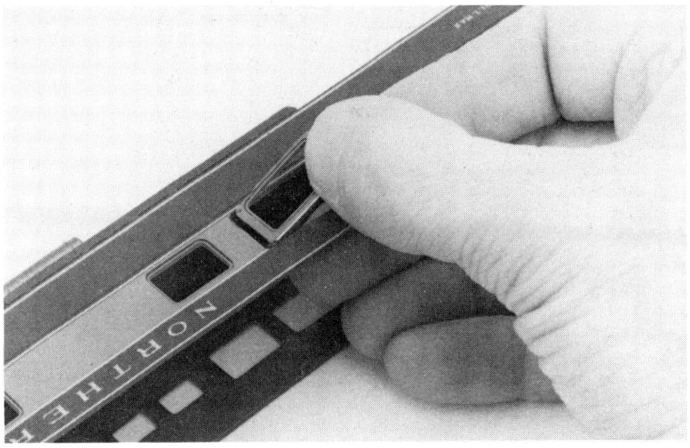

Enlarge the hole with files until the window frame drops in. Test-fit the frame often to ensure that it will line up with the adjacent windows.

Cement the window insert flush with the car side. If the insert is a loose fit, hold it in place with masking tape on the inside of the body until the cemented joints dry.

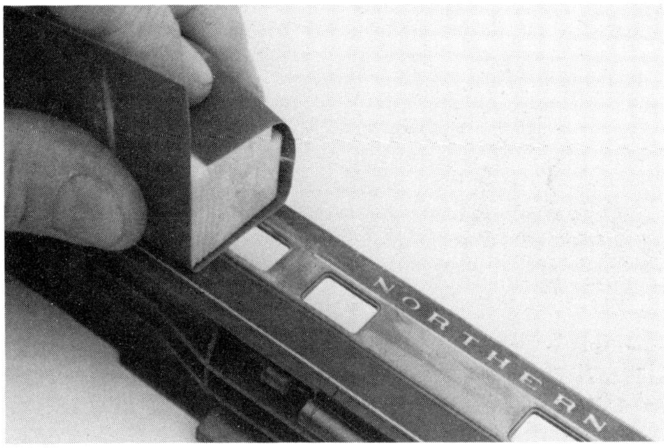

Let the cement set overnight, apply filler putty to the seams, and sand smooth after the putty hardens.

convert conventional streamlined cars to dome cars by grafting on a dome from another car. Heavyweight riveted-steel cars from the 1920's and 1930's can be modernized by installing air-conditioning ducts along the clerestory, by adding large oval windows taken from streamlined cars, or by blanking the tops of the high windows with thin plastic sheet. Arched roofs can be lifted from streamlined cars and fitted to other carbodies to dramatically alter their appearance. There are enough plastic passenger cars—particularly in HO—that you can duplicate almost any prototype car by using parts from available models.

Finally—and I'd rate these among the most challenging kitbashing projects—there's a type of passenger car for an entirely different type of passenger: railroad business cars and private cars. Business cars are used as traveling offices and homes away from home by railroad officials, and private cars were owned by railroad magnates and millionaires—Sanfords, Goulds, Vanderbilts, and Harrimans. Private cars make ideal kitbashing projects because each was custom built to satisfy its owner's needs or whims.

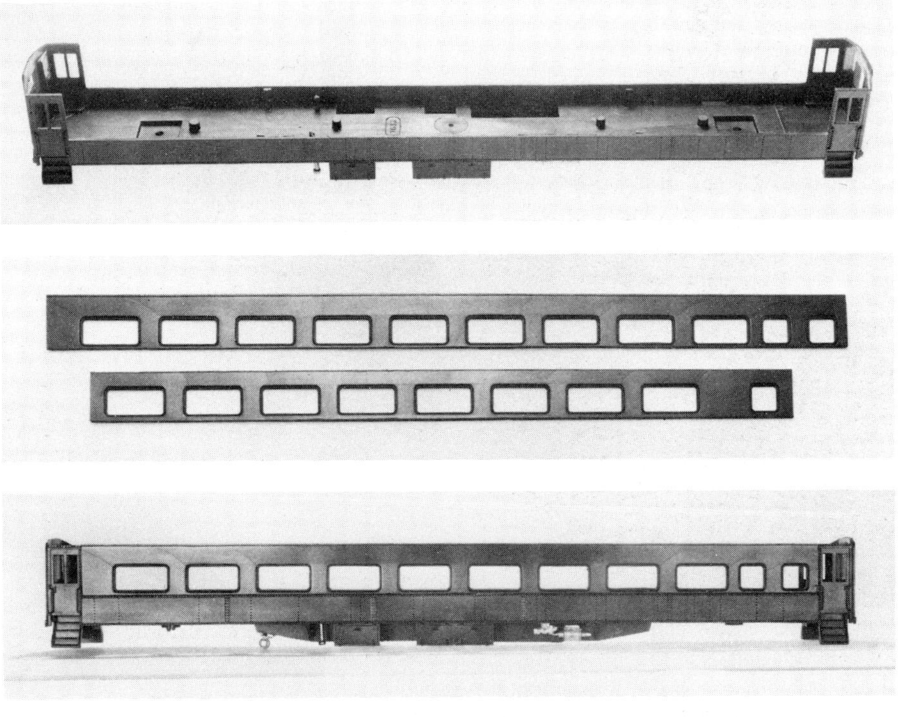

Modernizing a heavyweight coach involves replacing the entire window band with wide windows from a modern car. This AHM HO Pullman has had the old-style windows removed (top). An AHM streamlined coach provides a wide-window band (middle). The final step is to add the new windows to the underframe (bottom).

Kitbashing locomotives

Add personality to your locomotive roster

BECAUSE they combine animation with interesting detail, your locomotives are the most-seen and most-remembered models on your layout. Your visitors, especially other model railroaders, pay careful attention to your motive power, so it's worthwhile to make your roster memorable by including at least a few engines that are different from out-of-the-box versions.

Locomotive kitbashing projects—either diesel or steam—fall into three categories: upgrading, minor modification, and major modification. We'll examine each category and discuss how each applies to diesel and steam locomotives. You'll use the techniques discussed in the preceding chapters for locomotive kitbashing, so most of this chapter is devoted to illustrating the *kind* of kitbashing work that is possible, with only a few specific step-by-step discussions.

You can model nearly any diesel locomotive used by major American railroads by using parts from one or more inexpensive plastic diesels. There are over 50 different HO plastic diesels and over a dozen different designs in O and N scales. This variety is sufficient to provide parts to build most prototypes. Modifications necessary to model specific prototype units usually involve changes only to the superstructures; the chassis is left alone. Superstructure alterations range from simple headlight changing to major surgery. Most diesel kitbashing is quite similar to the operations on passenger cars described in Chapter 6.

There is a growing variety of plastic steam power in HO and N scales. Steam engines are slightly more difficult to kitbash than diesels because of their combinations of round and rectangular forms. Round boilers, square cabs, round cylinders, and boxy tenders must be carefully joined. There are relatively few plastic steam locomotives offered in O scale, but they are particularly easy to kitbash because most of their detail parts are separate items rather than integrally cast parts.

Let me add one note of caution: Don't jump into locomotive kitbashing until you've got some experience in the basic kitbashing techniques. Do at least one or two passenger and freight car projects before you begin sawing away on your locomotives.

Upgrading locomotives. Let's start by talking about locomotive *upgrading*. The simplest—and some of the most effective—detail you can add to any locomotive is to give it a lived-in look. This means adding crew members, cab arm rests, and cab curtains on steam engines or rearview mirrors on diesels. These small touches take less than an evening to install on most engines but they bring even a plain model to life.

The most noticeable flaw in the realism of plastic HO and N diesels is the out-of-scale size of the handrails and support stanchions. Replacing HO handrail stanchions with Kemtron brass substitutes or the newer Athearn wrap-around style is simple. Trim off the old stanchions, drill holes to fit the new ones, and press the new stanchions in place, securing them with a small drop of ACC applied from behind. The handrails themselves can be formed from steel music wire (see fig. 6-1 for correct sizes), using the original plastic pieces as patterns. Be sure to check photos of the prototype you are modeling to verify the correct handrails.

To superdetail the pilots of your diesels, add air hoses and MU cables using commercial castings, or make your own hoses and cables from partially stripped insulated electrical wire. Another upgrading detail item is a diaphragm for the B end of a cab diesel—early F's, E's, and PA's all wore diaphragms on their "back end," although the diaphragms were later removed from most units.

The only thing that distinguishes the appearance of an imported brass steam locomotive from that of a budget-priced plastic version is the wealth of free-standing detail parts on the brass engine. Many such details can be removed from one plastic locomotive to re-detail another, or they can be fabricated from plastic scrap and wire or purchased separately. Brass castings are expensive, but you can purchase a plastic locomotive and enough castings to superbly detail it for a fraction of the price of a brass model.

The techniques for removing unwanted details on plastic steam locomo-

Mantua's colorful HO "Dixie Belle" 4-6-0 Ten-Wheeler is based on a prototype locomotive of the late 1800's. To modernize his engine in much the same way that real railroads updated their older motive power, P.O. Putnam added handmade domes, cast metal detail parts, and free-standing handrails and piping. The tender was updated by adding a scratchbuilt sheet styrene fuel oil bunker, ladder, marker lights, and extra handrails. Figures complete the job.

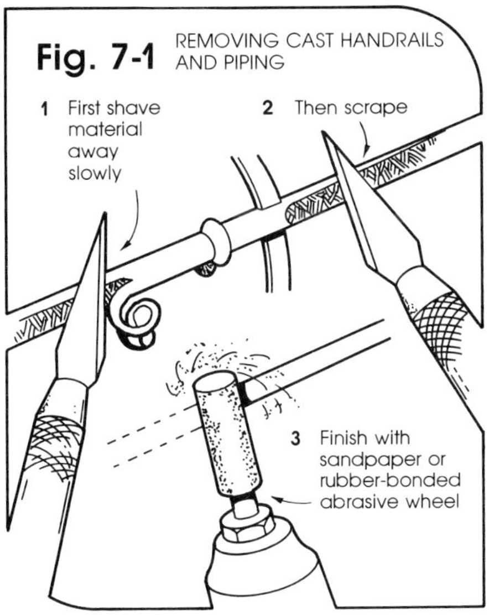

tives are similar to those employed to remove cast-on grab irons. Use a sharp knife blade and work carefully to avoid damaging nearby details. Piping should be scraped away a sliver at a time to prevent the blade from digging into the surface and to minimize the amount of filing and sanding, fig. 7-1.

You can upgrade a plastic tender by replacing the molded plastic coal pile with a thin shell of more realistic coal. You don't want to add a lot of weight to the tender, so if you start with an empty fuel bunker, use a block of Styrofoam or a few pieces of tape to take up most of the space, then pour on your scale coal. When the pile is a shape you like, moisten it with water from an eyedropper. Then flow in a solution of one part white glue and four parts water. When this

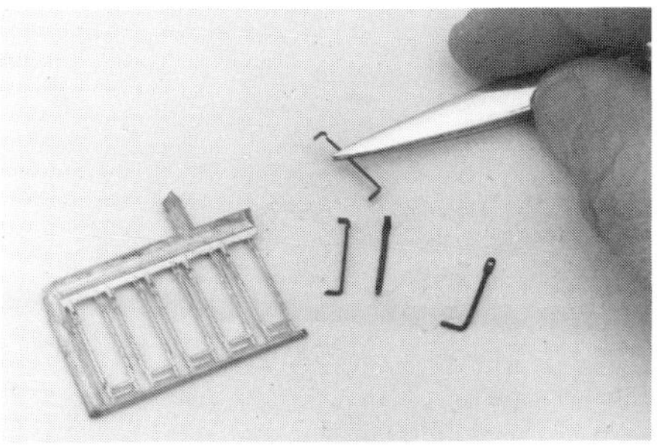

Replacement diesel handrail stanchions: left to right, Kemtron brass stanchions, Athearn wrap-around posts, older Athearn stanchion.

Note the difference between the .026″ handrails on No. 3624 (left) and the closer-to-scale .018″ wire on No. 3622.

Gordon Odegard

Ted Shrady

Diaphragms make interesting, easy-to-add details for cab-type diesels. Left, an E unit without a diaphragm, right, another E fitted with one.

AHM's HO Norfolk & Western 2-8-8-2 has excellent detail as it comes from the box. Anthony Sapienza replaced molded piping, added detail castings, and made minor changes to model one of the Y6b's that Santa Fe bought from the N&W.

Note the differences between the cast brass Cal-Scale bell (left) and the turned bell on this AHM HO Ten-Wheeler.

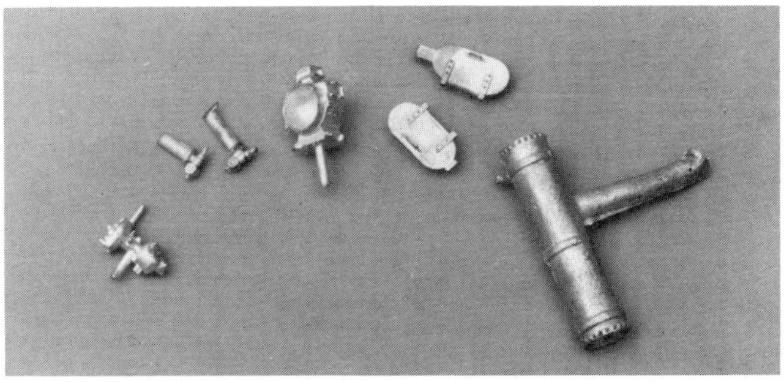

Left to right, Cal-Scale generator, Kemtron check valves, Cal-Scale headlight, Kemtron hatches and air tank.

This AHM HO tender has been repainted and decaled, but the biggest improvement was addition of a realistic coal pile over the molded plastic one.

Diesel detailing parts make it possible to modify any stock plastic unit to represent a specific locomotive from your favorite road. These HO scale parts are only a few of those available.

This HO snowplow pilot casting is the raw material for an easy one-evening diesel detailing project. Several types of snowplow pilots are available; mounting any of them requires removing interfering detail from the existing locomotive pilot beam area.

EMD

Many railroads have distinctive headlight preferences. This T. & N.O. (Texas & New Orleans) engine wears the extra "beer barrel" headlight specified on Southern Pacific road units.

sets, the coal will be held in place, but will still look loose.

Minor diesel modifications. There are dozens of details that can be altered on plastic diesels to match modifications on prototype engines. The specific road or specific unit that you want to model will determine the changes you must make. You'll have to make at least a few changes, even if the engine you want to model is an SDP40 and you start with an out-of-the-box HO SDP40. The pilots need extra detailing, and you'll want to add markings showing the locations of service openings (Micro Scale makes a decal set for these). There are usually several small details—headlights, fuel tanks, air horns—that should be changed to match a particular prototype locomotive.

Model manufacturers usually pattern their kits on stock-version factory blueprints from the locomotive builders, but when the railroads order new locomotives, they specify modifications to meet their particular operating conditions. For example, diesels that operate in mountainous areas where there is heavy snowfall often carry a snowplow pilot on one end. Several manufacturers offer HO snowplow castings, or you can fabricate your own in any scale from thin plastic sheet. Likewise, headlight preferences differ from railroad to railroad; you can purchase detail castings to replace the standard items on your plastic locomotives, or modify the existing headlights and housings with small pieces of plastic. The more you study prototype diesels, the more unusual and distinctive features you'll find.

Altering an SD-series six-axle locomotive to match the passenger-equipped versions is another easy-to-spot and easy-to-accomplish conversion.

Murray Sincoff altered the headlights of these Athearn HO U33C's to match Erie-Lackawanna units. At far left, E-L 3307 has no headlight, while E-L 3360 (center) has a single light in place of the dual headlight housing.

EMD

This brand-new EMD GP30 rides on traded-in Alco trucks. Modeling such a "kitbashed" unit in any scale would make a uniquely interesting conversation piece for your layout.

Murray Sincoff kitbashed Erie-Lackawanna GP7 No. 1224 from an Athearn HO GP9 by removing the dynamic brake bulges and raised winterization hatch, filling the openings, adding a fourth round fan, and relocating the horn.

A sampler of HO tenders: (left to right) top row – AHM 2-8-8-0, AHM USRA Heavy 4-6-2, AHM 4-6-6-4; center – AHM 0-8-0, AHM USRA Light 4-6-2, Roundhouse Vanderbilt type, AHM USRA Heavy 2-8-2; bottom – Mantua Mogul, AHM Bowker, Roundhouse HOn3 2-8-0, Mantua 0-8-0.

Simply swapping tenders can make quite a difference in a steam locomotive. Top to bottom: a Mantua HO 2-6-0 Mogul with its own stock tender, with a tender from a Mantua 0-8-0, and with a Roundhouse Vanderbilt tender.

The long hood on the SD40 and the SD45 must be stretched to accommodate a steam generator. This modification is particularly impressive on the SDP45 because the hood comes out square, not tapered. Some railroads have purchased SDP-series locomotives in order to mount larger fuel tanks on the longer frame. The hoods on these special units are longer than standard SD hoods, but the ends are tapered in the conventional pattern.

Minor modifications to steam locomotives. The tender is the place to start altering a steam locomotive. Changing the type of tender can radically change the appearance of most locomotives, as can the easy step of changing the fuel type, fig. 7-2. Tenders are usually available from the manufacturers as separate items, or can be procured at swap meets. Before you start on the boiler and cab, always see what can be done with the tender.

Steam engines underwent many modifications from the time they left the builders to the time they were scrapped. The USRA locomotives offer a good example. During World War I the United States Railroad Administration developed standardized designs to meet wartime demands for increased locomotive production. More than 5000 locomotives that were operated by almost 100 railroads were built from these plans. Because the railroads modified USRA-design locomotives extensively to suit their needs, these standard designs are ideal starting points for minor or major kitbashing projects. Several plastic models of the basic USRA designs are available in HO and N.

The steam locomotive changed greatly during the hundred years that it served as the prime mover for the world's railroads. Mechanical and trim details distinguish locomotives of one period from those of another. If you are interested in establishing a distinct time period for your model railroad, kitbashing is one way to add specific period details to a stable of inexpensive steam locomotives. Changing domes, head-

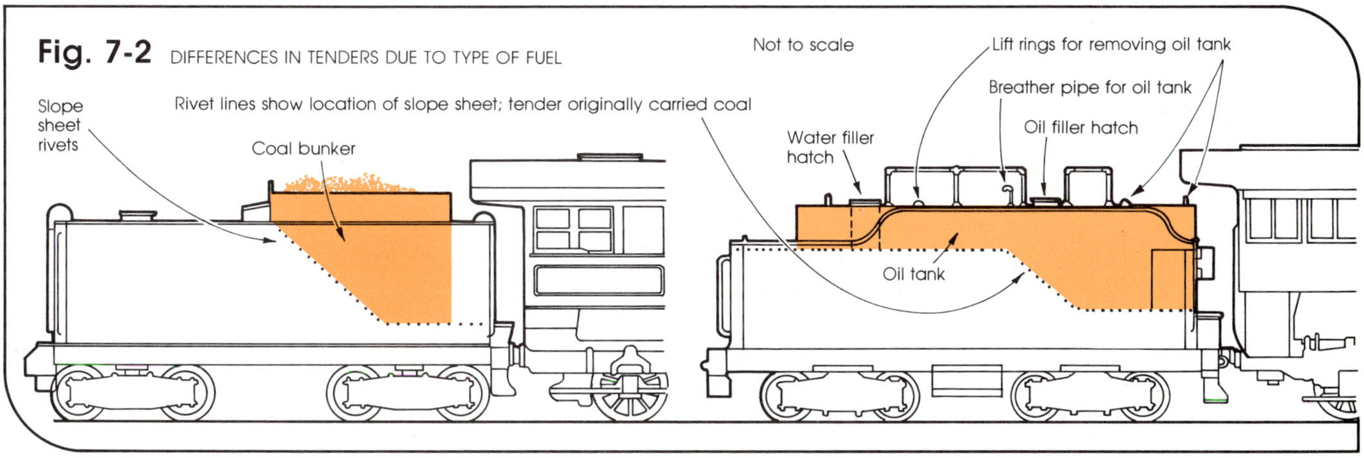

Fig. 7-2 DIFFERENCES IN TENDERS DUE TO TYPE OF FUEL

light, cab, and maybe the tender is usually sufficient to backdate a steam locomotive to the 1890's, or to update an older model to the 1920's or 1940's. Nearly every manufacturer of plastic steam locomotives offers models with domes, cabs, and tenders that date individual engines to the early, middle, or late steam periods. Other manufacturers sell individual parts—domes, headlights, bells, and so on—that can be used to establish the desired period.

Removing parts from one boiler or superstructure molding for use on another calls for several approaches. Small details—bells, generators, and some headlights—can be cut away neatly with a razor saw or jeweler's saw. Larger pieces—stacks, domes, feedwater heater housings, and air tanks—may require sacrificing some of the surrounding material. The photo sequence shows how a hot knife was used to remove a large part. The hole in the boiler shell is a lot larger than the finished part, but this is of no concern once a boiler casting has been condemned to

An E8 B unit

Union Pacific

A. Excellent EMD E8 A units are available in HO and N, but there are no matching E8 B units. Not all roads that had E8's ordered B units, but here's a UP example we can use as a reference for our easy kitbashing project.

B. Here's the basic idea: replacing the nose section on the A unit with the opposite end from a second body.

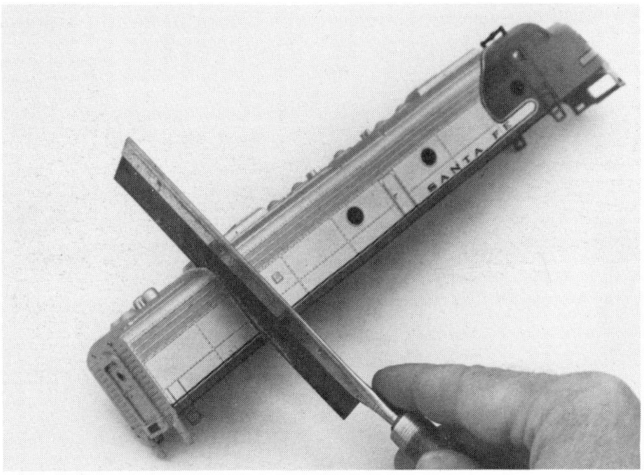

C. You can accomplish this kitbashing project in either HO scale or N scale. In HO, you'll need two AHM E8 A unit bodies. Make the first cut on the right side, 1/64″ forward of the third rib from the rear end of the body shell.

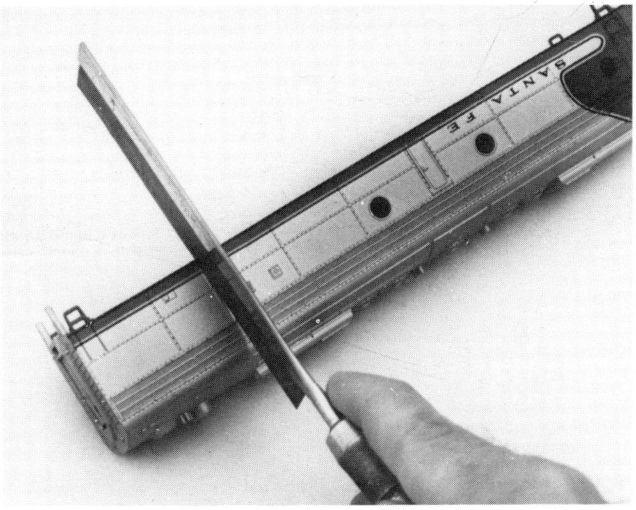

D. Next, rotate the body and make a second cut 1/64″ forward of the third rib from the rear on the left side.

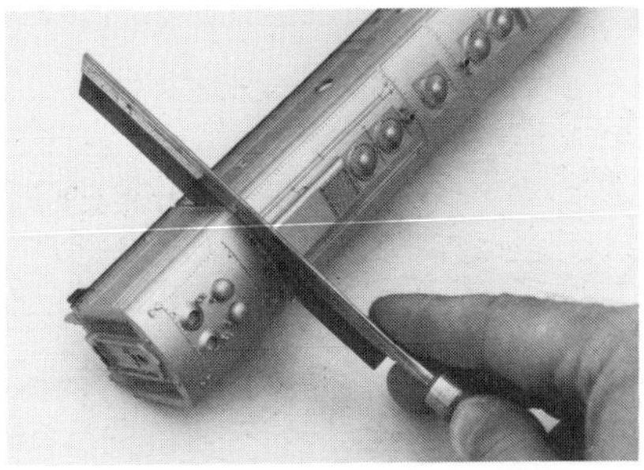

E. Using the side cuts to align the razor saw blade, make the final cut across the top of the first body.

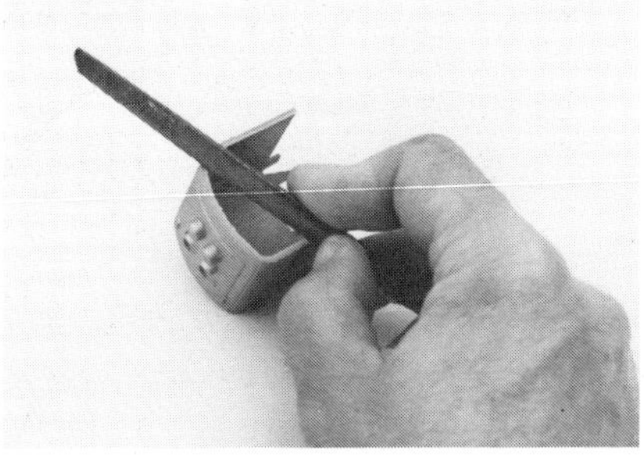

F. File the cut end to remove saw marks. Work carefully so you don't remove material from the vertical ribs.

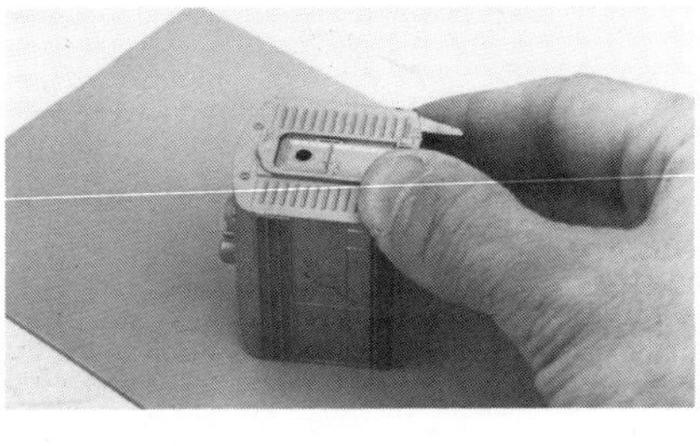

G. Rub the cut end on No. 600 wet-or-dry sandpaper cemented to a flat surface. The end must be at a right angle to the roof. Sand to within a few thousandths of the vertical ribs.

donor status. In some cases you can drill $^{1}/_{16}$" holes around the part to be removed, then cut through the thin plastic left between the holes to free the part.

Because so much of their running gear and plumbing is exposed to view, you must be cautious when you change the appearance of steam locomotives. Figure 7-3 shows some of the relationships between major functional parts that can't be altered. Use prototype plans or photos when you kitbash steam locomotives, but, as always, aim for plausibility rather than inch-for-inch duplication.

Major diesel modifications. Now we come to major modifications—true locomotive kitbashing. In a sense model railroaders are only following the lead of the prototype here, because real railroads kitbash engines too! Many railroads have shops where entire locomotives are built or rebuilt with parts from wrecked or scrapped units. ICG's Paducah rebuilds and Santa Fe's CF7's are examples of these "homebuilt" locomotives. Locomotive builders also ac-

H. Carefully scrape away the wispy plastic burrs raised during the filing and sanding operations. Don't remove even a trace of the body itself.

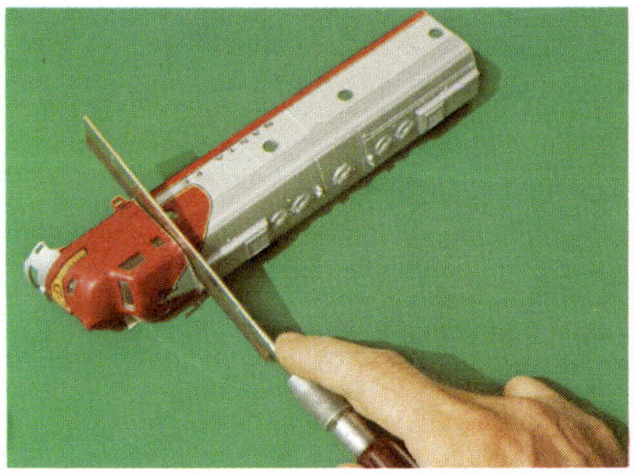

I. The short end piece we just finished will replace the nose on the second body to create the B unit. Cut the nose away next to the molded frame at the rear edges of the door. Make the same right, left, and top cuts as on the first body.

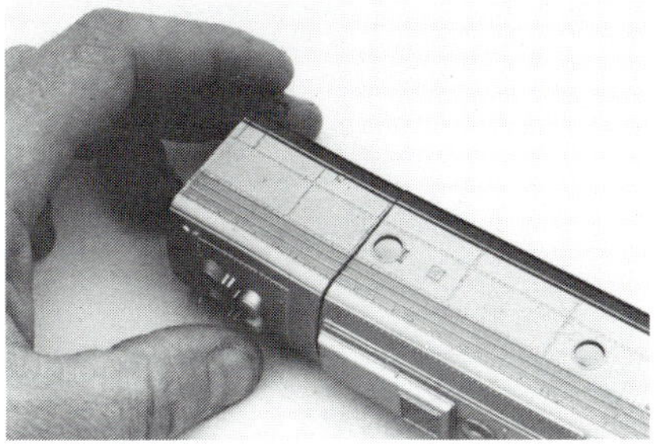

J. Hold the pieces together and sight down the sides and top to see where the cut ends must be filed to get all three surfaces in perfect alignment. Use files and No. 600 sandpaper until the joint is perfect. Remove the steam generator detail from the roof of the short end.

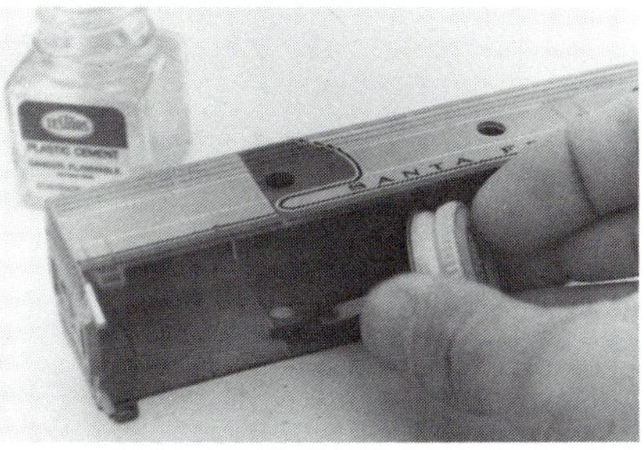

K. Apply cement to the cut surfaces, then squeeze together. Apply cement to the inside and squeeze until a pin-size bead of plastic oozes out. When the joint has dried, scrape the bead flush. If there are visible cracks, fill them with putty.

L. Apply primer, finish colors, and decals to match your E8 A unit. Add Walthers or MHP diaphragms to the ends, install .015" wire grab irons, and mount your favorite couplers. Note the blank plate where the steam generator has been removed.

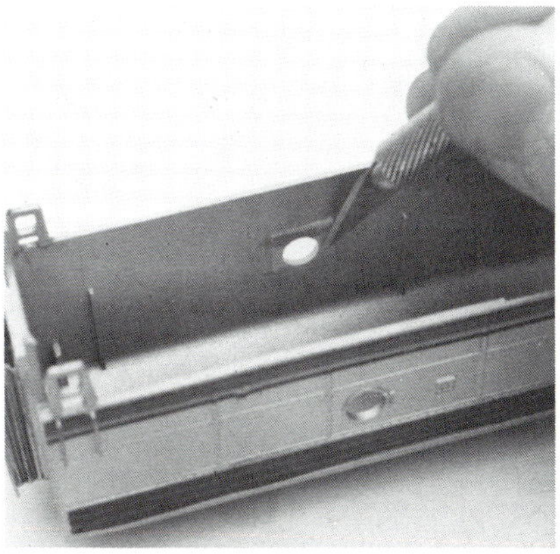

M. Install clear plastic behind each window with 5-minute epoxy.

N. The curve on the forward end of the AHM chassis must be filed flat to clear the new B unit body shell.

O. The grillwork was "opened" by applying a wash of nine parts thinner to one part flat black paint so that the black stuck only to the recessed areas. The completed B unit is sure to draw some compliments from your visitors.

Alco

Earl A. Yorke

Here's an example of the alterations steam locomotives underwent between construction and retirement—these photos show the same engine! Chesapeake & Ohio 133 is a USRA design built during WWI; C&O 543 is the engine years later after tender, headlight, feedwater heater, air compressor location, and even the number had been changed.

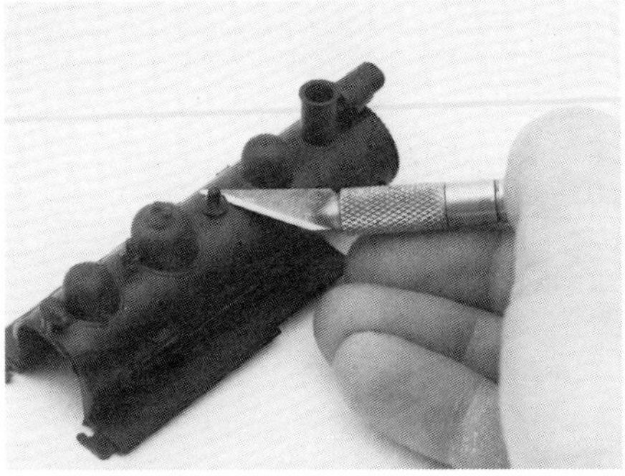

Plastic details to be replaced or used elsewhere can be removed with a knife or saw. Work carefully so adjacent detail is not damaged.

A hot knife speeds the job of cutting parts from a boiler shell—in this case, a steam dome. Make the cut at least 1/16" from the edges of the part and remove excess material with files or a motor tool to prepare the part for use.

cept trade-ins on new equipment and often use the trucks from the trade-in units under new locomotives. Thus, it's not unusual to see Alco or GE trucks under a locomotive outshopped by EMD. Such hybrids are fun to model.

The key to kitbashing diesels is the recognition that the builders—we'll use EMD as our example—utilize many standard items to build their locomotives, but arrange them to suit the mechanical requirements of specific units. Identical fans, grills, vents, stacks, cabs, lights, trucks, and even hoods are often used by a manufacturer for many years. A new model may have grills and fan housings of the same design as those used 10 or even 20 years earlier because the original design was sound and the manufacturer saw no reason to change it. Knowing this, you can look upon both prototype and model diesels as collections of standardized parts. You can model units that are not offered in ready-made form by using parts from a donor shell, repositioning them as they appear on the prototype you wish to model.

Suppose you want to kitbash a specific EMD hood unit in HO. You'll find that

W.G. Fancher

Replacing one set of drivers is an easy modification to a locomotive. This B&O Pacific sports Boxpok main drivers with spoked drivers fore and aft.

Stan Kistler

Anthony Sapienza reworked a Model Die Casting HO 4-4-2 into this super-detailed Santa Fe Atlantic. He replaced most of the detail parts and added more detail to modify the stock 1480-class kit prototype to an earlier 1400-class engine.

Santa Fe's own Cleburne shops "kitbashed" the road's 233 hybrid CF7 road switchers from older F units. The result is a locomotive class unlike any other.

EMD

How's this for a kitbashed prototype—an Alco road switcher rebuilt by EMD, with Alco trucks, cab, and short hood, but a long hood (and diesel engine) from a Geep!

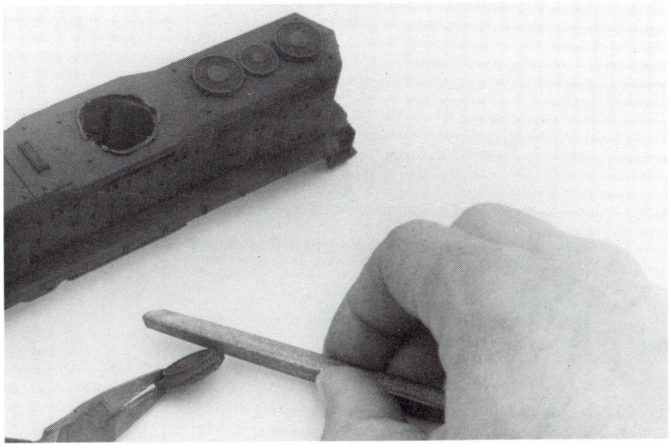

To obtain diesel parts that are not available separately, cut them from a spare body shell. Leave plenty of extra material around the edges of the part so you can cut, sand, and file it to the required shape.

almost any other EMD hood unit of roughly the same vintage can serve as a donor for most of the parts. In HO, the list of available units includes the GP7, 9, 18, 20, 35, 38, 40, the SD9, 24, 35, 40, 45, and the SDP40. You have your choice of early or late hoods and cabs, 4-wheel and 6-wheel trucks, and a wide range of standard details—the fans, dynamic brake housings, grillwork, and so on. Most plastic diesel shells are available separately for a couple of dollars so your parts supply of donor bodies need not be expensive.

Plastic diesel shells can be modified using the techniques we've already discussed; bodies can be spliced just as we did with passenger cars. Grills, fans,

Most manufacturers sell undecorated diesel body shells for a small fraction of the cost of a dummy unit. These shells can be used as replacement bodies for older models, or as parts donors for kitbashing projects.

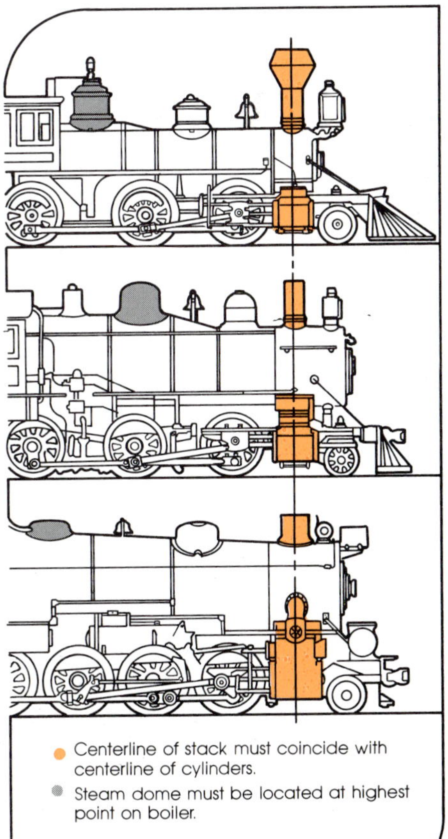

Fig. 7-3 THINGS YOU CAN'T CHANGE

Text continues on page 72

Updating an American

A. Models of locomotives from the very early and very late days of steam are abundant, but there are few examples of turn-of-the-century power. AHM's "Casey Jones" 4-6-0 is a good starting point for developing a roster of 1900-era steam power. This 4-4-0 is one engine on that roster.

New York Central: TRAINS Collection

B. This project does not aim to duplicate this chunky NYC 4-4-0, but rather to match its proportions.

C. I used two AHM HO locomotives: one Casey Jones Ten-Wheeler and one Genoa 4-4-0. AHM has offered both engines in O scale.

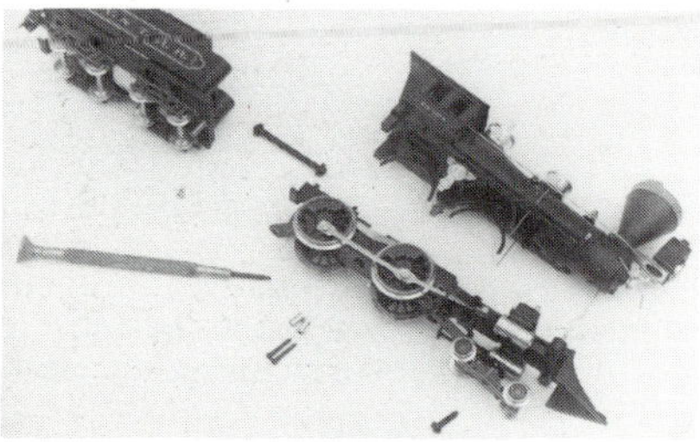

D. Start by disassembling both models, keeping parts separate. Four screws hold the body to the chassis on the Genoa.

E. The screws that hold the Casey Jones superstructure are located beneath the pilot truck and at the rear.

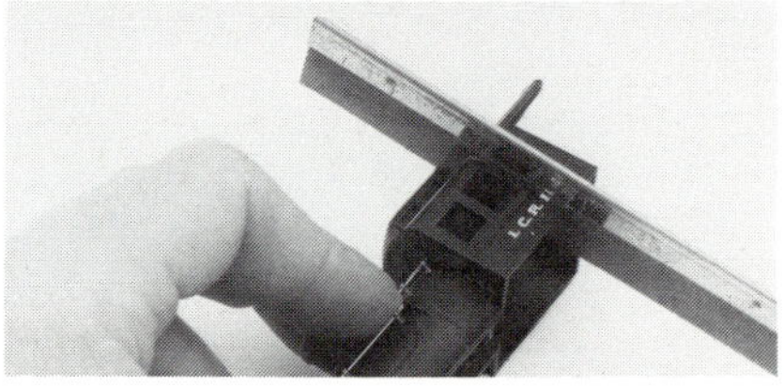

F. The 4-6-0 cab is too large for the 4-4-0. Removing one window makes the cab correct.

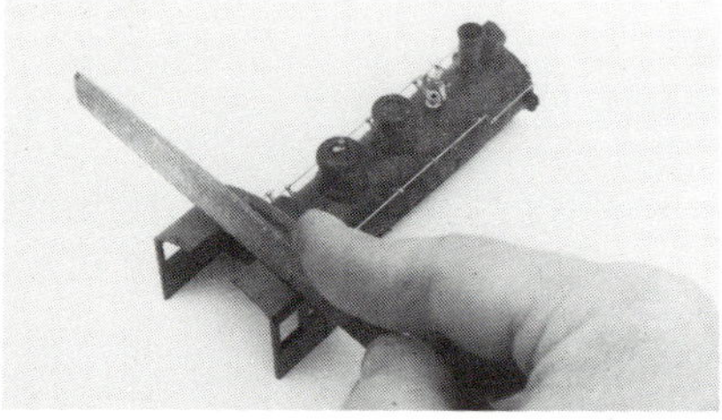

G. Carefully remove the raised panel lines on the cab and the clerestory on the roof. File the roof to match the front.

H. To make a cab back, saw away the sides on the piece cut from the cab. Remove the remaining portion of the roof.

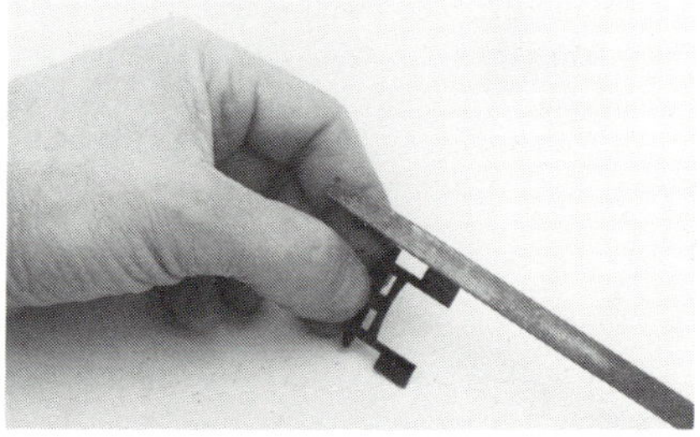

I. File the cab back so it will fit inside the shortened cab. Check the fit and cement the back in place.

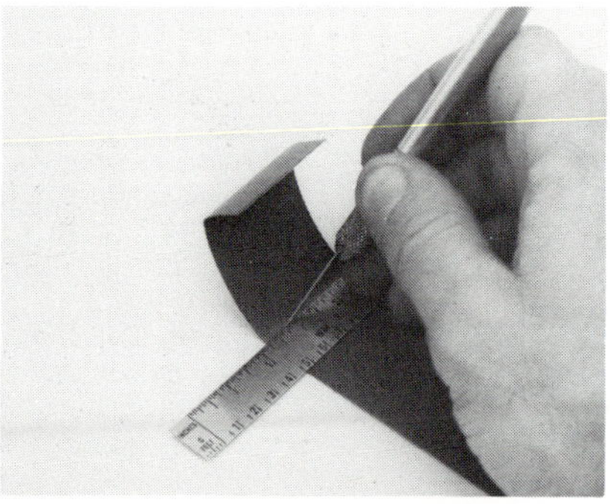

J. Roll a piece of .010″ plastic sheet over a round knife handle until it conforms to the shape of the roof. Use a piece that is 1/2″ wider than necessary and trim it to size after shaping. Cement the new cab roof in place with liquid cement.

K. Fabricate flip-up vents from plastic sheet and cement them to the new cab roof. Cut running boards from .010″ plastic sheet. Cover the bottom of the sides of the cab with the .010″ plastic sheet, too.

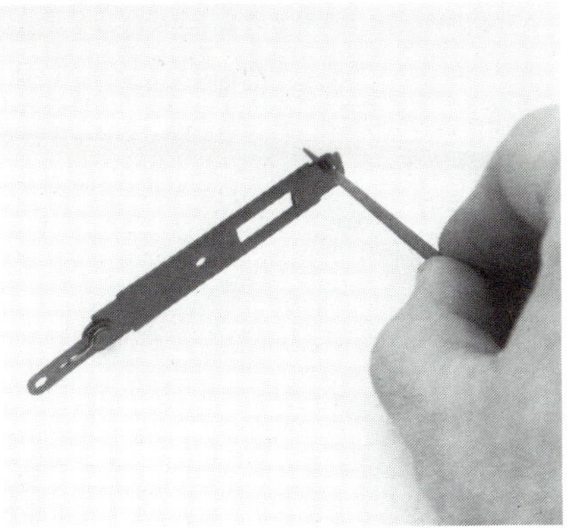

L. The tiny pilot wheels on the Genoa look out of place with the modern superstructure. I replaced the pilot truck with the one from the 4-6-0. File or drill out the rivet that retains the 4-4-0 pilot truck.

M. Next, enlarge the rivet hole in the retainer plate to accept the screw that retains the Casey Jones pilot truck. Either tap the hole or glue the screw in place with Walthers Goo or 5-minute epoxy.

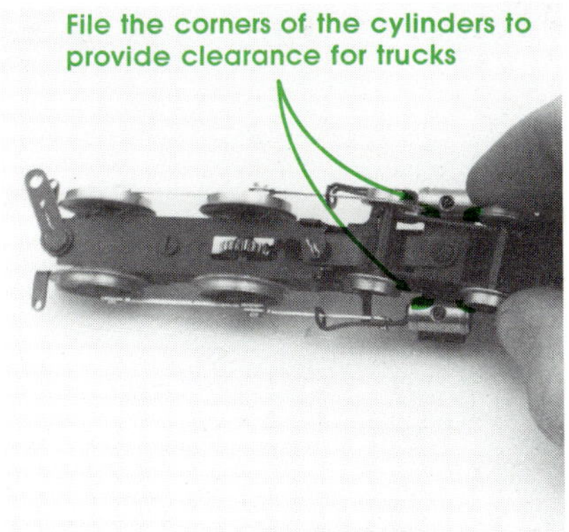

N. The pilot truck wheels strike the inside of the Genoa cylinders. File to provide clearance for the engine to negotiate curves. The bottom of the smokebox must be filed round to rest on the 4-4-0 cylinders.

O. The wood pilot on the Genoa is too old-fashioned for our modernized American. Slice it off just in front of the cylinders. Cut the modern pilot and pilot deck from the Casey Jones.

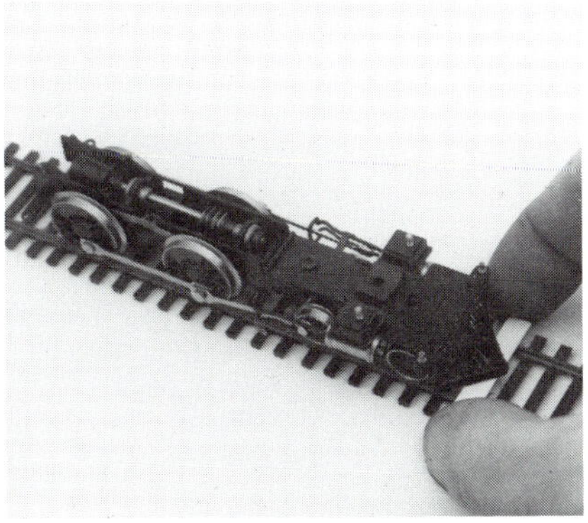

P. Cement the new pilot in place on the Genoa frame. Insert a shim of .040″ plastic between the bottom of the pilot and the tops of the rails to hold the pilot and deck at the correct height while the joint dries thoroughly.

Q. Remove the wood load from the Genoa tender by drilling away the plastic rivets inside. Fill with masking tape, with enough bulge to clear the tender-mounted motor. Test-fit the shell on the chassis.

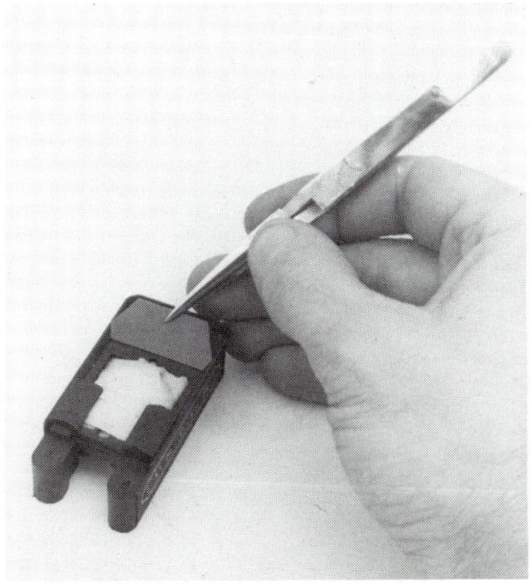

R. Make an extended coal slope sheet for the tender. Cut a paper pattern first. When the lower angles are an exact fit inside the top of the tender, transfer the pattern to .010″ plastic. Cement the extension piece in place at a 45 degree angle.

S. Remove the brass handrails, bell, and whistle, and mask the headlight lens when you paint the superstructure. You can paint the brass cylinders or leave them unpainted. You'll have to drill new holes for the cab grab irons and the pilot-deck braces will have to be shortened to fit. I used a cast metal air pump because the 4-6-0 pump was left with the chassis.

and louvers can be blanked or grafted in just as passenger car windows are filled or shifted. The most obvious, and perhaps the easiest, diesel shell modification is changing the short hood of a road switcher from high to low or from low to high. In HO, you can replace a low nose like that on Tyco's GP20 with a high hood from an Athearn GP9 shell. A low-nose conversion for an Athearn GP9 or an AHM GP18 requires removing a section to lower the hood. Several steps of the latter conversion are illustrated in Chapter 10 (don't let the lathe frighten you; you can make the same cuts with a razor saw).

Tyco's GP20 (right) features some toylike detailing, but has correct louvers for the GP18 and GP20. Grafting louvers from a Tyco shell into an Athearn GP9 (left) is a good first step toward an accurate GP18 or 20 – and an interesting project.

To kitbash a low-nose road switcher from a high-nose version, saw the top from the short hood (above), remove a section of the hood (below), and reassemble the remaining sections.

Richard Fleming

Bob Foster

G.M. Best

Guy L. Dunscomb

It is very important to keep the segments of a kitbashed body shell properly aligned. Horizontal or vertical misalignments look awful on locomotives; they are dead giveaways of sloppy workmanship. If a new hood or some other body portion doesn't ride at the proper height on the locomotive frame, use thin plastic shims to bring the shell to the correct height.

In extensive cut-and-join work much of the original strength of the one-piece body may be lost. If there is room, cement a .035" or .040" or thicker styrene reinforcing strip between the two hoods or along the entire underside of the shell roof. If there isn't room for such a splint, use epoxy fillets to restore strength and rigidity.

When modifying locomotives, it's a good idea to reduce the size of the chassis lugs that retain the snap-on body shell. This allows mounting and removal with less flexing of the shell, reducing stress on the body joints.

One way to achieve family resemblance among your steam locomotives is to fit the same superstructure to several wheel arrangements. The cab and boiler from the MDC HO 0-6-0 (top) could easily be used on 2-6-0, 4-6-0, and 4-4-0 mechanisms. Compare the overall size of the MDC superstructure to the AHM 4-6-0 body, and note how it looks on an AHM 4-4-0 chassis (below).

G.M. Best

Family resemblance in motive power was common in the steam era. These Southern Pacific locomotives share cab style (with awnings), dome type, bell location, and (except the switcher) headlight location and number boards. You can achieve a similar effect on your railroad by kitbashing.

Extensive steam locomotive modifications. Major changes to steam locomotives are among the most ambitious plastic kitbashing projects. The work isn't tricky, but you should start with a small locomotive—our modernized 4-4-0 is a good example—to gain experience in swapping superstructures, running gear, and tenders before tackling larger locomotives.

The easiest and most visible steam locomotive conversions involve mating a superstructure from one locomotive to the running gear of another, perhaps adding a tender from a third locomotive to finish the job. In this way you can build up a stable of locomotives with a variety of wheel arrangements, but with a strong family resemblance. You'll often have to make modifications to the superstructure and frame, but little or no mechanical work is required on the operating parts. If a superstructure must be shortened or lengthened to fit new running gear, try to obtain the required shells separately.

Let's take a look at some of the possibilities in HO scale, where there's the greatest variety of plastic locomotive models and the widest range of fittings. Suppose you want to build a family of engines along the lines of Model Die Casting's 0-6-0 switcher, the one with the slope-back tender. You could use the chassis from an AHM 4-4-0, an AHM 0-4-0, or an AHM 4-6-0. You might then add a two-wheel pilot truck to the stock 0-6-0 mechanism to make a slim-boilered 2-6-0. In that way, you could make five or six light steam locomotives, each different from the other, but each clearly on the roster of the same railroad. With even less work, you could create a similar effect by grafting only the cab from the 0-6-0 to any of several boilers and superstructures.

Streamlining a steam locomotive is obviously a major modification, but it is made easier because of the smooth surfaces and intentional lack of detail on the prototype. Railroads usually added streamlining to existing non-streamlined engines, so your aim is to duplicate their efforts in miniature. Most of the work can be done with sheet styrene and filler putty.

When kitbashing locomotives, keep plausibility in mind. Use the many available reference books to see if your project could have been used on a real railroad. Stay away from outlandish combinations. Otherwise, if you can justify what you want to do, have at it. Happy kitbashing!

Structure kitbashing

Make your structures unique by altering and combining well-detailed plastic kits.

RAILROADS don't exist just to run trains, they carry commodities and people from one place to another. In miniature we can't do much about loading or unloading cars or ushering scale passengers on and off our trains, but we can lend a suggestion of these activities by providing sources and destinations for passengers and freight. While industrial buildings and stations are obvious sources of traffic, dwellings and stores suggest that there are people to work in the industries and to ride the trains. Locomotive servicing facilities such as water tanks and sand houses suggest that our model locomotives really are serviced and repaired; ice houses and car washers suggest the same for rolling stock.

When your pike needs structures, don't just buy and build kits. Kit structures are made for general locations so that they will fit on any layout. Kitbashing allows you to make structures fit specific situations on your layout, and to increase their realism by fitting them between tracks and into existing scenic contours. Simple changes—repainting, weathering, or the addition of a smokestack or lean-to office—are enough to make your buildings, and your layout, different from anyone else's.

Several firms offer plastic sheet stock with molded surface detail such as shingles, stonework, bricks, and corrugated metal roofing. Others offer cast windows, doors, and detail items, and many of the castings used in kits are sold separately for scratchbuilding and kitbashing, fig. 8-1. You can combine these materials and parts with parts you make from kits to produce a structure of any size, shape, or purpose.

Simple additions can substantially alter the appearance of a structure. A tall stack, a water tank on the roof, or a splashy billboard can help hide the

Albert Hetzel reversed the roof panel, shortened the cooling tower, and omitted an addition on AHM's HO Casket Company to make his structure unique.

Allan Simmons built this enginehouse for his HOn3 layout from two Revell No. H995 enginehouse kits. He replaced the peaked roof with a flat one, added another arched panel to each side wall, and replaced the doors to make a structure that only vaguely resembles the original kit.

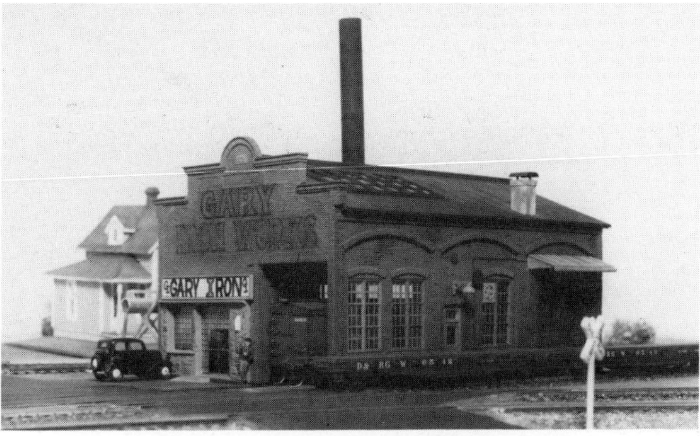

Another Allan Simmons conversion – a small factory built from Revell's No. H996 HO Weekly Herald. The biggest change here was adding a track door to the front wall.

Fig. 8-1. Several manufacturers offer extensive lines of plastic and metal doors, windows, and detail parts for structures. Excellent variety is available in O, HO, and N scales.

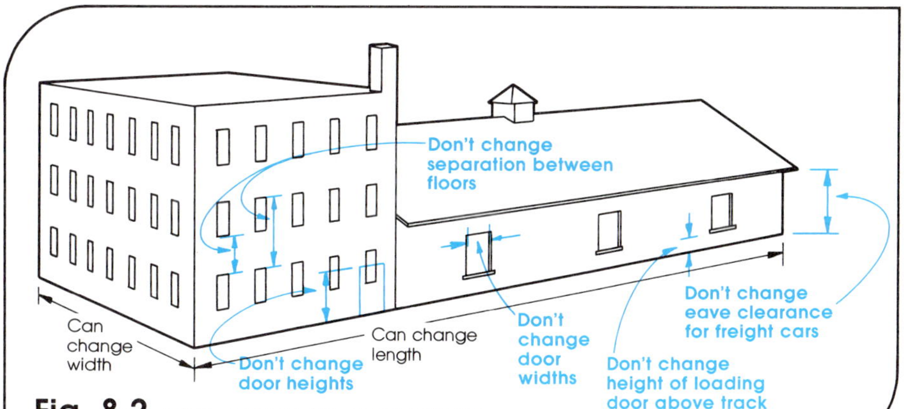

Fig. 8-2 WHAT YOU CAN AND CAN'T CHANGE

Train yourself to eliminate cast details that tend to give away kitbashed structures.

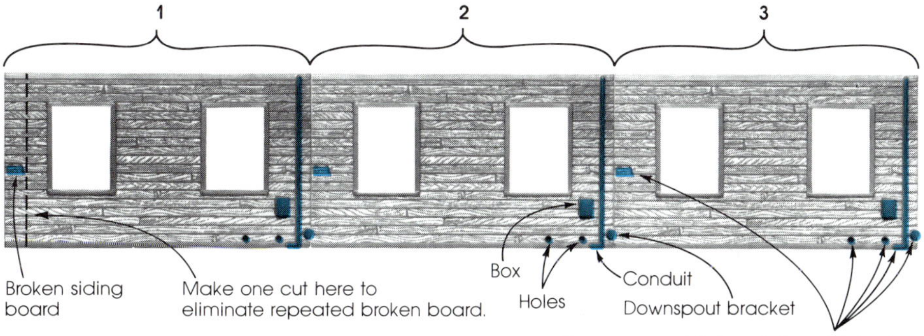

Fig. 8-3 ELIMINATING REPEATED DETAILS

sameness of the building. Another easy project is joining several separate industrial structures together with conveyors, piping, and enclosed walkways to achieve the busy look of a manufacturing complex.

To build unique structures from plastic kits, you must stop considering them as kits at all. Instead, look at them as boxes of parts that can be reworked and combined to produce buildings of your own design. Plastic structures have

Roundhouse HO "Module Pack" components are interchangeable wall, roof, window, door, and detail parts that can be assembled into any size or shape. All three buildings were pieced together from Roundhouse modular sections.

Paul Kepner used two HO Rico stations to build this station. He replaced the baggage end with a waiting-room end and modified the rear roof to match the front.

Another HO Rico station conversion, this one by Albert Hetzel. His Trinidad depot is less ornate than the kit, and features roof lines revised to resemble Santa Fe practice.

intricate detailing—bricks, cracked boards, pipes, conduits—that would take hundreds of hours to scratchbuild. We put all this detail to work on our layouts when we use the kits as large detailed *parts* to build our own structures.

Some model railroad manufacturers have already put the idea that kits are parts to work. Locomotive roundhouses with add-on extra stalls are available in several scales. The HO modular structures offered by Ulrich, Roundhouse, and Jouef work on the same principles as toy building blocks. Each wall section has the same overall dimensions; some include doors or windows. By assembling these modular "blocks" side by side or on top of one another, you can build a unique structure of any size.

The walls of almost any plastic building can be considered as modules to be used to build longer and wider structures. An example of this concept is the low-relief factory project built with walls from Pola HO "Gruesome Casket" kits. This modular thinking requires

Low-relief background buildings

Linn H. Westcott

A. Layouts with mountains owe much of their effectiveness to the ability of vertical scenery to suggest additional space. The back of the mountain is implied to the viewer, making the layout seem larger. We can also take advantage of this effect by modeling tall cityscape buildings that line the tracks. Here's a likely prototype on the Milwaukee Road at Milwaukee, Wisconsin.

B. This low-relief structure is assembled from Roundhouse brand "Module Pack" HO wall and window sections, except for the foundation sections, which are leftovers from another kitbashing project. If you are starting without an extensive scrap box, use narrow sections of Roundhouse parts to bring the freight doors to the proper height to match your rolling stock.

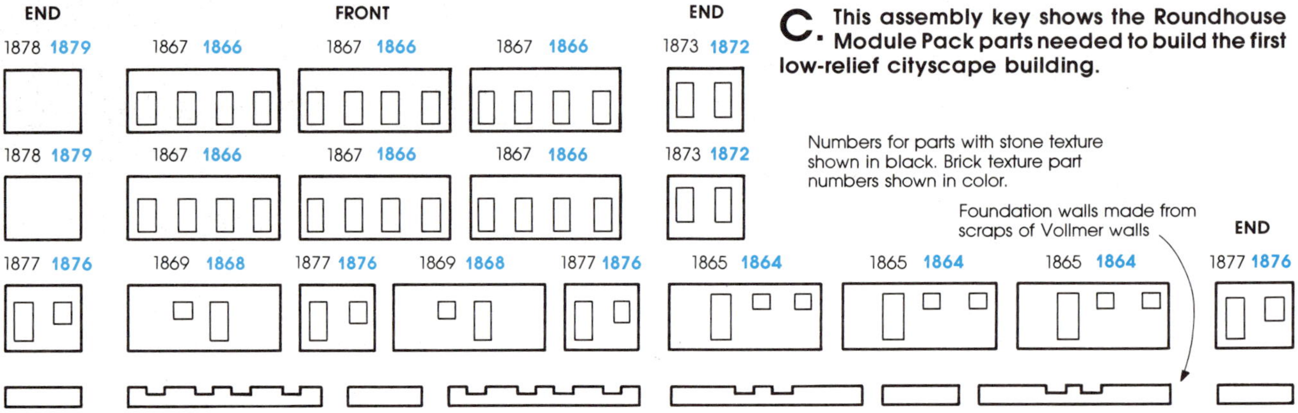

C. This assembly key shows the Roundhouse Module Pack parts needed to build the first low-relief cityscape building.

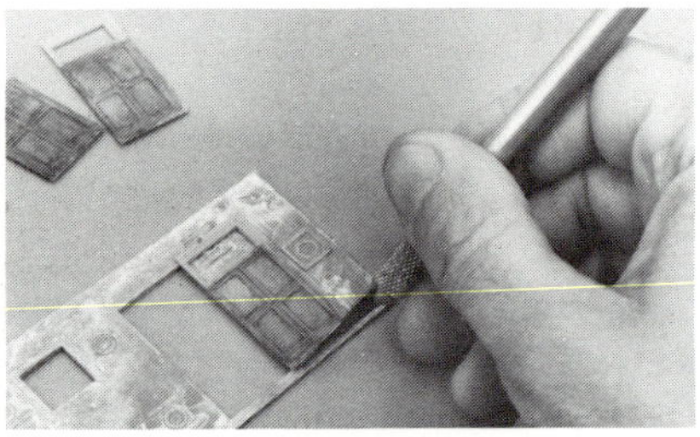

D. Two double doors from the No. 1851 Door & Window pack are used for each freight door. Trace the outline of the door, not including the flange that goes inside the wall, on the back of the wall.

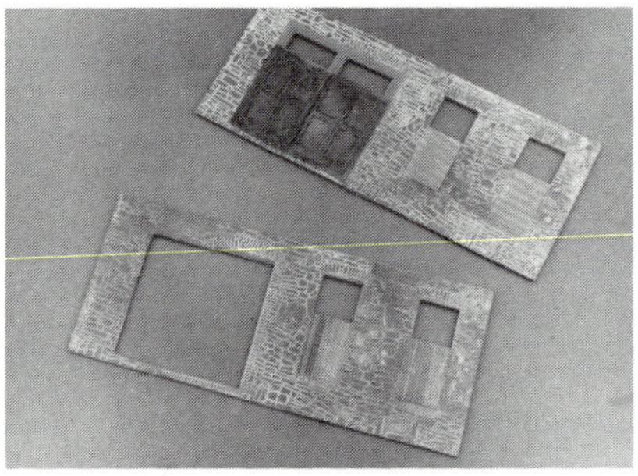

E. Use a motor tool or jeweler's saw to cut the larger door openings. Trim the burrs from the edges with a hobby knife.

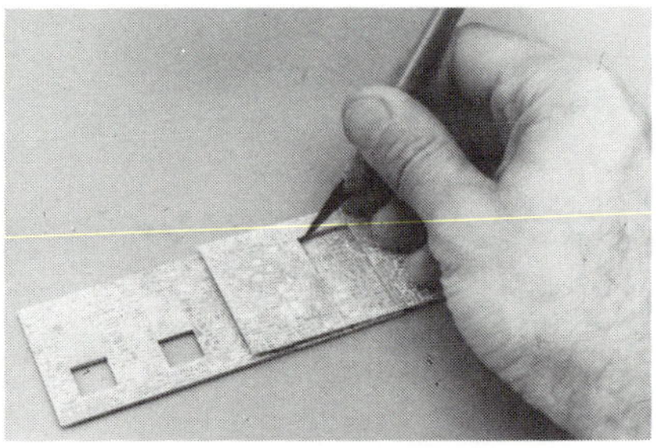

F. The door openings in the No. 1865 walls must be filled with stone cut from an extra wall section. Trace the outline of the required plug on the stone.

you to consider doors and windows and the inch of wall that surrounds them in the kit as your parts. This gives you more freedom to match a structure to your available space than if you limit yourself to complete kit walls.

There are two kinds of structure models that aren't all there. They are intended to be placed against the layout backdrop to *suggest* larger structures. *Flats* are simply structure walls with no three-dimensional quality other than the thickness of their material. *Low-relief* buildings have short side walls that may or may not be at right angles to the wall that faces the viewer of the scene. Both types of structures are "tricks" that depend on the same illusions used to design stage scenery for plays.

Planning modifications to walls. There are a few limitations to what you can do to a building, fig. 8-2. You must allow adequate separation between floors in multistory structures, and you must provide doors large enough for people and freight to move in and out.

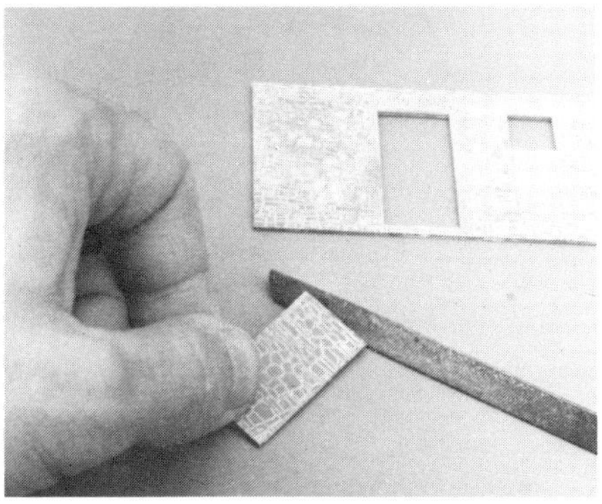

G. Cut the plug with a razor saw. Make it $^1/_{32}''$ oversize all around. File the edges to fit.

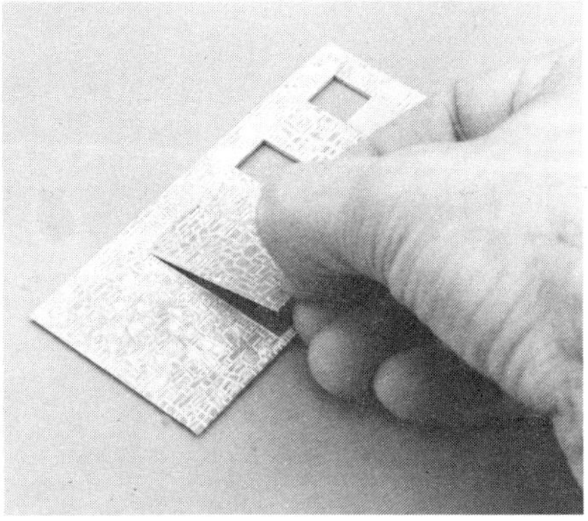

H. Install the plug and apply liquid cement from the back.

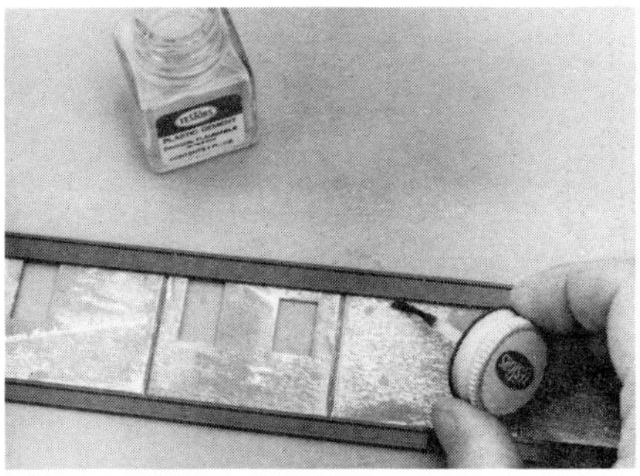

I. Use Plastruct No. 308 $^1/_4''$ channel to back the butt joints between the wall modules. Hold the wall pieces face down on a sheet of glass and apply cement from the rear.

J. Three Plastruct strips join the walls to make the front. No vertical reinforcing is necessary.

K. The cornice pieces are cut to fit from Roundhouse No. 1857 cornice moldings. The ends must be cut square so the pieces can be cemented end-to-end.

L. The single-story section is made in the same manner as the rest of the structure. Note how leftover cornice molding was used to brace the interior. Lengths of flat sprue would also work here.

M. The completed low-relief structure is deep enough to simulate a complete building, but it only occupies a few inches of layout space between the track and the back wall. The interior should be blocked with cardboard partitions to hide the lack of detail and the fact that the structure ends abruptly at the wall.

Project continues on page 78

Don't worry whether or not there is a specific prototype for your structure, because prototype buildings come in every conceivable size, shape, and combination of materials, and if you adhere to sound prototype *practice*, chances are you'll come up with a model that's similar to a building that exists *somewhere*!

Before you start sawing, reworking, and assembling the structure parts, it helps to lay out all the kit pieces to see just what you have. Familiarize yourself with the walls, roof, and details, and see how they fit together to make an unmodified model. Note where joints are made by butting edges together, and where beveled edges are used for the joining surfaces. If parts interlock in a complex manner, note their positions so they won't pose problems for you later on. Walls can be cut so molded-in details on the corners are preserved, or they can simply be cut and the corners beveled to match the angle on the kit parts.

Sometimes, there is too much cast-in detail. This is especially true where the details are non-structural items such

N. Our second building is built from a kit from which we make our own "modules." This structure is built on an angle to suit its particular viewing situation.

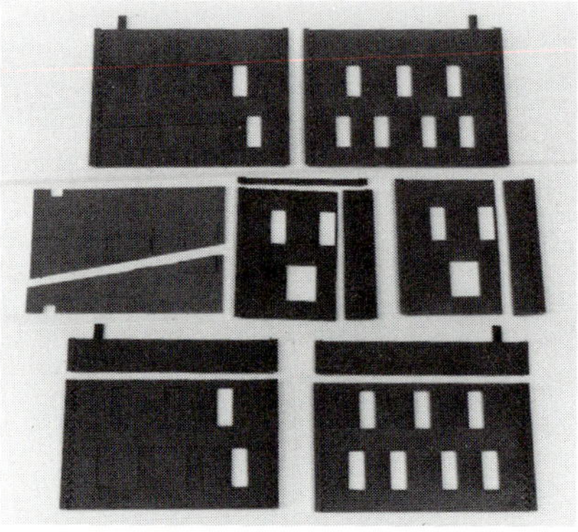

O. Two Pola Gruesome Casket, Railroad Hotel, or Ramsey Journal kits are required. Cut the side walls from one kit above the second-story windows. Make vertical cuts in the rear walls 1/16" from the sides of the upper-story windows.

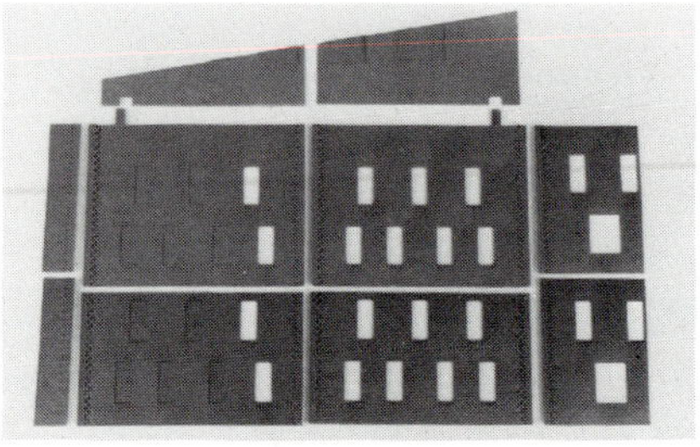

P. Make all cuts along mortar lines, using them to guide your blade. The modified walls and roof parts fit together as shown. Note how the shorter second story allows equal vertical spacing of the second-, third-, and fourth-story windows.

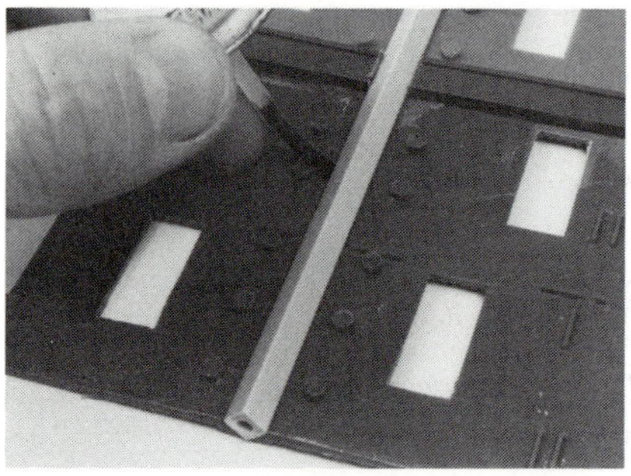

Q. Use 3/16" Plastruct square tubing as reinforcing strips behind the kits' mitered corners. File the sharp edge of each corner so there is 1/32" of flat surface to butt together. Lay the walls face down on glass and install the square tube from the rear. Use 5/16" Plastruct channel as horizontal reinforcement.

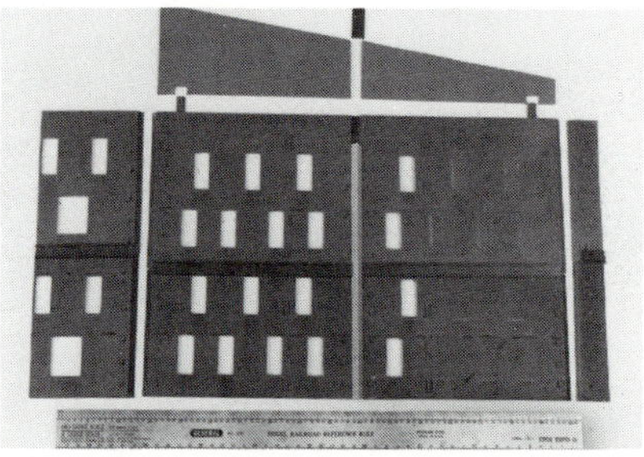

R. There is no need for a rear wall. Do not cement the 5/16" Plastruct channel reinforcement to the roof until the roof has been fitted into the end wall angle.

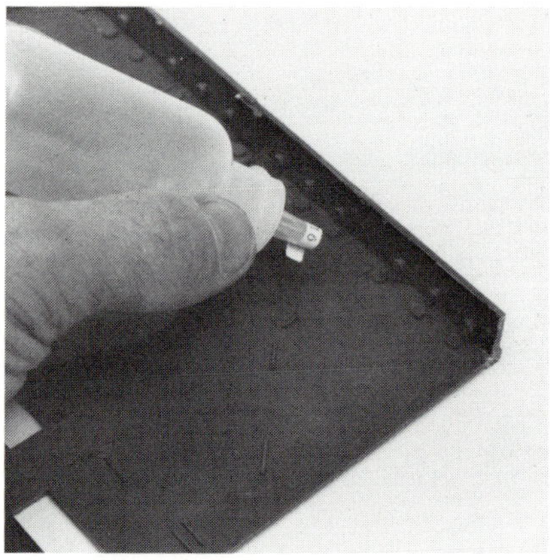

S. Use liquid cement to join ends to front. The corner will be slightly sharper than 90 degrees. Cut the roof to match.

T. After the corner joints have set at least overnight, remove the unneeded chimney tabs that project from the top of the front.

U. The roof sections will be 1/16" too short. Glue the roof halves to the walls, then install 5/16" Plastruct channel to span the gap.

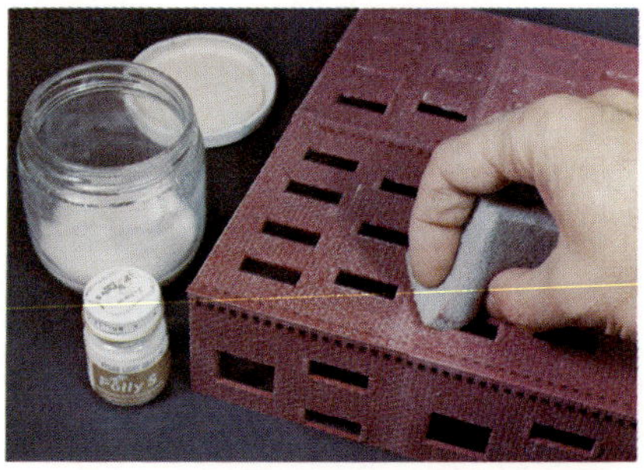

V. Use a wash of one part Polly S reefer gray to nine parts water to simulate mortar between the bricks. Wipe the wash over the surface of the model with a sponge. The gray will stick to the mortar lines, filling them.

as electrical conduits, fire alarm boxes, and so on. When you splice several identical pieces together to make a long wall, these details are repeated. This repetition is a giveaway, and the best thing to do with this sort of detail item is to remove it from all but one wall section, fig. 8-3.

I've mentioned this before, but it's worth repeating: you'll want to remove many, if not all, of the alignment pins and lugs on the back of structure wall and roof parts. This will make the parts easier to handle and assemble, because they will lie flat for cutting and truing and because there will be no interference at the joints. If removing these lugs seriously weakens the assembly, add reinforcing braces and gussets.

Structure kits that include a base are designed so the base will provide structural support to keep the side parts flat and hold the corners in proper alignment. Rather than go through the job of hiding the base when the structure is installed on the layout, most modelers leave them off. When you assemble a structure without the base, you may need extra bracing inside to keep the walls aligned at the corners. Pieces of sprue that include right angles can be used as shown in fig. 8-4.

When planning a building larger than the standard kit, keep in mind that combining two kits will not yield a structure twice as long as the original, because you'll usually lose several scale feet—sometimes more—in splicing the walls. When you are piecing together complex structure walls, dry-assemble opposite wall units, measure them, and trim the longer one to fit. This practice ensures your structure will come out rectangular.

Try to plan vertical cuts so the edges of trim boards or pilasters will cover the joints. If possible, try to have one section overlap the joint to hide it completely. This is especially important in masonry structures. Try to plan horizontal cuts so the joints can be covered by signs, porch decks and roofs, or near-horizontal downspouts.

Cutting wall sections. For initial cutting and shaping on structure parts use heavy, coarse tools, then shift to finer cutting tools and abrasives as you near the finished shape of the part. For example, many plastic structure walls are quite thick, and you can save time and effort by making the major cuts with a fine-tooth hacksaw. Don't cut too enthusiastically, or you'll melt the plastic. Likewise, to bevel the edge of a wall, consider using a coarse wood file or Surform tool to remove material quickly, shifting to files and sanding blocks to make the finished joining surface.

After you've completed the sectioning and joining, but while the walls are still flat on your workbench, think ahead to the other operations that will be performed on the walls. Are there holes that will have to be drilled to mount lights, signs, or loading-dock roof sections? If you can locate and drill them while the walls are flat, you'll avoid handling the model when it is near completion.

Unwanted door or window openings can be filled with matching pieces cut from another wall. In brick buildings,

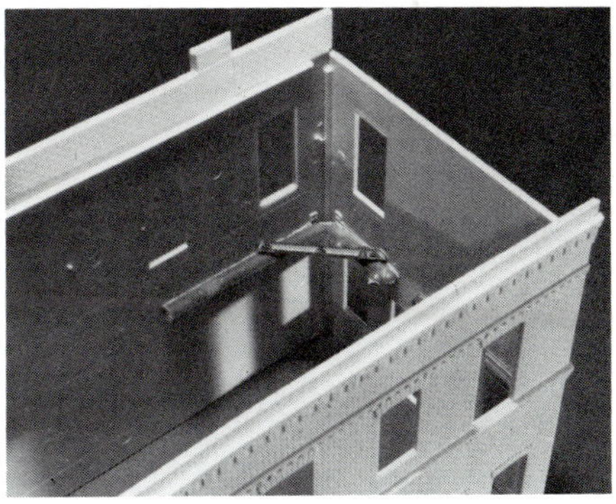

Fig. 8-4. Right-angle sprue sections can be used as interior bracing. This bracing is also floor support.

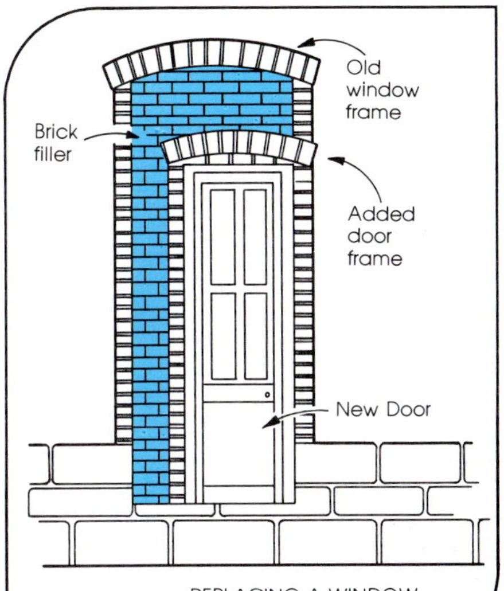

Fig. 8-5 REPLACING A WINDOW WITH A DOOR

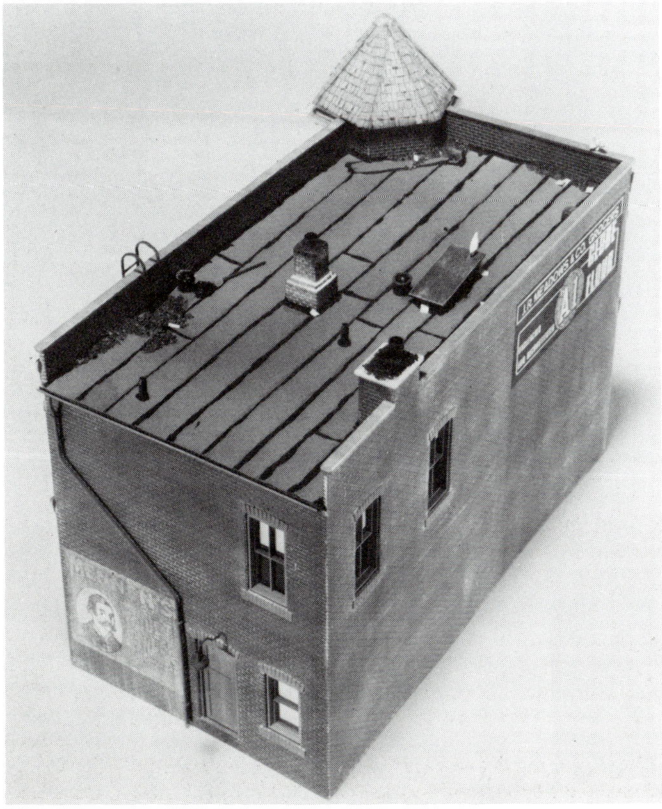

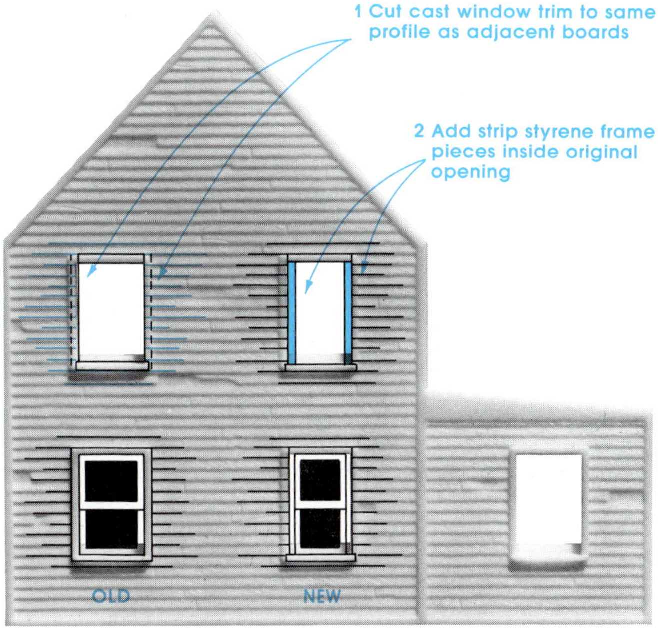

Fig. 8-6 NARROWING CAST WINDOW OPENINGS

This Heljan HO restaurant roof was surfaced with sandpaper and the cupola covered with paper shingles. A hatch, leaves, papers, and pigeons were added.

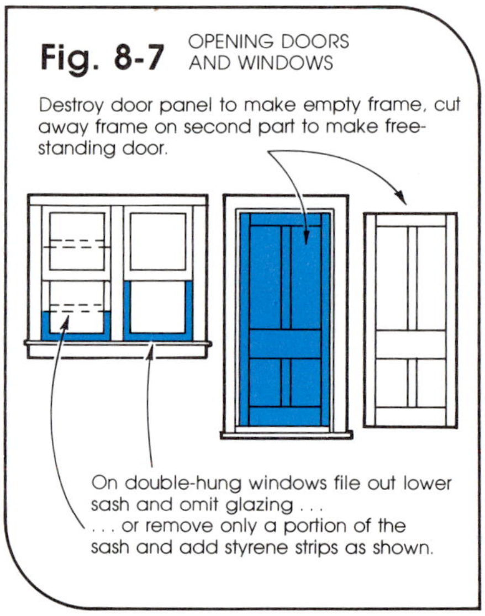

These Vollmer HO structures feature several distinctively European details, among them tile roofs and the extensive use of decorative wrought iron. By omitting some of the iron grillwork trim parts, repainting or replacing the tile roofs, and making other minor, easy changes, these excellent plastic structures will add much-needed variety on any North American layout.

Paul Kepner built both these structures from Vollmer No. 5610 HO factories; Deyo's Tools required two kits, Bill's Warehouse, only one. Paul replaced the peaked roofs with flat ones, replaced the tall ground-floor windows with brick plugs or freight doors, and omitted most of the decorative wrought iron trim details.

Trace the outline of each new window and door on the back of the wall. If the castings include trim that overlaps the wall material, deduct the width of the trim from the size of the opening.

Enlarge the openings using a jeweler's saw, motor tool, or coarse file. Cut to within $^1/_{32}''$ of the layout lines, then finish the openings with fine files. Test fit the castings frequently as you remove material.

The modified wall section (left) is less ornate — more appropriate for a typical North American factory structure. It's also almost unrecognizable as coming from the original kit.

openings can be filled with brick pieces without removing the molded-in frames, so the model looks like a real structure that has had some of the windows or doors bricked up. Larger openings, such as freight doors, can be filled and a smaller door or window cut in, another practice common on older prototype structures, fig. 8-5. Plain sheet plastic can be carved to match the brick, stone, or wood surface of the kit walls if you can't find a kit piece large enough for the opening you want to fill.

One of the fundamental techniques in structure kitbashing is changing and rearranging windows and doors. Once you have decided what new parts you will use and where you will place them, mark the outlines of the required openings on the back of the wall sections with the tip of a knife blade. Be sure to allow for the trim or lip that will cover the edge of the opening when the casting is in place, and don't make the new opening too large.

Use a coarse file, jeweler's saw, or cutting bit in a hand-held motor tool to enlarge existing openings or to cut new ones. Cut only to within $^1/_{32}''$ of your layout lines, and use files to trim to the lines, test fitting with the window and door pieces as you go.

Altering roof parts. Unless your rail-

To quickly Americanize the windows in European-prototype kits, trim away extra window mullions with a sharp knife. Smooth remnants of the removed mullions with a file.

Some European kits furnish windows and trim as separate castings, a feature which makes the windows especially easy to modify. Here, a window is shortened to fit a smaller frame.

After rough-cutting the window insert to the smaller size, use a file to straighten and smooth the cut edge. Always leaving extra material to trim for a final fit is one of the rules of kitbashing.

Here, the separate window trim molding is trimmed to fit the shortened window insert. Separate window trim and inserts make painting European-prototype plastic structures an easy job.

Fig. 8-8 COVERING UP POOR JOINTS

road is at eye level, the roof is the part of a model building that you see the most. Roof texture and detail are worth extra effort and special attention. Changing the roof angles even slightly makes an otherwise commonplace structure less familiar, even to knowledgeable viewers.

The roof is usually the most difficult part of the building to piece together successfully from kit parts, and in many cases you'll find it easier and faster to build a new roof from styrene sheet or commercial texture materials. The trick where roof angles are complex is to make trial-and-error fitting templates from scrap cardboard. Work with these until you have the correct shapes, then transfer the patterns to the plastic parts.

To disguise joints in kitbashed roofs, try adding tar paper patches over the existing roof texture, or consider tar-papering the entire roof surface. Use strips of No. 400 sandpaper, construction paper, or masking tape to simulate tar paper. Where the discrepancy is small, consider hiding it with an add-on element such as a sign, water tank, or ladder.

Tricks with windows and doors. Windows and doors from one kit can be fitted to others once you've mastered the techniques of filling, enlarging, or cutting new openings to match the new parts. Careful selection of windows and doors and repetition of these elements in several structures can yield a prototypical family appearance to your railroad service structures (sand houses, stations, section houses, yard offices, and so on). To reinforce and enhance this effect, select and use a standard color scheme for walls, roof, and trim.

Some kits have very bulky window and door trim, and this oversize trim gives the model a puffed-up, toylike look. This is especially true of many N scale structures. Consider placing the window and door castings behind, not in, their openings. If necessary, add thin styrene strips around the opening on the outside of the wall. On frame structures, it's possible to narrow window frames, especially cast-in window frames, with a minimum of fuss, fig. 8-6. The opening size can be reduced by cutting away the window trim to continue the siding boards to the edge of the window opening. Then, new trim pieces can be added inside the opening, flush with the outer edges of the siding boards.

Another trick with windows and doors is to open some of them to add a lived-in look, fig. 8-7. Saw and file away the framework on one door casting, and place it into a frame made by removing the door panel from a second casting. For open windows it's often sufficient to simply remove the lower sash of a double-hung window. Omit the clear glazing material in open windows.

Americanizing European structures. Structure kits manufactured in Europe are often patterned after distinctly European prototypes, and they don't look quite right on North American layouts. There are several minor details that can be changed to make these structures fit right in. This work is well worth the effort because of the

Kitbashed Victorian station

A. This station was built from three Kibri No. 8310 HO Banks. Occupying a space only 5″x10″, it gives the impression of a larger structure.

C. Parker

B. Here's a "near prototype" for our station, a building on the Maine Central RR. at Bangor, Maine. We don't have the room – or time – to model it brick for brick, but we can capture its spirit in plastic.

C. You'll need three Kibri Banks. Stone walls and large windows are right for a 1900-era depot.

D. The Bank fronts make the station front and sides, rear walls the station rear, and ends the station tower.

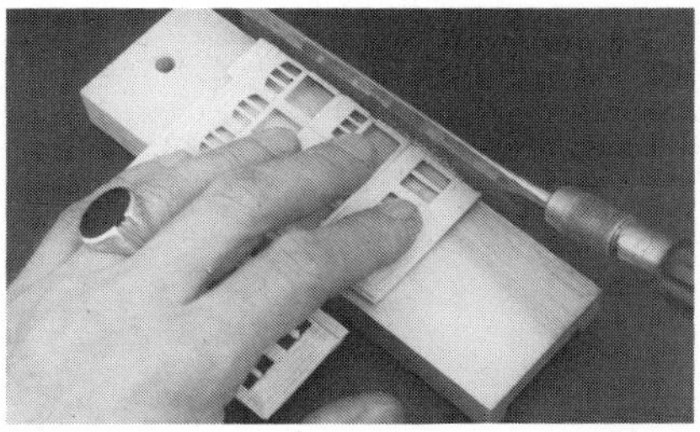

E. Trim the stone corner strip from one front and one rear wall. The front and rear walls must be filed flat where they butt in the center of the new wall units.

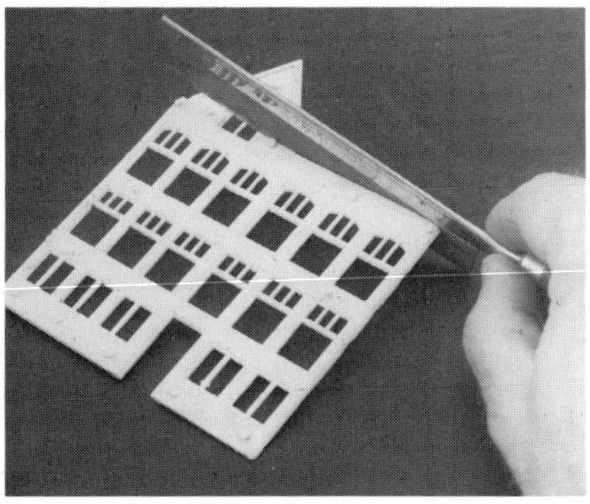

F. Keep the peaks on the right half of the front and rear walls, but cut all others flush.

G. File the edges where you removed the peaks flush with the tops of the main wall sections.

H. Check that the front and rear will be the same length.

great variety of European-prototype structures available in both HO and N, and the excellent detailing of the models. They usually have too much trim —wrought iron grillwork, ornamental brick, "gingerbread" eave detail, and ridgepole trim.

The first major area to alter—again, because you and your visitors see it first—is the roof. You can replace tile roofing with sheets of plastic shingles, or, if the building will be far enough from the edge of the layout, repaint the tiles a shingle color such as green or gray.

Some arched openings can be enlarged to accept rectangular doors or windows as shown in the photo sequence. Excess ornamental detail can be left off when the building is assembled, or it can be trimmed away. Painting to tone down the often-gaudy color contrasts provided in the kits helps immensely. Finally, adding American signs and posters to a European building can make it seem right at home with your other structures.

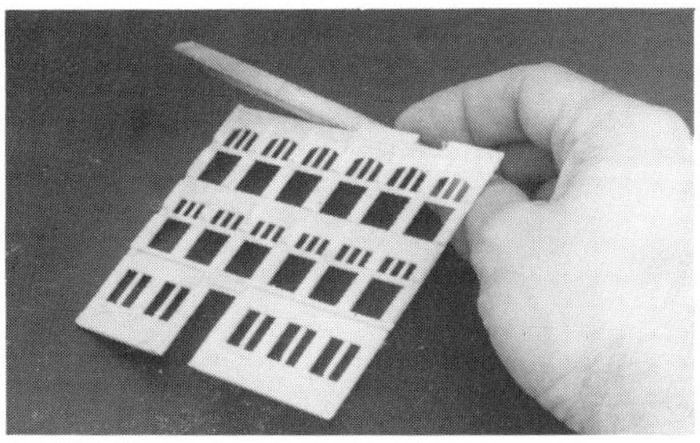

I. Remove the windowless first story from three of the end walls. The sawcut should be even with the top of the second-story window sills. File notches as shown here in the right corner of the front wall and in one end wall to accommodate the outside walls of the corner tower.

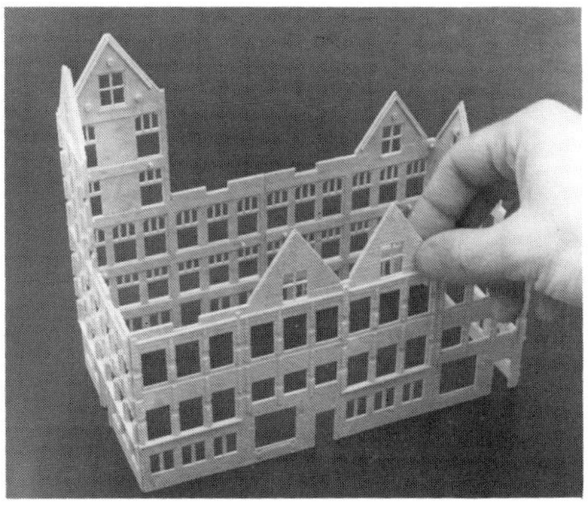

J. Cement one peak to the front corner of the left end wall and another to the right rear wall. Assemble the walls.

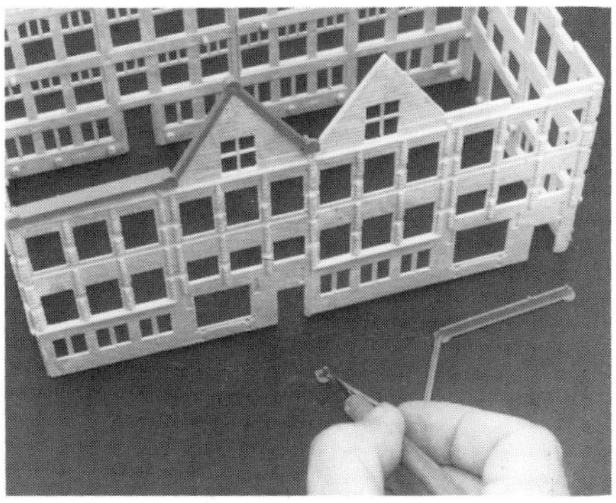

K. The cornice pieces must be fitted before the roof panels. Some of the kit cornices can be used as is. The others must be trimmed to fit by removing the end tabs.

L. Add the inside tower walls. One end wall must be trimmed so only the upper-story windows remain. The bottom is then filled in with a solid end wall. The blank tower wall is another solid end wall. Remove its first story so it matches the others.

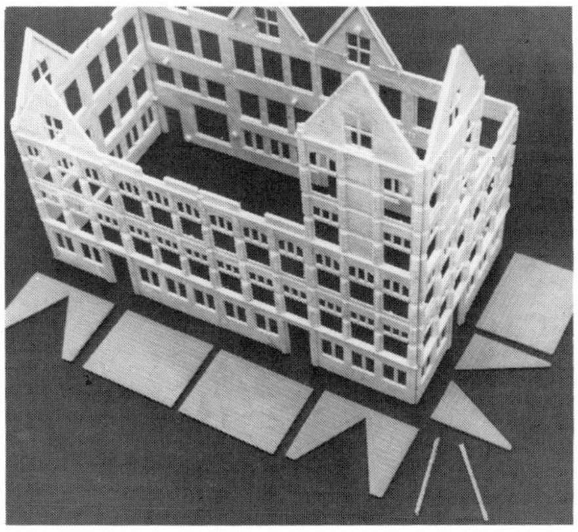

M. Cut one set of kit roof sections on the shingle side of the vertical groove to make the two roof pieces for the front and rear of the tower. Four triangular roof sections must be used for the tower roof. Saw each of the remaining roof parts on each side of the smooth groove. Remove all grooves so you have a total of 12 shingle roof sections (two for the tower).

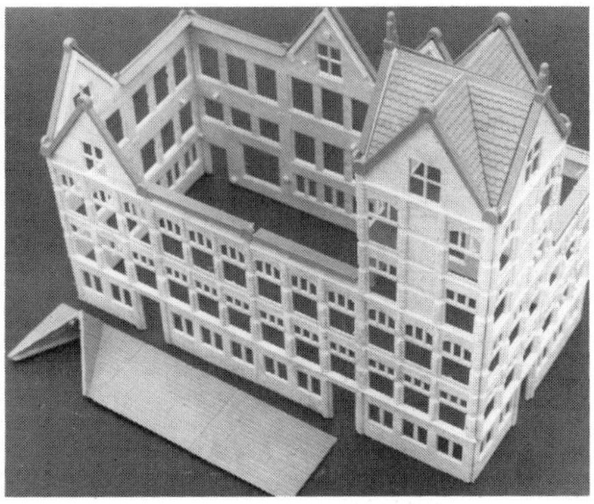

N. Three roof pieces, one with and two without the "V" notch, butt together to form the front roof. Reinforce with plastic sheet.

O. Four shingle pieces make the two rear corners of the roof. Make two right and two left sections.

P. Bevel the edges of the roof sections where required, test-fitting frequently.

Q. The beveled roof sections fit the back corners and two notched sections fit over the dormers.

Project continues on page 84

Doors and windows of European kits often have smaller panes of glass than their American counterparts. These can be modified by slicing out some of the intermediate mullions, or by replacing the windows and doors entirely. To enlarge the size of the glass panes, start by using a sharp hobby knife to cut out the unwanted pieces. Don't try to remove every bit of the mullion with one cut or you'll nick the part that you want to leave intact. Instead, cut out the major portion, trim away most of the remaining plastic, and carefully file the last remnant of the mullion smooth.

Assembly hints. Assembling kitbashed structures is not significantly different from assembling kits. As I've emphasized before, strive for strong, neat joints, and use reinforcing pieces where needed for strength and rigidity. Where necessary, camouflage poor joints with add-on details, fig. 8-8. Use white glue to hold parts that you expect to remove later on. A good example is a roof. On most buildings, the roof can be cemented to all the walls. The resulting

R. Cement the triangular roof pieces from the kit to the notched roof pieces to fit over the dormers. Cut the V-shaped vertical roof trim (No. A107) in two to fit the modified roof. Cut .020" sheet plastic to fit inside the roof.

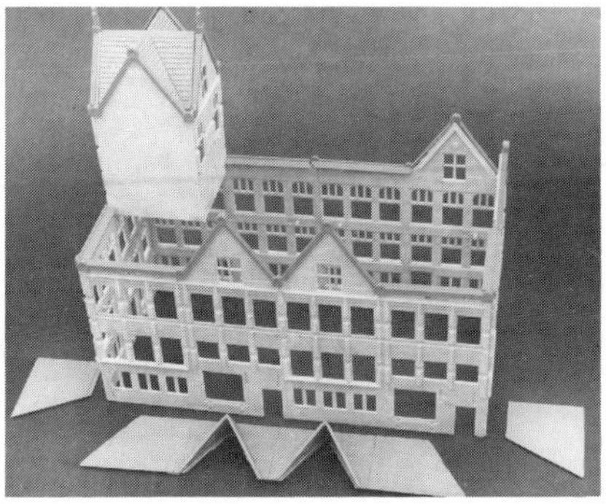

S. Cement all cornice pieces in place, but do not add the roof pieces yet. Check the entire roof for proper fit.

T. Use two scrap wall peaks as braces where the main roof sections touch the inside tower walls.

U. Position the plastic sheet ⅛" below the upper edge. Cover with No. 600 sandpaper painted flat black.

V. Now add the plastic trim stones and strips. It's easier if you hold the small pieces with the tip of a hobby knife.

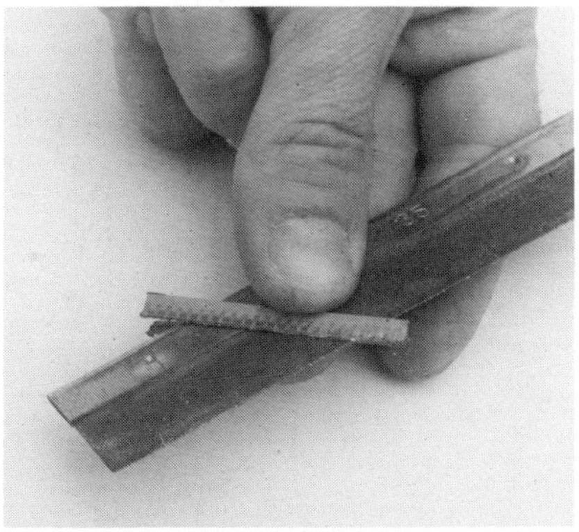

W. Five roof peak trim pieces must be split down the middle so that you will have enough. Work slowly to ensure the saw blade doesn't wander off center.

X. The trim over the peak of the tower roof must be notched. Cement shutters to the rectangles on the roof panels in place of the round European dormers.

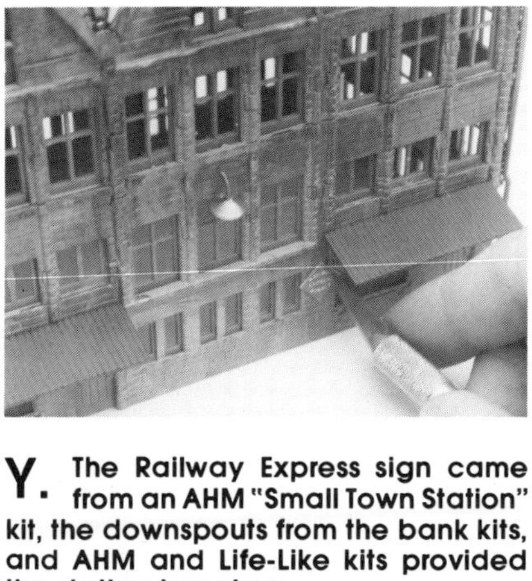

Y. The Railway Express sign came from an AHM "Small Town Station" kit, the downspouts from the bank kits, and AHM and Life-Like kits provided the station benches.

Z. The concrete platform base is thick cardboard painted gray and marked with a ball-point pen to simulate expansion joints and cracks. It completes the station.

assembly is very difficult to disassemble later if you should decide to re-kitbash the structure or need to replace a light bulb. White glue will hold the structure together and keep the roof from falling off, but the joints can be fractured easily with a little prying.

Give some thought to structures that you intend to light before you assemble them. A single coat of paint on the exterior usually isn't enough to seal the plastic against light transmission. To make sure the light only shows through the windows, paint the interior walls flat black, or line them with aluminum foil.

Structures that are to be lighted should be built with provision for changing the bulbs. Sometimes this is impossible. Where the structure will not allow disassembly, install two or even three bulbs in parallel, fig. 8-9, to guard against the possibility of burned-out bulbs undoing all your effort. Light bulbs should be positioned high inside the building to hide them from view, fig. 8-10. To keep down heat and prolong bulb life, bulbs should be run on a voltage substantially lower than their rating. For example, 12-volt bulbs should be run at 6 to 8 volts.

Finishing touches. There are a few things that you should do to every building on your layout—kitbashed or not—to make it more realistic. First, flat paint is essential, and your structures should be weathered to varying degrees to bring out their detail and to make them fit in their settings. All structures should look like they are resting in the surrounding earth, not on it, fig. 8-11. Run your scenery right up to the building foundation and work your texture material—ground foam rubber, sawdust, flock, or "zip" texturing—around the structure's base. Don't worry about the surrounding earth and bonding solution cementing the model to your layout forever—you'll find it's fairly easy to pry the structure loose to replace a light bulb or to move the building to another location. Paved concrete areas around your structures can be simulated with cardboard or sheet plastic.

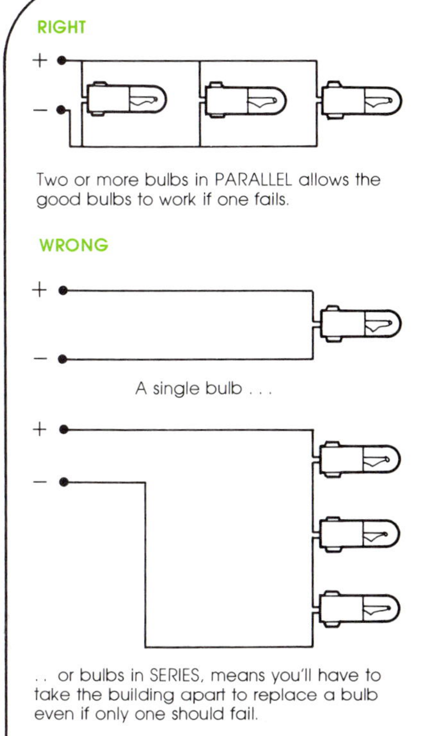

Fig. 8-9 LIGHT BULB WIRING

Note how scenic texture material has been worked up to the base of this water tank. The wood strips glued to the tabletop hold the building in place, but allow it to be removed for cleaning or alteration.

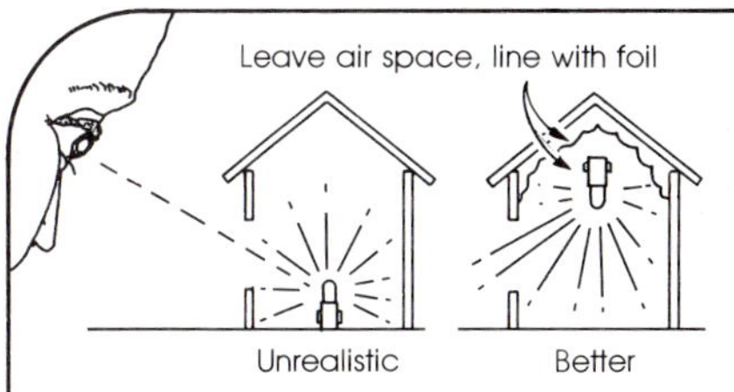

Fig. 8-10 LIGHT BULB PLACEMENT

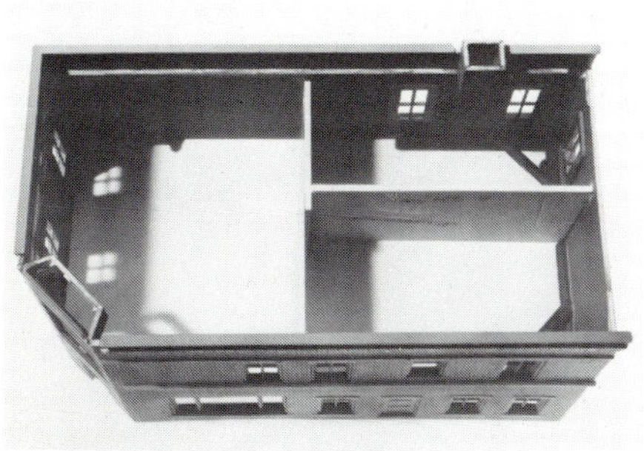

Simple sheet styrene dividers have been positioned inside this structure to prevent light from showing through. The dividers will be painted flat black.

Fig. 8-11 BLENDING STRUCTURES INTO THE LAYOUT Not to scale

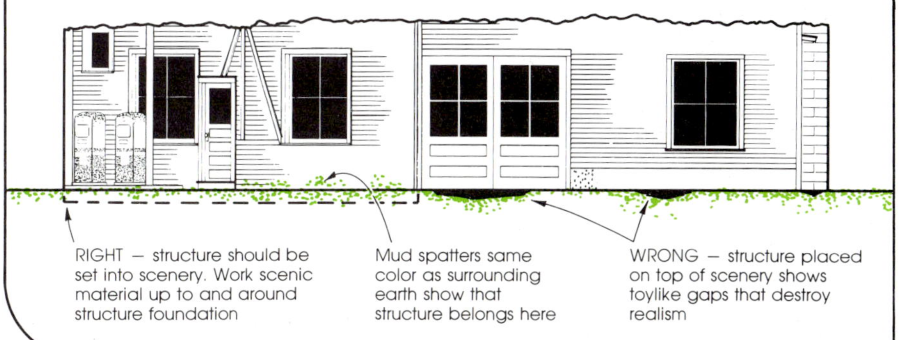

Advanced finishing

Here are more painting skills to add to your bag of modeling tricks.

PREPARATION, PRACTICE, AND PATIENCE are the keys to successful model painting and finishing. Advanced finishing techniques are based on these same principles, and, in general, are simply refined basic techniques rather than radically different ways of doing things. Airbrushing, for example, is simply a refined method of spray painting, and in discussing airbrush techniques we'll reemphasize many of the things we said in Chapter 3 about aerosol can painting. In this chapter we'll also cover methods for removing unwanted paint and provide information on blending and caring for your paints.

Removing unwanted finishes. As I've said several times, you'll usually be able to purchase plastic locomotive and car bodies undecorated. When you are unable to find unpainted bodies, or when you want to use painted bodies because you have them on hand, you'll need to know about removing paint. If you try to apply new paint over old, you'll obscure detail. The added paint coats will fill seams and make rivets and other raised details look bulky. Removing paint from parts to be used for kitbashing helps to bring out detail and helps you to see such features as panel joints and engraved lines. In the same vein, paint removal is often necessary to provide clean surfaces for cementing kitbashed parts. Be aware, however, that there is always a good chance of damaging the model while removing the paint, and that removing paint isn't much fun. Paint removal should be considered a last resort to be used only when you can't find an undecorated model.

Lettering, numbering, and striping on locomotives or cars are relatively easy to remove because they are often ink rather than paint. If you want to reletter a car or simply change the numbers without repainting the entire model, try removing only the factory lettering without damaging the paint. Lettering can often be removed by rubbing gently with a cotton swab dipped in water, alcohol, or decal setting solvent. Touch the swab to the lettering and give it a few seconds to soften the ink, then use the clean end to swab away the residue. Try both isopropyl and denatured alcohol. If they fail, try one of the decal setting fluids or lighter fluid. The best way to control the process is to barely dampen the cotton swab with the solvent and hold it against the lettering to see if it will work.

The biggest problem in removing all the paint from a model is that the same solvents that dissolve paint may dissolve plastic, too. Manufacturers use such a wide variety of paints that it is impossible to say exactly what will remove each of them. Some paint removers are not compatible with certain plastics, so it pays to test the remover on the inside or back of the model before using the agent on the entire model surface. Some removers will cause the plastic to craze just as solvents would, others will soften or embrittle it. Some paint removers may cloud the surface of clear plastic parts such as windshields and other windows.

Certain paints can be removed by soaking the model in denatured alcohol and prodding at stubborn areas with a pointed toothpick. Products sold especially for removing model railroad paint include Scalecoat Wash Away and Accu-Paint Accu-Strip. Many modelers have used automobile brake fluid for a paint stripper, and it presents a workable substitute if you are not able to find a commercial paint stripper intended specifically for plastics. If you can obtain the correct stripper, use it. The best general rules for selecting and using a paint removing agent are to use the mildest agent that will remove the paint, and to use it only as long as absolutely necessary.

All paint removing agents are bad for your skin, so wear rubber gloves—the kind used for dishwashing are fine—and consider wearing safety goggles. They don't cost much, and they can prevent a painful or debilitating eye injury.

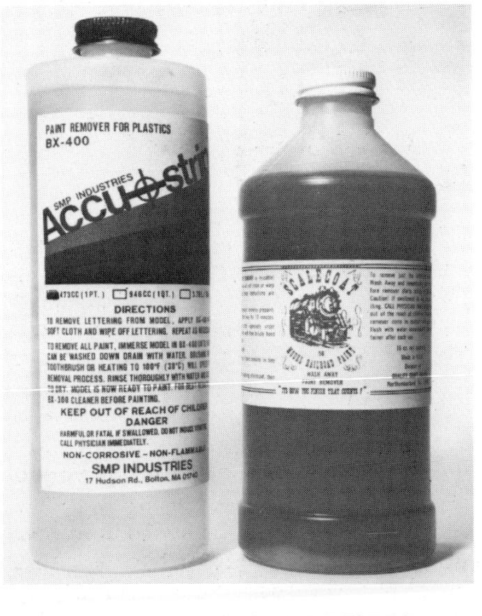

Because they are formulated for styrene plastic, paint removers sold specifically for model railroad use are safest. Left, SMP Accu-strip, right, Scalecoat Wash Away paint remover.

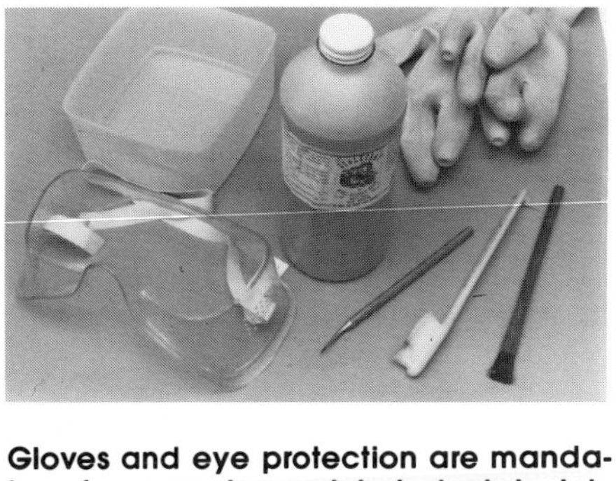

Gloves and eye protection are mandatory for removing paint. A dental pick, toothbrush, and acid brush also help.

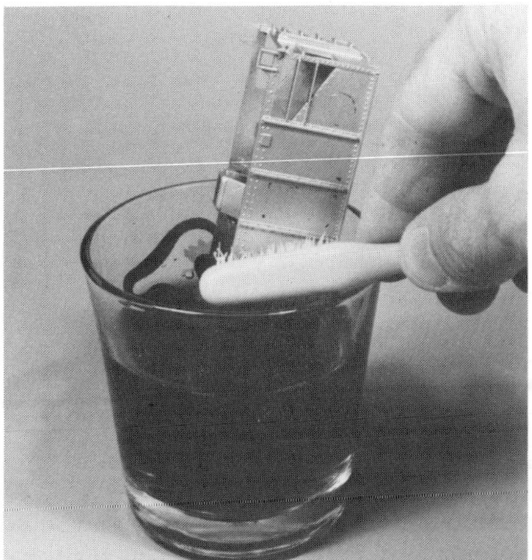

A glass makes a handy container. Immerse the part to be stripped and scrub gently with a toothbrush.

Remember that you're working with volatile, flammable fluids. Work well away from flames in a well-ventilated room. Cover your work area with a thick pad of old newspapers to protect it from the paint remover.

Depending on the consistency of the paint remover you are using (some are watery, some paste-like) you can either decant the remover into a bowl or tray and dip the model in it, or brush the agent onto the surface of the model. After the remover has had 3 to 5 minutes to work, use a toothbrush to scrub away the old paint. Pay particular attention to recesses such as those around diesel fans and grills and freight car framing. Prod stubborn areas with a pointed toothpick or Popsicle stick. A metal tool will scratch the plastic, but the decal pricker tool, fig. 4-3, does come in handy if you are careful.

After stripping, wash the model with warm soapy water to remove all traces of the stripping solution. Be sure to clean the model thoroughly and give it a complete rinse in running water. This rinse is important; it ensures that you won't get paint remover residue on your fingers when you work with the model and that traces of paint remover won't remain to destroy fresh paint.

Using an ultrasonic cleaner. Complete paint removal requires time and effort, and the best method is also the most expensive, requiring the use of an ultrasonic cleaner. These cleaners use high-frequency sound energy to agitate the cleaning solution and the object being cleaned. This agitation quickens penetration of the paint remover and shakes the paint free from the surface of the model once it is loosened. The biggest advantage of the ultrasonic cleaner is that the vibration and tiny bubbles created in the cleaning solution can penetrate into crevices and openings where no scrub brush or tool could ever fit. If you purchase an ultrasonic cleaner, be sure the tank is big enough to accept the largest model part you expect to clean in it. Keep in mind that it is possible to immerse one end of a model at a time for treatment, so the tank need not hold the entire model, but it must accommodate the cross section of the model.

Follow the manufacturer's instructions for using the ultrasonic cleaner. Use a toothbrush to help the cleaner do its work, and don't leave the cleaner running unattended. During operation all ultrasonic cleaners become hot and heat the cleaning fluid and the model. Run the machine for short periods—15 to 25 minutes—letting it cool between cycles. Because of heat buildup, flammable cleaning agents should *not* be used.

Never immerse your fingers in the cleaning solution when the ultrasonic cleaner is running. The ultrasonic action drives the cleaning chemicals into the pores of your skin, and even brief exposure can result in a serious chemical burn or infection.

Painting with an airbrush. An airbrush is an essential tool for improving the overall quality of your finishing. It is a small version of the spray guns used in industry to paint automobiles, furniture, and many other items. Most airbrushes are designed for use by artists, but their characteristics are well suited for applying the finishes we use in model railroading. The airbrush is not a magic method of applying paint. It offers full control of paint application, control that allows you to apply enough paint to color the model without hiding detail or creating sags or runs. You also have complete freedom to mix and thin paint colors and coatings. The airbrush has three distinct advantages over the aerosol can: air pressure can be adjusted to provide either a "wet" or "dry" spray, paint flow can be adjusted to provide a broad or narrow spray pattern, and you can mix paint to any color you wish.

There are two different uses for the airbrush in model railroading. First, there is simple application of paints and coatings where the airbrush is used to apply a finely dispersed spray to achieve complete coverage with a thin coat. Using the airbrush for special effects, where it excels because it can be adjusted to very fine spray patterns, is the second use. These two uses require different techniques, so we'll discuss them separately.

Most hobby shops, mail-order houses, and art-supply stores stock several brands and models of airbrushes. There are two basic types: single-action and double-action, fig. 9-1. On single-action airbrushes the finger button regulates the flow of air or propellant gas, and the paint flow adjustment is independent. This means that you adjust the paint volume before painting, and normally the setting is not changed. On double-action airbrushes, gas flow and paint flow are regulated by a single button. The usual arrangement is that you press the button down for air and pull it back for paint.

Both types of airbrush are satisfactory for our purposes. Double-action airbrushes are more complex and more expensive, but they offer additional control, especially when used for weathering and other special effects. Most brands of airbrush offer different paint flow adjustment ranges. If the airbrush you choose has several sizes, choose the middle one—No. 2 if the sizes are 1, 2, 3; B if the sizes are A, B, C; medium if the choices are fine, medium, and heavy.

When you purchase an airbrush, you'll also have to decide which type of paint container to use with it. Color *cups* are open-top containers that plug into the side or bottom of the airbrush. They have the advantages of light weight and quickly changing from one color to another, but the disadvantage of spilling paint if you tip them too far to the front or side. Color *bottles* have screw tops that make spilling less likely, but they are heavier and more cumbersome.

Low-cost spray gun sets are also available, and several of them are labeled "airbrush." These sprayers can not match the fineness of spray or the range of adjustment of true airbrushes. They do offer the advantage of being able to mix your own colors and to vary the proportions of paint to thinner for better flow and coverage, but their spray patterns and working characteristics are more like those of aerosol cans than airbrushes.

Ultrasonic cleaners speed and simplify paint removal. Larger units (above) hold an entire model; smaller tanks (below) can treat only one portion of a body shell at a time.

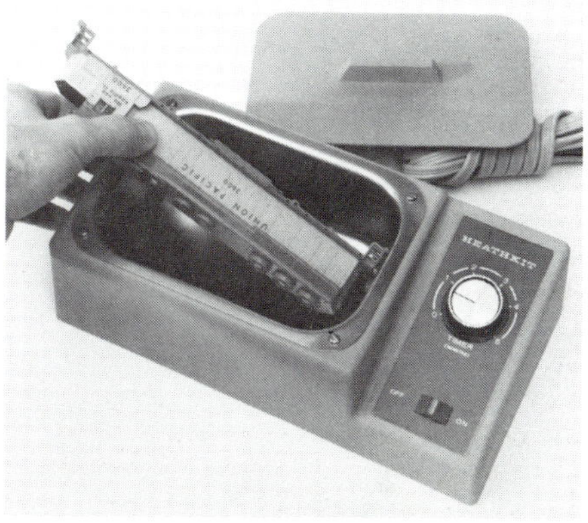

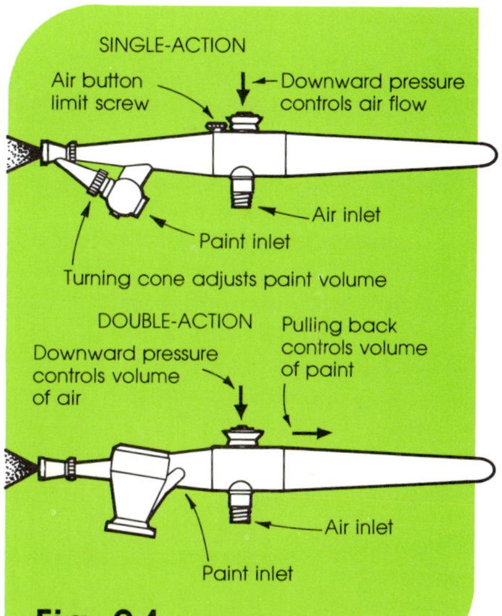

Fig. 9-1 TYPES OF AIRBRUSHES

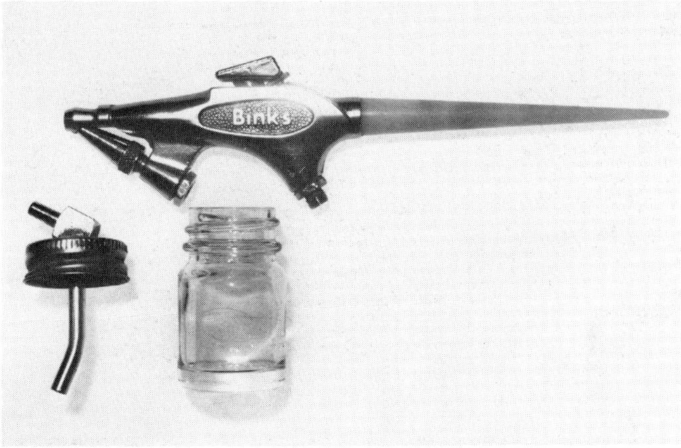

This Binks "Wren" airbrush is a single-action, external mix type that will handle most model railroad painting tasks. It comes with a color bottle paint supply.

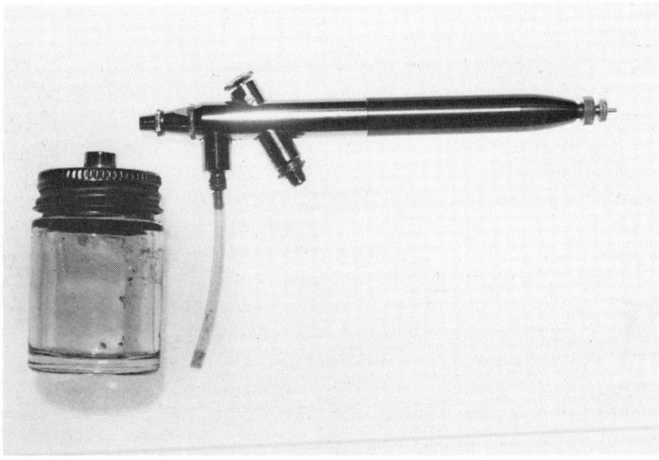

The single-action, internal mix Badger airbrush also utilizes a color bottle and siphon arrangement.

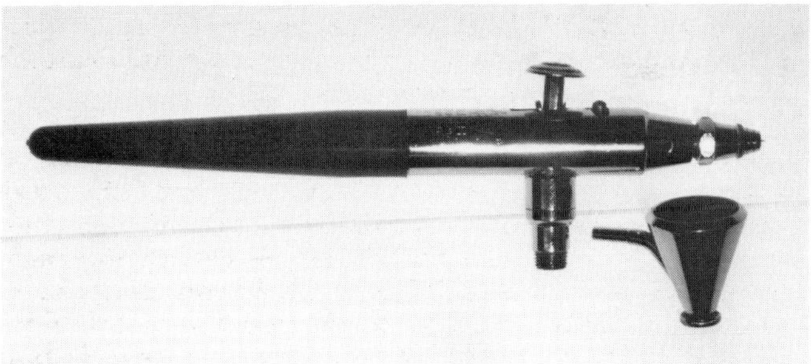

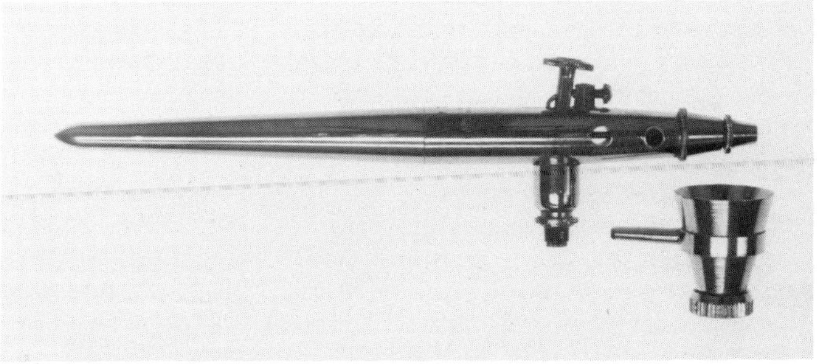

Double-action airbrushes such as the Paasche "V" (left) and the Thayer & Chandler model (right) are more expensive than single-action machines and offer more control over paint. Both are shown with open-top color cups.

Pressure sources. In addition to an airbrush, color cups or bottles, and hose, you'll need a supply of compressed propellant gas. There are several alternatives. Small cans of propellants similar to those used in spray cans are available with fittings to adapt them to the airbrush. These have the advantage of low initial cost, but the disadvantages of pressure drop as the can becomes cold or starts to run out of propellant, and of having to purchase new cans frequently.

Larger refillable compressed carbon dioxide cylinders are available, fig. 9-2. This type of gas supply will accept a pressure-regulating valve. The cylinders are heavy and bulky, and you do have to pay for refills. Gas cylinders have the habit of always running out on a weekend when you can't get them refilled.

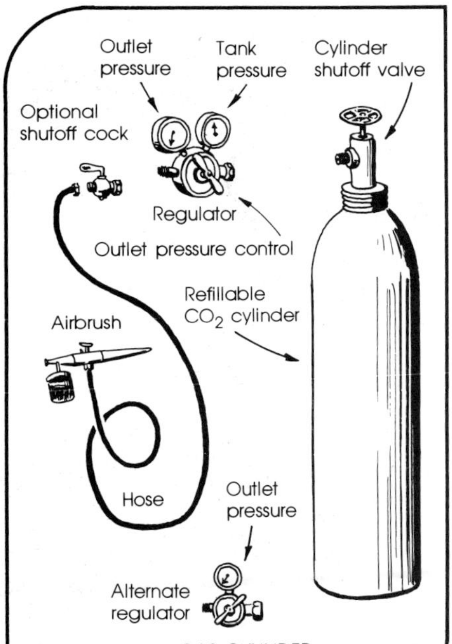

Fig. 9-2 GAS CYLINDER PRESSURE SYSTEM

Small containers of spray-can propellant offer an inexpensive way to get started in airbrush painting. If you find that you do a lot of airbrushing you'll want to shift to a non-disposable source of pressurized gas.

The best source of compressed gas for your airbrush is a small air compressor. Any compressor will do as long as you can regulate its output pressure from 12 to 40 pounds per square inch. If you intend to use it only in hobby applications, I'd suggest purchasing a compressor specifically intended for airbrush work. You'll need a moisture trap for the outlet of the compressor. This will keep water out of the air line and off your models. It's particularly important during humid weather.

Whether you use a compressor or a refillable gas bottle, you'll need a regulator to adjust the output pressure, and a gauge to indicate what the pressure is.

Using your airbrush. The first step in airbrush painting is preparing the paint. All paints must be thinned, and paint manufacturers usually provide thinning recommendations for airbrushing. If you have no other guidance, thin the paint from 20 to 25 per cent with the proper solvent; mixtures of 3 or 4 parts paint to one part thinner provide good starting points for determining what thinning ratio will work best with your equipment. Some brands of paint are intentionally made thick and must be thinned even for brushing. These paints can require as much as 1 part thinner to 1 part paint for proper airbrushing.

All paint should be thoroughly stirred or shaken, then strained. An inexpensive tea strainer and a small funnel, both purchased at a supermarket or dime store, are sufficient straining equipment. Straining is important, because it eliminates oversize paint clumps that can clog the paint passages in the airbrush and cause spotty painting. You'll be surprised what you can strain out of a brand-new bottle of paint.

Each brand of airbrush comes with its own instructions, and all the general rules that apply to aerosol-can painting apply to airbrush spraying. Since there are several things you can vary, start by adjusting the spray pressure. If you have an air regulator, adjust it so the air pressure from the compressor is about 25 pounds per square inch. Paint right from the bottle can require pressures as high as 40 psi for application, while very thin paints go on smoothly with only 12 to 15 psi.

Different paint colors require different air pressures to generate the same spray patterns and coverage. Light-colored pigments are usually heavier than dark ones, and there is a higher proportion of pigment in white or yellow paint than there is in brown or black. This is to provide more covering power. In general, you'll need more pressure to lift and spray light colors than dark colors.

Small compressors appropriate for airbrushing include the Binks diaphragm type (left) and a larger W. R. Brown 1/3 h.p. unit (right). The Brown compressor includes a tank that smooths out pulsations in air pressure.

Next, adjust the paint control so the spray pattern is about 3″ across when the airbrush is held 6″ from the model. Practice on newspapers or white cardboard until you are comfortable with the spray pattern. If the paint flow adjustment doesn't give you the spray pattern you want, go back to adjusting the pressure regulator or try varying the distance from the airbrush to the work. If the paint splatters, try reducing the pressure all the way down to 15 psi in 5 psi increments. You may have to hold the airbrush closer to the model or add more thinner at lower air pressures.

The important thing to realize is that you must experiment with your airbrush to see what it can do. Try many different combinations of paint consistency, paint supply, air pressure, and working distance. When you find a combination that's comfortable, jot down the settings so you can duplicate the conditions later on.

Now let's try actually airbrushing some paint. Start the spray off the model and sweep across the model quickly enough to provide even coverage. Never start or stop the spray on the model. For most painting, hold the airbrush 6″ to 12″ from the model. Try to keep the airbrush the same distance from the model and at a right angle to the model as you sweep the paint pattern across. Do not pivot the airbrush, move it in a straight line. Do not try to control the spray pattern by how hard you press on the air button; you should

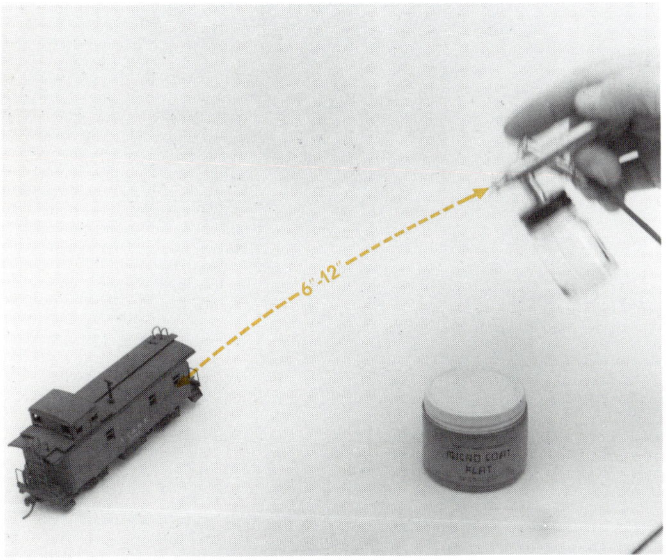

The correct spraying distance for most paints and coatings is from 6″ to 12″. It's very easy to forget this while you are airbrushing; in fact, it often seems as though the airbrush is constantly drawn closer to the model. Discipline yourself to check the distance frequently.

Straining every drop of paint to be used in your airbrush eliminates many airbrushing problems. Use a small funnel and an inexpensive tea strainer (shown in use here) or other fine-mesh sieve such as the smaller enamel-washing strainer in the foreground for straining.

Airbrush care and troubleshooting

YOUR AIRBRUSH will be one of the most expensive tools in your shop, so it pays to understand how to care for it. Scrupulous cleanliness is necessary for your airbrush to perform properly, and more trouble comes from improper or incomplete cleaning than from any other source. Nothing will ruin your airbrush as quickly as leaving it loaded with paint — even for half an hour — or not cleaning it thoroughly after painting.

The best — and most specific — advice for caring for your airbrush comes from its manufacturer, since he designed the brush and knows how to keep it working. If you don't have an instruction booklet, write and request one. Be sure to include the model and serial numbers of your airbrush.

CLEANING PROCEDURES

You must clean your airbrush every time you use it. When you finish spraying, load the color cup or bottle with clean thinner and spray into a rag. Then move the rag close to the tip of the airbrush to deflect air back into the nozzle. Some air will find its way into the paint passages, bubbling the thinner in the color cup. This backward flushing action will remove most residual paint in the airbrush and make the rest of the cleanup job easier.

Getting all paint out of the airbrush before you put it away involves partial disassembly of the airbush. As a minimum you must remove the color control, either the cone-shaped color control on an external-mix airbrush, or the needle on an internal-mix type. Most airbrushes come with a wrench which will loosen all major fittings. The other tools you may need are a small screwdriver, pipe cleaners, pliers, cotton swabs, and a few rags. Wrap masking or electrical tape around the serrated jaws of the pliers to loosen fittings that don't have flat faces for a wrench.

Use a pipe cleaner dipped in thinner to soak paint from the needle bearings and paint passages in the airbrush, then wipe the exterior of the airbrush with a soft rag dipped in clean thinner. Pass air through the brush for 20 or 30 seconds to blow out residual thinner and dry the internal parts.

Next, clean the color container. Rinse it with thinner and wipe clean with a rag and cotton swabs. Clean the siphon passages with a pipe cleaner and make sure the vent hole in the top of a bottle-type color jar is not clogged.

While cleaning be careful not to distort any holes, jets, or openings. The shape of these openings is crucial to the proper operation of the airbrush. Always keep in mind that your airbrush is a precision tool. Never try to poke a pin or needle in the nozzle of the airbrush to remove paint. A special reamer to clean the needle tip area comes with some airbrushes. These reamers are also sold separately. The cleaning reamer is used to remove hardened paint from inside the tip. It is the same diameter and shape as the needle. It should only be used to remove material from the tip if all other methods fail.

REASSEMBLY

Before reassembling the airbrush, check that there is no paint on the threads. Inspect all parts by holding them up to a light to ensure both paint and air passages are clear. Be gentle when tightening, finger-tight is usually sufficient for everything but the air hose connection. If the airbrush is a needle type, do not reinsert the needle all the way into the tip. Leave it loose and remember to remove, reinspect, and insert the needle all the way into the tip before the next use.

Any airbrush will last a lifetime given proper cleaning and care, but there are parts which will wear out. If you airbrush frequently, examine the color control, needle, needle bearings, and nozzle tip while you have them apart. All airbrush manufacturers offer repair parts.

Store your airbrush and hose away from dust. Whenever you attach the air hose to your pressure source run air through it to blow out accumulated dirt before you attach the airbrush. Always replace the protective cap on the end of the airbrush. This cap prevents damage to the end of the needle or color control.

TROUBLESHOOTING

Properly cleaning your airbrush and always straining the paint will eliminate most airbrushing problems. Here's how to solve some of the common ones:

- **No air.** First, look for an obstruction between the gas source and the paint nozzle.
  (a) Is there pressure at the source?
  (b) Does air come out of the air hose when the airbrush is detached?

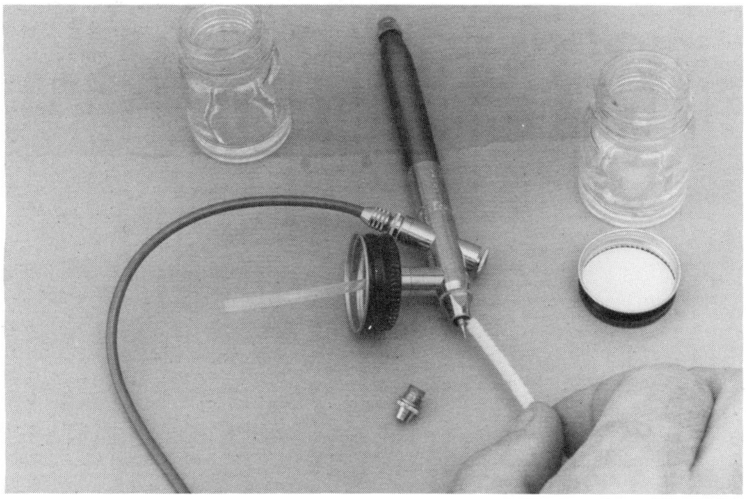

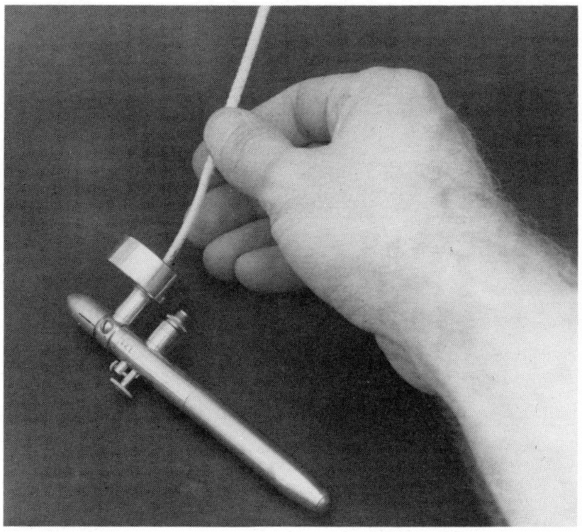

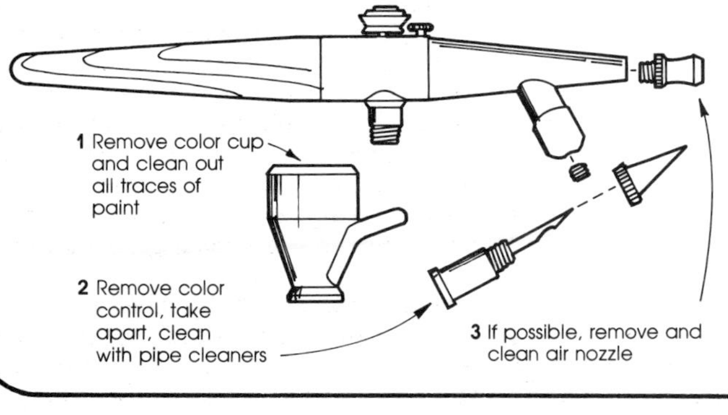

CLEANING AN EXTERNAL-MIX AIRBRUSH

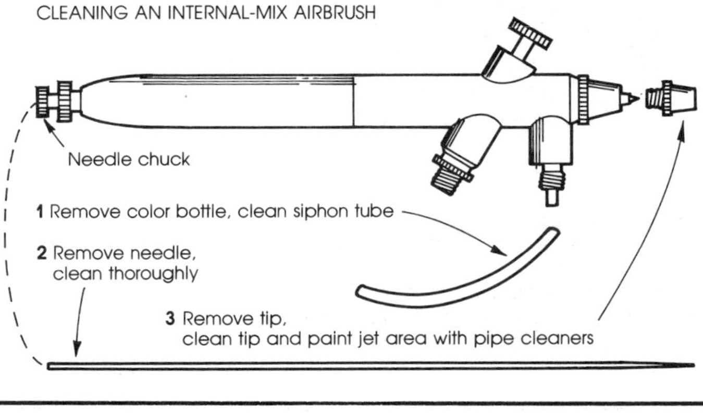

CLEANING AN INTERNAL-MIX AIRBRUSH

(c) Are you standing on the hose?
(d) Disassemble the airbrush and look for dirt or other foreign matter in the air valve.

- **No paint.**
  (a) Is the vent hole in the color bottle cap open?
  (b) Is the paint tip clogged?
  (c) Is the paint thin enough?
  (d) Is the air pressure too low?
  (e) Check that nothing is deflecting the air stream away from the paint tip.
- **Dirt.** If there is dirt in the paint spray in spite of careful cleaning and paint straining:
  (a) Check the hose. If it is old, rubber can break off from its inside walls.
  (b) If the compressor is in a dusty area, it should have both intake and output filters. If you have a moisture trap it will usually serve for an output filter.
- **Erratic paint spray.** In a needle-type airbrush the needle is the source of several potential problems:
  (a) Is the needle bent or distorted?
  (b) Is the needle point centered in the tip?
  (c) Does the needle mate perfectly with the tip?
  (d) To straighten a bent needle, roll it back and forth on a glass sheet. Use your fingernail or a wood stick to gently work the tip of the needle straight. Remove burrs by drawing the needle across an oilstone with a twisting motion.
- **Paint runs and sags.**
  (a) Is the spray too close to the work?
  (b) Is the spray being held on the model too long?
  (c) Is the paint too thin?
  (d) Hold the airbrush farther from the model, move it more quickly, or thicken the paint.

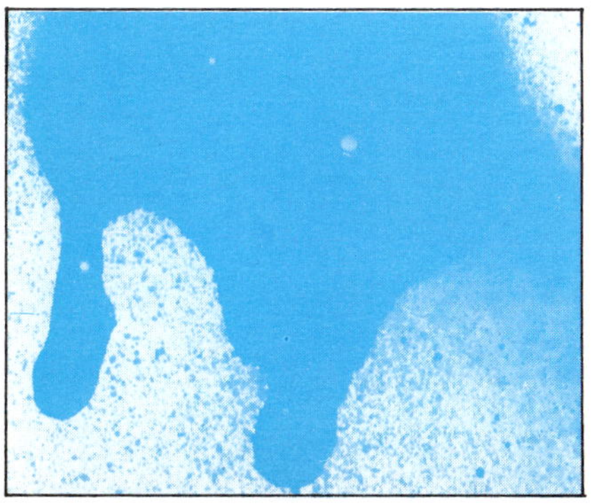

- **Uneven paint pattern.**
  (a) Is the airbrush too close to the work?
  (b) Is there too little pressure?
  (c) Is the nozzle partially clogged?
  (d) Hold spray farther from the work, clean the nozzle, or increase the pressure.

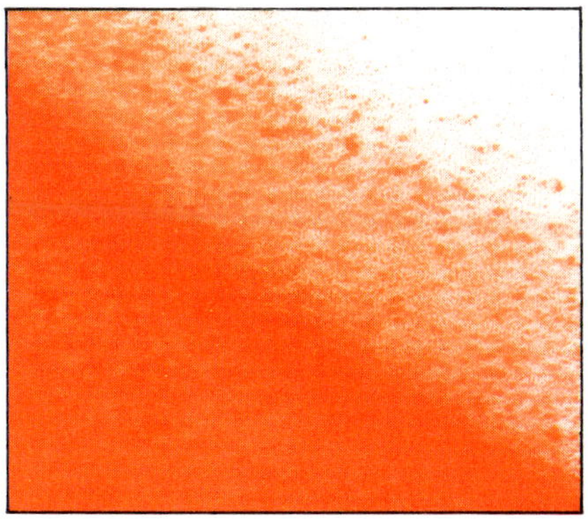

- **Paint appears rough, peppery.**
  (a) Is the spray too far from the work?
  (b) Are you using too little thinner?
  (c) Is there too much air pressure?
  (d) Hold spray closer to work, thin the paint, or decrease the air pressure (in that order).

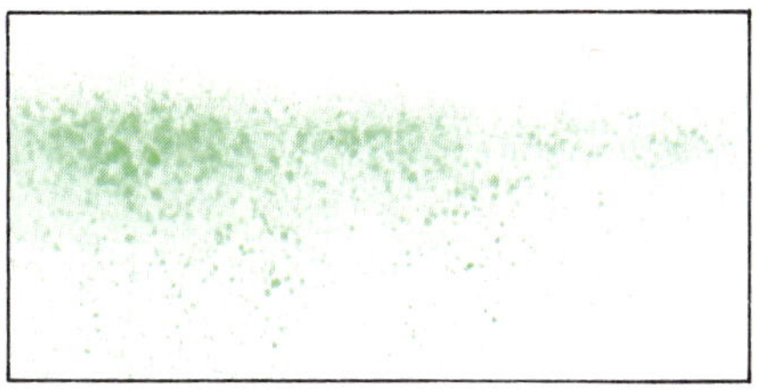

- **Paint spray irregular.**
  (a) Is the nozzle partially clogged?
  (b) Is the paint thoroughly mixed?
  (c) Clean nozzle in thinner, mix and strain paint thoroughly.

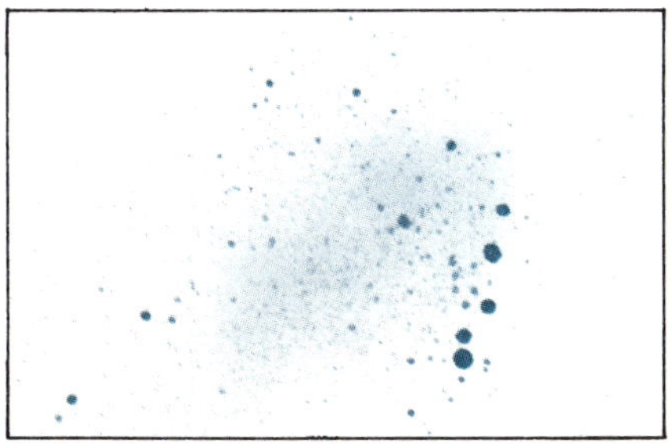

- **Proper paint pattern.** No problem at all!

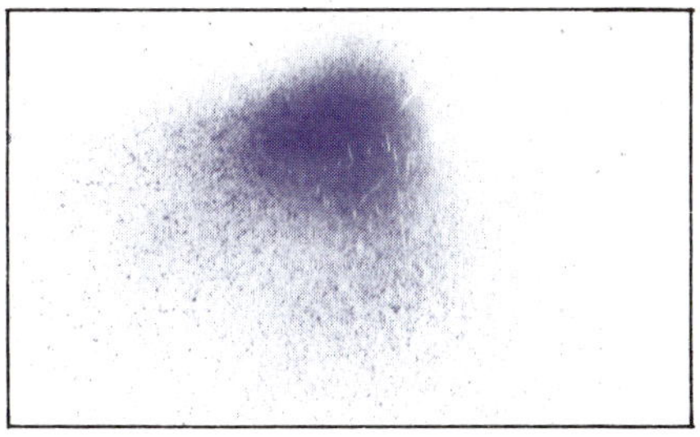

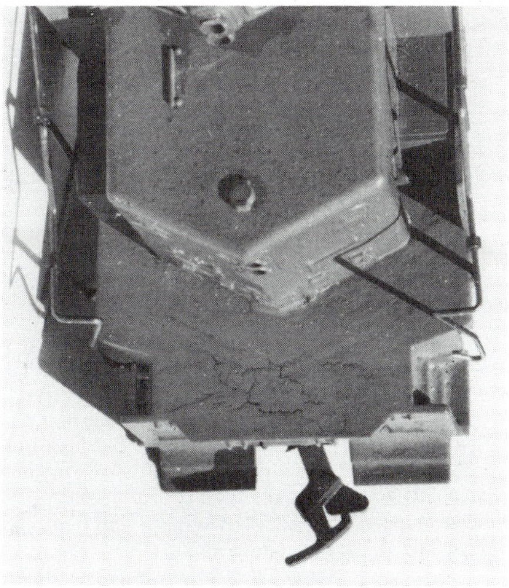

The ruined end platform on this diesel looks like a mud-cracked dry creek bed because the plastic-incompatible paint airbrushed on it was still quite wet when it reached the model.

push the button all the way down and control the air and paint flow with the pressure regulator and paint flow adjustments.

The flexibility of the airbrush allows us to use plastic-incompatible paints on plastic models, and this is valuable for several reasons. Most plastic-incompatible paints dry quicker and harder than plastic-compatible paints. Also, there is a greater variety of railroad colors available in incompatible paints.

Incompatible paints can be airbrushed on styrene without fear of crazing by what is called "dry" spraying. To do this, manipulate air pressure, paint supply, and spraying distance so that the paint is applied in a thin coat that is nearly dry when it hits the model. I say nearly dry, because if the paint is entirely dry when it gets to the model, it will form a powdery deposit that will rub off easily. When the paint droplets hit the model they must still be liquid, but enough of the solvent must have evaporated during the trip between airbrush and model that the remaining solvent will not have a chance to craze the plastic. Practice on an old carbody and you'll get the hang of it in no time.

While airbrushing, keep a jar of thinner ready to clean the airbrush every time you set it down and every time you change colors. Spray clean thinner through the brush until color stops coming out. When you are through painting for the day, disassemble and clean the airbrush according to the manufacturer's instructions. You will ruin your airbrush if you fail to clean it completely. See the Toolbox on Airbrush Care and Troubleshooting for more information on cleaning.

Airbrushing for special effects. The special effect that makes an airbrush worth its cost is weathering. Increase the air pressure setting to above 35 psi, set the paint flow to minimum, mix 10 to 20 parts thinner to one part paint, and use your airbrush to dust your locomotives, rolling stock, and structures just as nature does. The paint should hit the surface of the model just wet enough to grip, but it should look dry. Practice on newspaper or scrap cardboard, holding the airbrush 3″ to 6″ from the model.

Keep the airbrush moving while you spray dust effects. It may seem that nothing is coming out of the nozzle, but if you linger in one area you'll cause an unrealistic paint buildup. For your first airbrush weathering projects, concentrate on the trucks and bottom edges of rolling stock bodies and around the bases and eaves of structures.

Often you'll want to dust a completed model with a weathering color, while keeping the spray off certain areas. A good example is any model with windows, where you don't want dust and grime over the shiny glazing. One way to guard against overspray is to use a hand-held mask. Don't hold the mask too close to the model, or you'll come up with an unrealistic sharp edge. To make a soft-edge hand-held mask, tear a sheet of cardboard with a wrenching, twisting motion. This will produce a feather edge, fig. 9-3.

With a little experience and experimentation, dozens of special effects will suggest themselves. For example, you can airbrush light-and-dark contrasts to make parts appear larger or smaller. When painting locomotive handrails, use a lighter color than the body, but spray only the upper portion of the handrail, fig. 9-4. This technique will make oversize handrails appear thinner.

Airbrush safety. The safety precautions applicable to airbrushing concern the flammable paints and thinners that you will spray with the airbrush. The importance of adequate ventilation to carry away hazardous fumes cannot be overemphasized. Thinners contain hydrocarbon compounds which are both flammable and hazardous to your respiratory system, so ensure that plenty of air is flowing through your work area before you start to paint. Keep open flames and other sources of ignition away from the workbench.

Because an airbrush does such an excellent job of atomizing paint, some solid particles will become suspended in the air while you paint. These particles can irritate your nose, so wear an inexpensive foam filter mask while airbrushing even if you have an exhaust fan in your workshop area.

Finally, compressed gas in cylinders requires strict safety procedures. The cylinders must be stored where they will not be subjected to high temperatures or physical abuse. If you choose this source of propellant gas, be aware that the cylinders are heavy and bulky, and that they must be moved with extreme care. They must never be dropped.

Mixing and storing paint. Although dozens of different colors are on the market, you'll often need a shade that is not offered. Your solution is to mix the color from the available paints. The three primary colors, blue, yellow, and red, can be used to mix almost any other color, fig. 9-5. Use black or white to darken or lighten the mix you have made from the primary colors. Usually, it is easier to start with a commercial color close to what you want than it is to work with primaries. Start with the lightest colors and add the darker colors slowly. Stir the blend frequently to evaluate the color.

When you mix a color of your own, keep a record of the paints you used and the quantities of each that went into the blend. Add the paints to the blend with a consistent measuring device such as an eyedropper so you can accurately count the number of drops. Clean the eyedropper with thinner immediately after measuring each color. Some modelers use a Popsicle stick or coffee stirrer as a measuring device. Dip the stick into the

Adding realism to plastic track

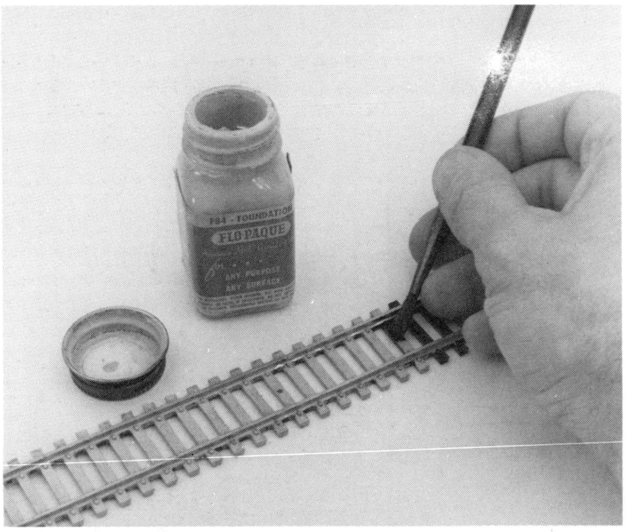

A. The detail on plastic track is exceptional, and we can improve its appearance by painting the ties to bring out the detail and match the appearance of weathered, sun-bleached wood. Start by painting the track – rails, ties, and all – a light beige or tan. This color provides a base for staining. If you mix your own color, try to match a piece of unpainted pine or plywood.

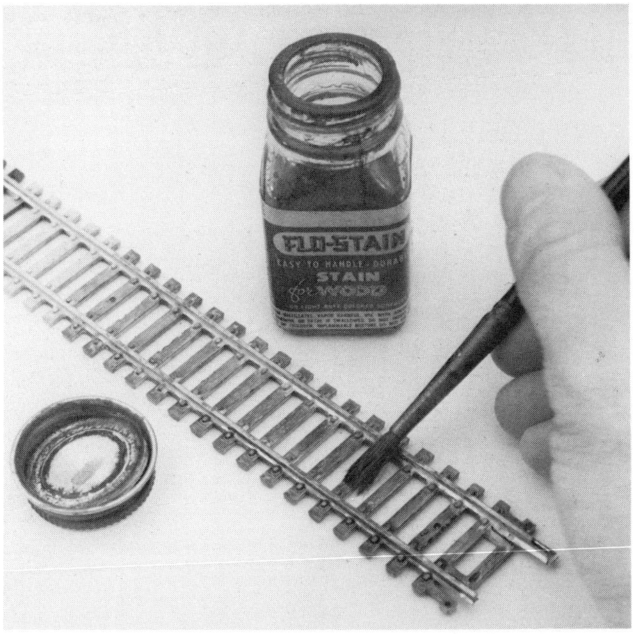

B. Let the base color dry for about an hour, then streak stain over the base color in varying quantities. You can use a commercial stain, as shown here, or mix your own. If you mix your own stain, mix nine parts thinner to one part brown, brownish-red, or brownish-black paint, depending on the type of wood you wish to simulate. Allow only the tip of the brush to touch the surface so the pattern of the stain will be grainlike streaks.

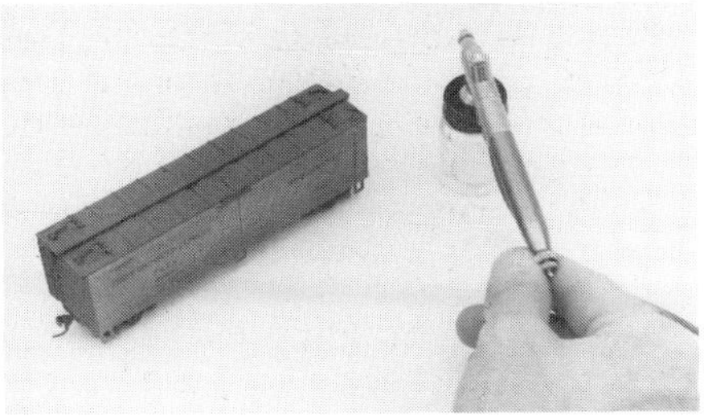

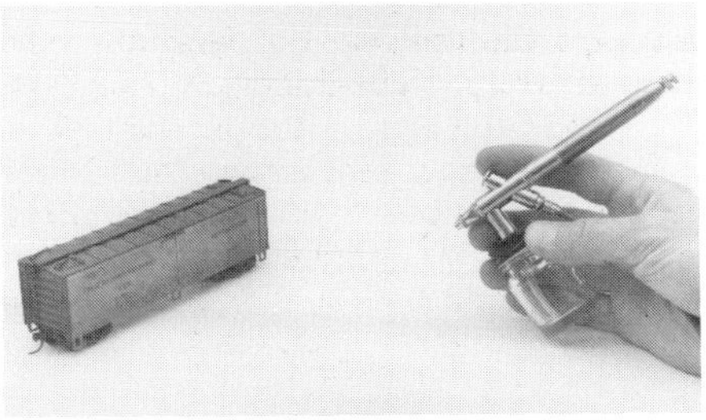

Use greatly thinned paint and high air pressure to dust the lower edges of the carbody and the trucks to simulate dirt picked up from the roadbed.

paint jar, allow the heavy flow of paint to run off, and drip paint into your blending jar while you count the number of drops.

Keep empty paint bottles and caps on hand to hold thinned paint. This way, you can save thinned or specially blended paints for future airbrushing instead of pouring them back into the bottle and diluting your "stock" paint. Keep leftover unthinned paint in the original bottles so it can be used for brushing, touchup, and mixing.

Sooner or later, you'll find a paint, primer, or other coating that is sold only in aerosol cans. It may seem wasteful, but it's actually worthwhile to discharge the contents of the spray can into a bottle so that they can be airbrushed for best results. Several types of metal-flake transparent paints and Testors Dullcote are in this category.

As you do more and more modeling, you'll probably settle on one or two brands of paint for the majority of your finishing needs. This is not to say that one particular brand is better than all the others, or that one brand will have all the colors you want. What you will find is that by standardizing on one brand, you'll have to keep less paint and fewer types of thinners on hand, and you'll develop a feel for how the paint behaves.

Standardizing on one or two brands of paint will save you money, as will adopting good paint storage habits. Keep your paint where it will not get warmer than room temperature, and where it will not freeze. When you open

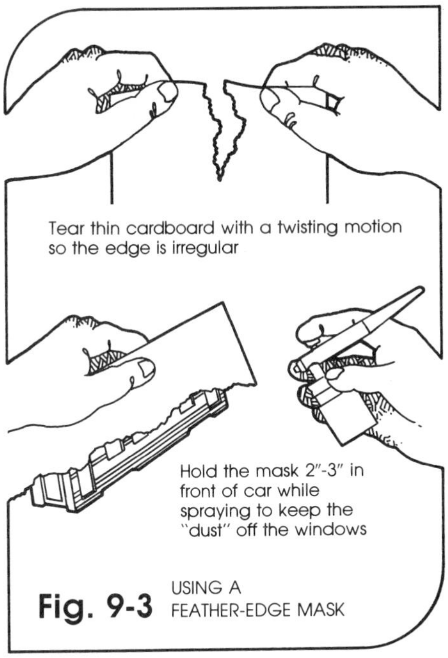

Fig. 9-3 USING A FEATHER-EDGE MASK

a bottle of paint, keep it covered as much as possible during use. Even setting the cap loosely on the bottle helps prevent solvent evaporation and keeps air away from the paint. Before putting the paint away, add about an eyedropperful of solvent but don't stir it in; allow it to float on top of the paint to further pro-

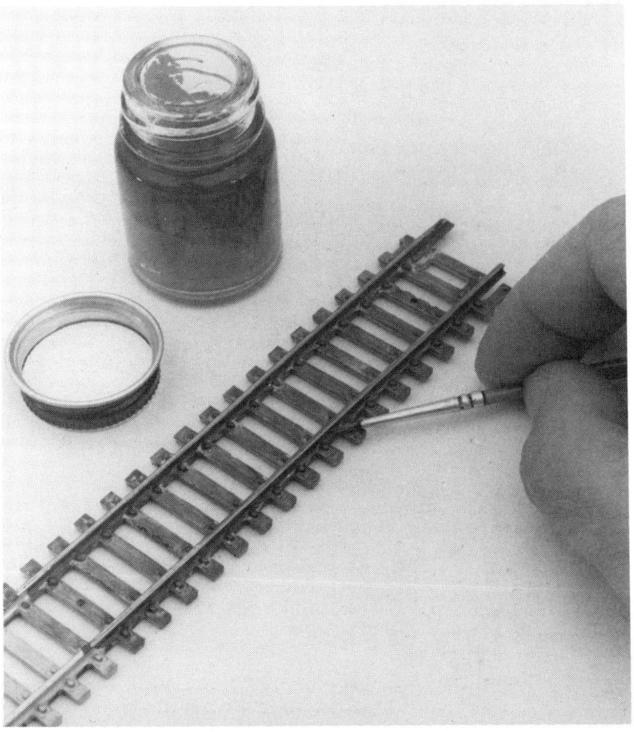

C. Painting the rails is easier than you might think; use a round No. 1 brush and don't worry if some of your rust color splashes onto the ties – it will simulate rust on the tie plates and spikes.

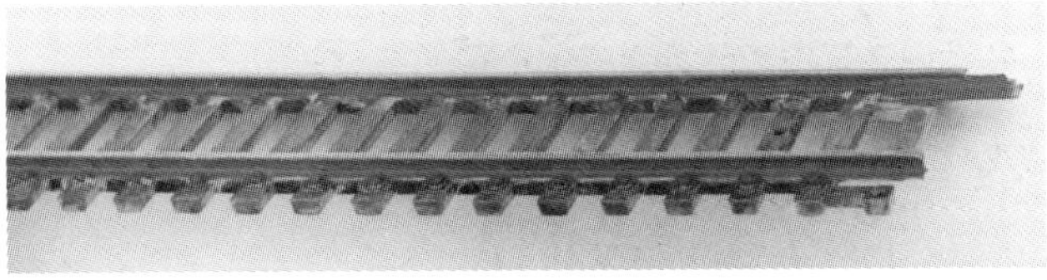

D. Treat the track with a light gray wash to complete the weathered appearance. Paint on the rails can be wiped off with a rag dipped in thinner – only the tops and inner edges provide electrical contact.

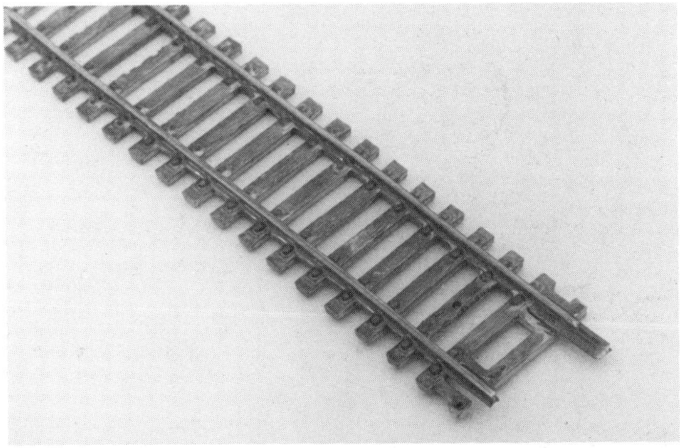

E. The improvement in the realism of plastic track is striking. This technique can be applied to track already in place, but you have to be careful to keep the foundation and stain off the surrounding ballast.

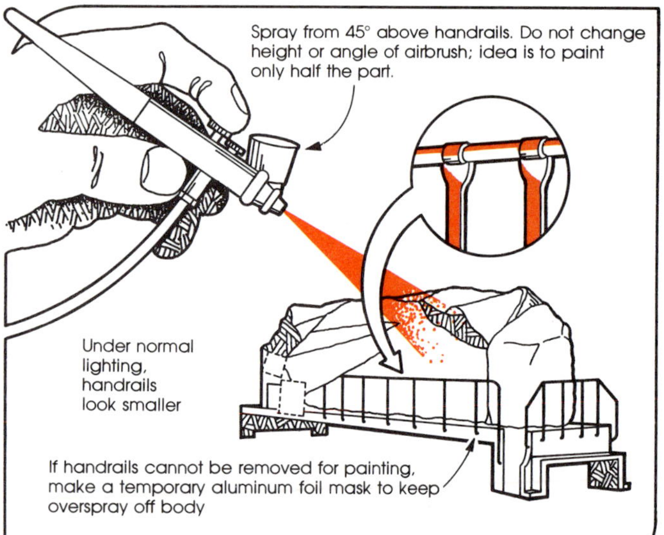

Fig. 9-4 HIGHLIGHTING HANDRAILS

All three of these cars have been airbrushed to effectively simulate prototype dirt and grime.

tect the paint from the air in the bottle.

When you reseal the bottle, wipe the neck of the bottle and the inside rim of the cap clean and screw the cap down tight. When the bottle of paint is more than half used, store the remaining paint in a smaller container with little or no air space. You'll find that these simple precautions will make your paint last longer, which means you'll have the right colors on hand when you need them.

Albert Hetzel brushed rusty red paint onto the frame and trucks of this car and added gloss black oil spills. He airbrushed with Floquil Grime to blend the effects.

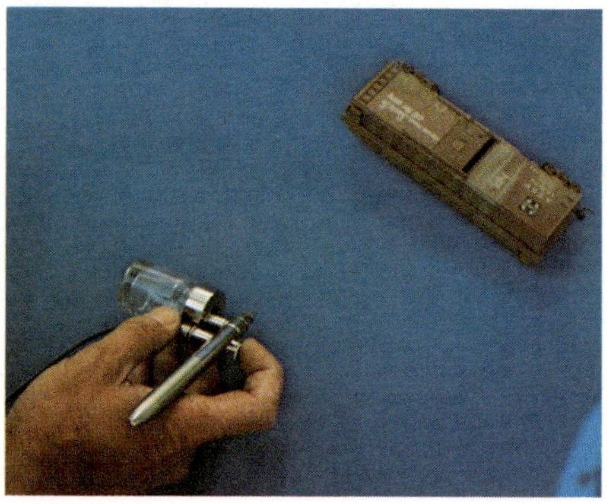

Overspraying brush-applied streaks and splatters tones them down and suggests they were made long ago.

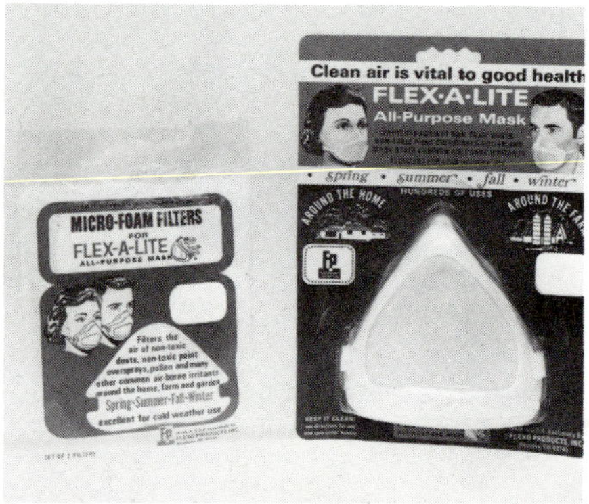

An inexpensive filter mask will keep paint solids out of your nose while airbrushing.

Mixing the primary colors of red, yellow, and blue creates orange, green, violet, and brown. As a rule, it is best to combine as few colors as possible to mix your own colors.

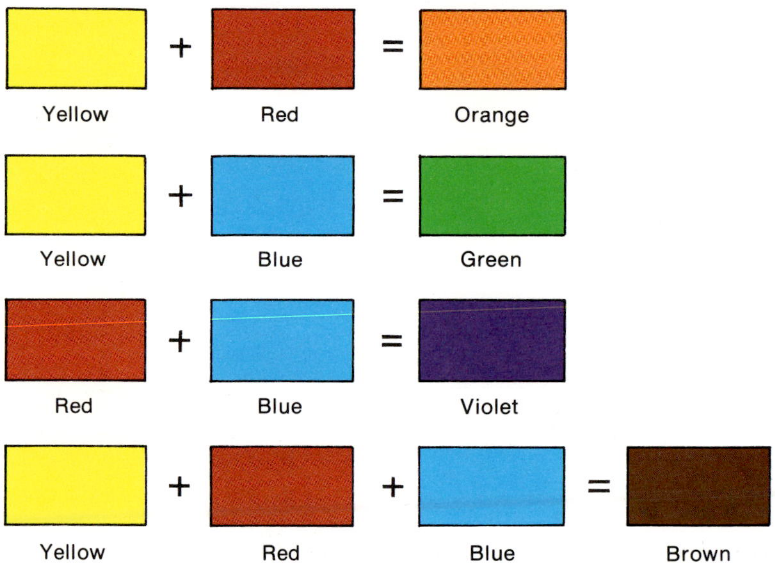

Fig. 9-5 BASIC COLOR MIXING

Advanced kitbashing

Improving your skills and applying them to ambitious modeling projects is the continuing fun of railroading with plastic.

JUST AS advanced finishing techniques are not completely different ways of doing things, advanced kitbashing techniques are more often refinements of basic techniques than radical departures from them. As you gain experience, you'll gradually improve your skills in three ways: through the use of special tools, through learning tricks of the trade, and through changing the way you approach your projects.

Adding tools to your workshop. Don't make the mistake of equating improved modelwork with expensive tools or exotic gadgets. There are several modestly priced tools such as the airbrush we discussed in Chapter 9 that can help speed individual construction steps, but others are simply gadgets that can hinder you. You should be able to write down what tasks you will use a tool for *before* you purchase it. Skill is something that you develop through practice and error, not a commodity you can buy in a shiny plastic case.

The first tool that you should consider adding to your workshop is a hand-held motor tool. It is a medium-cost labor saver that can speed up many model-building operations. The Toolbox on pages 96 and 97 provides information on the types of motor tools and their uses. There are dozens of attachments, but you'll find that you do most of your work with just a few of them.

Some of the jobs that the hand-held motor tool can do best are filing and sanding. While the motor tool is inferior to a file for making close-fitting joints, it can save you tedious work by quickly removing excess material.

Many modelers own small lathes that can be used to section plastic parts with far more accuracy than a hand-held razor saw. Multipurpose machines such as the Unimat and Machinex 5 can serve as lathes, milling machines, and drill presses. Their micrometer adjustments allow for precise positioning of holes, rivets, and sectioning cuts. The precise cuts necessary for locomotive kitbashing become simple once the machine is set up. What most sophisticated tools offer is precision; remember that you can achieve similar accuracy with a good working surface, a machinist's square, a steel ruler, dividers, and extra care on your part.

When using machine tools on plastic, low speeds are an absolute must to keep the plastic from softening and gumming up the tool. For sawing, use repeated applications of Vaseline petroleum jelly on the blade to lubricate it and the work.

Laminating. Occasionally you'll need a thick, solid plastic block $\frac{1}{4}$" to $\frac{1}{2}$" thick. Such heavy thicknesses are not widely available, but you can laminate them from sheet stock. Cut the pieces considerably oversize, and plan to trim them to size after laminating. You'll need to apply more solvent cement than a small brush or precision needlepoint applicator can deliver, so use a larger brush, a needlepoint applicator with a large tip, or an eyedropper. After applying the solvent, weight or clamp the lamination to squeeze excess solvent out of the joints and hold the pieces together.

Let laminated pieces dry thoroughly before shaping them. Because the solvent must migrate to the edges of the joints to evaporate, it may take up to a week for the lamination to harden so that it can be cut and shaped. Leave it for at least two days. If you try to work a laminated piece too soon, you'll encounter rubbery joint layers that you won't be able to finish properly.

Embossing rivet details. Most rivet detail on kitbashed models comes from the kits that we start with. Sometimes, though, you'll want to add rivets to scratchbuilt parts. Thin plastic .005" or .010" thick can be embossed from the back to provide acceptable rivet detail. If only a few rivets are needed, you can make them with a drilled metal plate and a punch or scriber, fig. 10-1, but for jobs requiring extensive rivet detail, you'll need to build or buy a rivet machine.

The first step in making rivets is to lightly scribe the centerline of the rivet

A hand-held motor tool is at its best when performing roughing-out jobs such as cutting window openings. Always remember that motor tools save time; quality is still up to you.

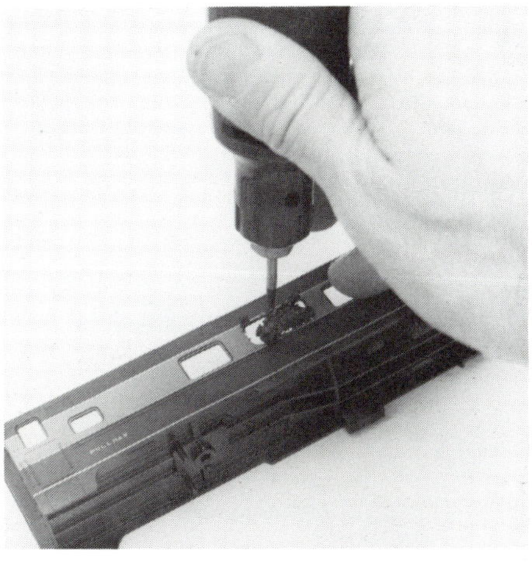

Always leave $\frac{1}{64}$"–$\frac{1}{32}$" of material to be removed with hand tools when you are cutting with a motor tool.

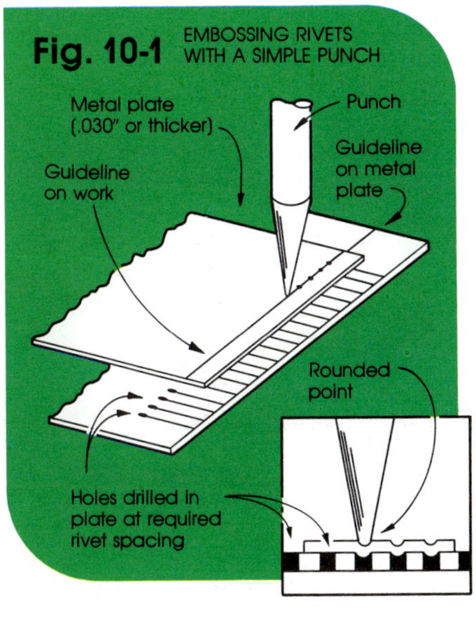

Using motor tools

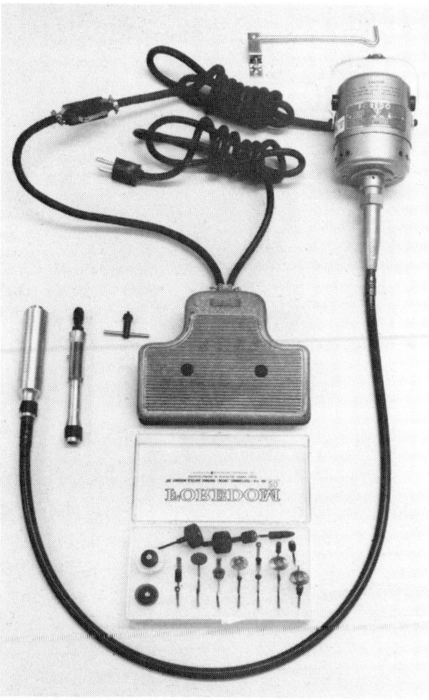

A Foredom flexible-shaft motor tool with a foot-treadle-operated speed control and accessory tool bit set.

A HAND-HELD MOTOR TOOL is the most common power tool in modelers' workshops. You'll find it useful for drilling, carving, and sanding, but its most frequent use is in rapidly removing excess material.

There are two basic types of motor tools: self-contained and flexible shaft. On the self-contained type you hold the motor right in your hand. Flexible-shaft tools have a separate motor that drives the handpiece through a flexible cable similar to an automobile speedometer drive. The self-contained models can be mounted in a bench stand or drill press stand to use them as miniature lathes or drill presses. The big advantage of the flexible-shaft motor tools is that only the slender handpiece is brought to the work. The handpiece is smaller and lighter than the self-contained tool, and it is easier to maneuver in tight places.

SPEED CONTROL

Motor tools run fast, usually too fast for the work we do. Most operate at speeds from 14,000 to 25,000 rpm. These speeds produce smooth, rapid cuts on metal and wood, but are much too high for plastic. Plastics are softened by the heat generated by high speeds, so to make a motor tool a useful addition to your workshop, you'll need a speed control.

At least one self-contained motor tool has a built-in speed control, but most controls are separate units, either a foot treadle or a small box with a control knob. The chief advantage of a motor tool with a built-in speed control is that it is handy for work on the layout. Both types of separate speed controls have advantages and disadvantages. The foot-operated unit allows you to start, stop, and vary speed without putting down the work or the tool. The bench-top box has a graduated dial that allows presetting the speed (2, 3, etc.) required for a certain job. An arrangement that combines the advantages of both is to use a bench-top controller and a foot-operated on-off switch.

ATTACHMENTS AND ACCESSORIES

Motor tool sets include an assortment of cutting, grinding, and polishing tools. Some of these are very useful, but others are needed once in a lifetime or not at all. The most economical plan is to purchase attachments when required for individual projects and specific tasks. Here are some of the most useful ones:

- **Steel cutting bits.** These sharp-toothed rotary cutters are handy for plastic because they do not clog as abrasives do. High-speed steel cutters last much longer than carbon steel but do not cost as much as tungsten carbide or vanadium steel. The barrel-shaped cutter 1/4" in diameter is especially useful. When cutting an opening, use a cutter for removing most of the material, then work to your layout lines with files. Toothed cutters work very fast, and the tool can get away from you. There's a tendency for the tool to grab and feed itself into the work. Where possible, hold the work in a vise. Engraving cutters and dental burrs are smaller versions of standard toothed cutters. They are handy for removing unwanted detail.
- **Sanding drums** mount cloth bands with abrasive grit glued to them. The replaceable bands are mounted on a mandrel that has a rubber drum. Drum diameters range from about 1/4" to 3/4"; several grit sizes are available. Sanding drums are useful for rapidly removing large amounts of material, but don't try to use them for finishing to joint lines.
- A **drill chuck** is a pin vise with a shank that fits in the motor tool. Intended mostly for drilling, it is also handy for making small turnings.

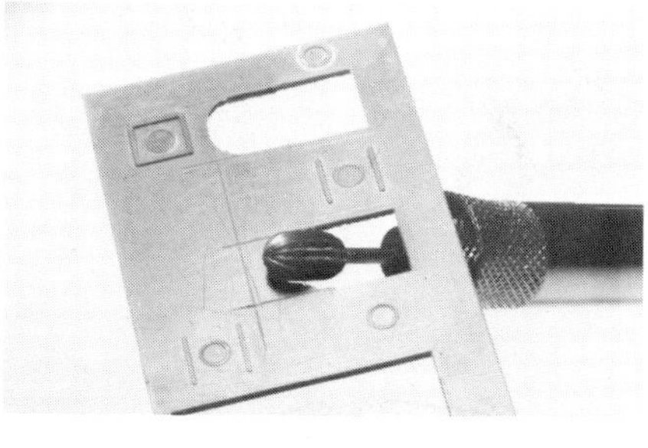

A toothed steel cutter can be used for rough cutting operations such as enlarging window openings.

- **Rubber-bonded abrasive wheels** are eraser-like rubber wheels impregnated with emery grit. They are excellent for polishing away traces of removed parts because they leave a smooth, flawless surface and because their action is very controllable. They should be used only to polish, never to remove large amounts of material. The two handiest sizes are 1" diameter by 1/8" wide and 1/4" diameter by 1/2" long.
- **Abrasive cutting wheels.** These hard, thin disks of bonded emery grit range from 1/64" to 1/32" thick. They are handy for cutting rail and steel music wire, removing detail, cutting sheet material, and slicing through heavy structure wall or carbody sections. They must be mounted on a screw-type mandrel. These wheels are delicate and easily shattered by side pressure.
- **Wire brushes** are made of brass or steel. They can be used to add wood grain to such parts as flat car decks.
- **Slitting saws** are small circular saw blades that mount on a mandrel. They are useful for slicing flat parts and for cutting off thin sections, but because they often grab and run across the work, they are among the most dangerous attachments. Always use a vise to hold the work; if that is not possible, forsake the motor tool and use a razor saw instead.
- **Collets and chucks.** Some motor tools come equipped with a key chuck, but most use collets to grip the attachments. You'll need a full set of collets from 0-1/8"; 3 or 4 sizes usually make up the full range.

Accessories are also available to hold the motor tool so you can have both hands free, or to turn it into a drill press or router. These are occasionally handy, but by no means required.

USING YOUR MOTOR TOOL

Before you reach for your motor tool, make sure that your work area is clear of small parts that could be inadvertently picked up and flung around. Rags are particularly dangerous. Ensure that the collet is

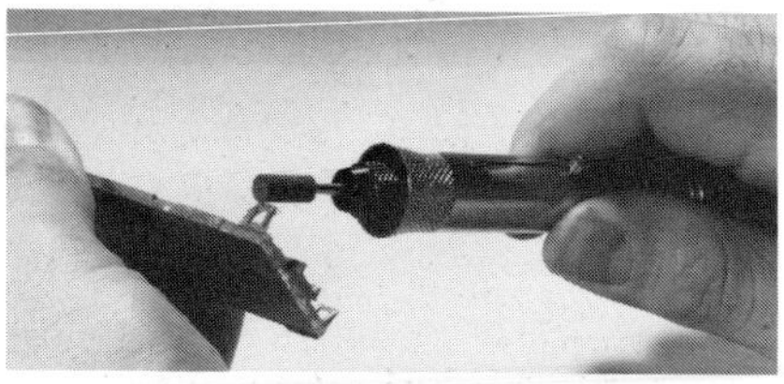

Only the light, slender handpiece of the flexible-shaft motor tool is brought to the work. It's easy to maneuver.

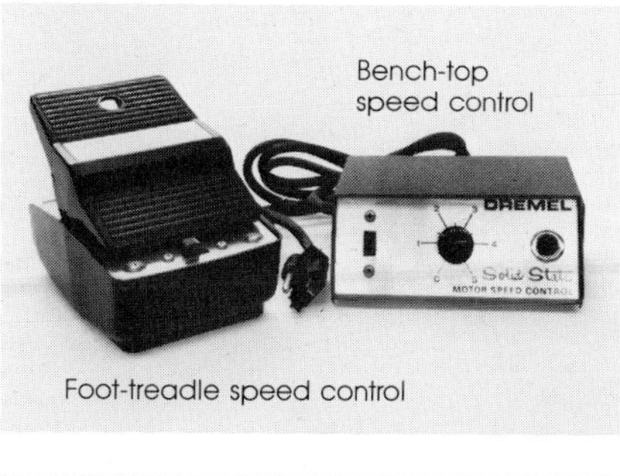

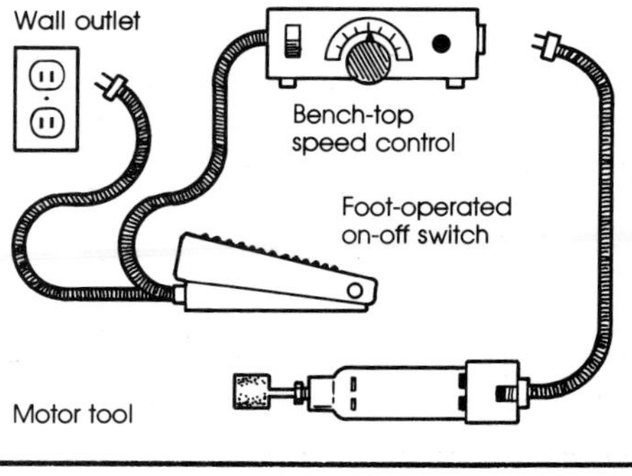

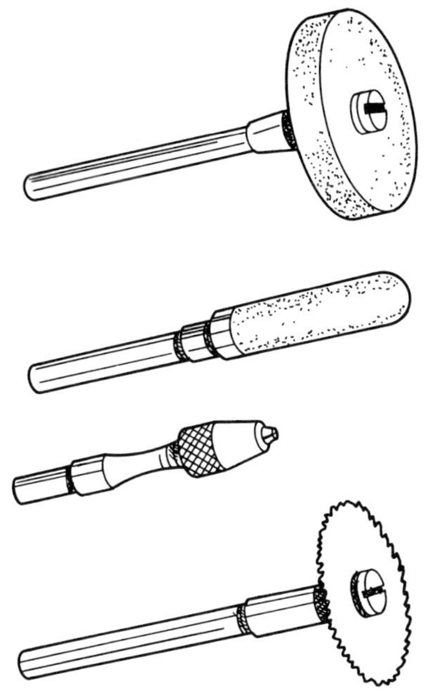

the correct size for the attachment you intend to use, and that the bit is firmly held in the chuck or collet. If possible, use a vise or clamp to hold the work. This is much safer than holding it in your hand, and leaves both hands free to manipulate the tool.

Adjust the speed of the tool. Keep the speed low enough that the cut is clean, and back off immediately if you detect the plastic starting to soften. Keep the tool moving to help prevent heat buildup.

Hold the motor tool with your whole hand – not just your fingers. This grip provides greater control over the tool and causes less finger fatigue. Where possible, support the heel of your hand on the bench top or brace your arms on the edge of the workbench. Keep your fingers as far as possible from the cutting action and train yourself to keep your fingers out of the path the cutter will take should it grab the work and get away from you.

If the tool is creating fine dust or chips, pause frequently to dust off the work so you can see what you are doing. Feed the work to the tool or the tool to the work against the rotation of the cutter whenever possible. This makes it less likely to snag. Use light cuts rather than trying to force the tool into the work. If the tool does not cut, the speed is wrong, the cutting bit is dull, or you are trying to make the machine perform a task beyond its capacity. Avoid overloading and overheating by using a light touch and letting the speed of the tool – not the pressure – do the work.

SAFETY

Eye protection is required AT ALL TIMES, with all attachments. Purchase inexpensive clear plastic safety glasses and force yourself to reach for them before you reach for the motor tool. If your safety glasses are scratched or yellowed to the point where you are tempted to work without them, buy another pair. Safety glasses are inexpensive; your eyes are irreplaceable.

Use the right tool, and don't force one attachment to do the job of another. Don't use a small tool where a large-diameter

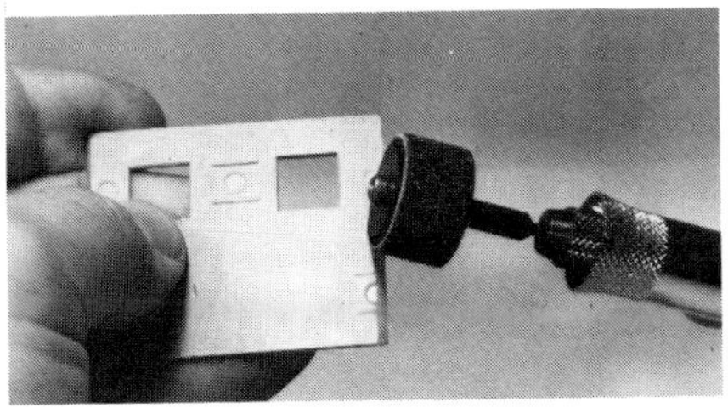

This coarse abrasive drum is handy for quickly beveling the edge of this structure wall section.

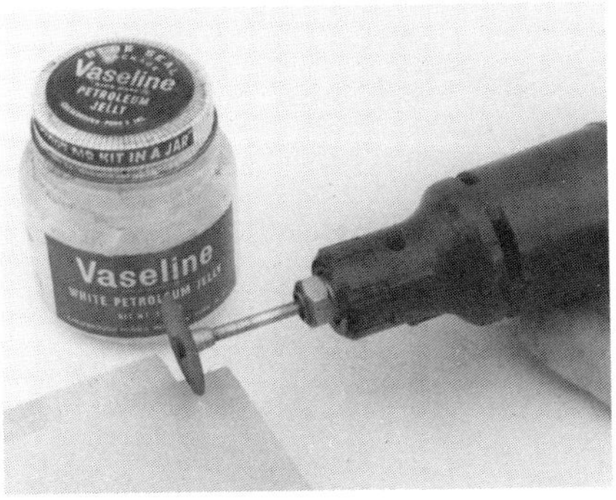

Slitting plastic with a thin abrasive cutoff wheel requires low speed, lubricant, and safety glasses.

one is correct. Disconnect the motor tool while changing accessories. Form the habit of removing the chuck key or wrench immediately after tightening the chuck. Starting the tool with the chuck key in place can throw the key out with great force. If your tool has a three-prong line cord, make sure it is plugged into a grounded outlet. If the cord becomes worn or damaged have it replaced immediately by a qualified repairman.

CARE AND STORAGE

Have a sturdy hook in your work area where you can hang your motor tool. Always remove the cutting tool before storage. Keep tools where children can't get at them – under lock and key if necessary.

Check the instruction manual to see if the tool requires periodic lubrication. Don't overlubricate; excess oil will get on your hands, on the cutting bits, and on your models. Use a vacuum cleaner with a narrow nozzle to draw debris out of the motor ventilation slots. Periodically, check the motor brushes for wear (this is one of the few parts you can service yourself). Consult the manufacturer's instruction booklet for specifications on brush wear and replacement.

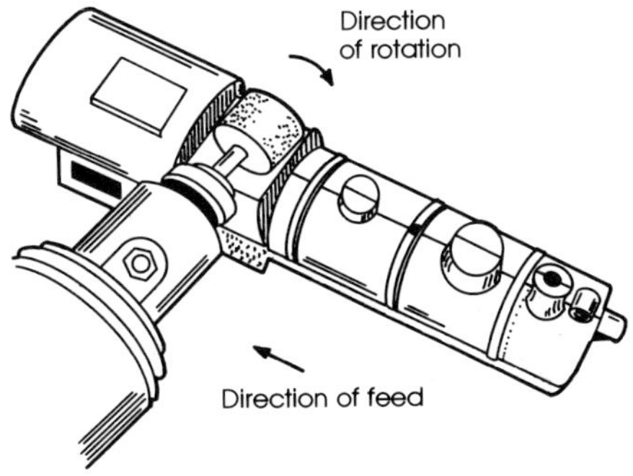

To laminate thick plastic sections from thin sheet, spread liquid cement on the surfaces to be joined, weight or clamp the pieces together, and apply additional cement at the edges. Be sure to let the cement dry thoroughly before working with the laminated piece.

row on the back of the stock. Then walk off individual rivet locations with dividers. Often, you can tape or rubber-cement a scale drawing right to the plastic and use it as the rivet positioning guide. Punch the rivets right through the paper and remove the drawing when you cut off the formed piece.

Next, practice making rivets on a scrap of the same plastic you will

Many modelers have built rivet machines from sewing machines, arbor presses, or other devices. This rivet embosser is an offering of Precision Manufacturing Co. of San Antonio, Texas.

Any rivet-making technique requires considerable practice before you are able to make neat rows of uniform rivets. Once you get the feel of the process you'll be able to turn out something as complex as a locomotive tender side in less than an hour.

use. Make several rows so you develop an understanding of how the process works. Whatever tool you use, practice until you have a feel for how much pressure is needed to make a pleasing round rivet rather than a hole or bump in the plastic. Finally, turn to your finished work.

To emboss rivets on a curved surface such as an oil tank, do the layout and embossing on the wrapper while it is flat, then carefully bend the wrapper to shape. To prevent splitting the plastic during the forming process, cut thin strips after the rivets are embossed.

A tall steel trestle

David Orosi

A. Most model railroads feature a timber trestle but few include modern steel trestles which are just as impressive. This prototype is on the Louisville and Nashville near Independence, Kentucky.

F. The girders will be placed underneath the rails. Don't cement the parts together yet, but go ahead and test-fit all the parts. Keep filing until everything fits properly.

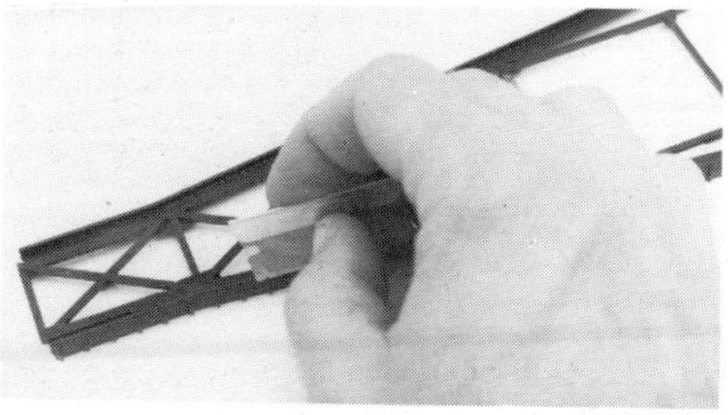

B. Required parts for HO: 5 AHM No. 2590D girder bridges, 2 Bachmann/Plasticville No. 1815 O signal bridges, 6 each Plastruct No. 303 and No. 306 3/32" and 3/16" channel, and plastic sheet or gussets from a Kibri truss bridge.

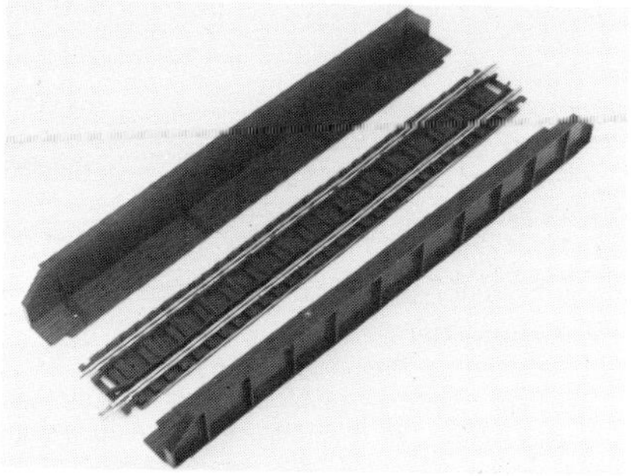

D. Bend the girders upward to snap them off along the cuts. File the sides of the plastic deck section.

G. Two short girder sections rest on top of each of the support towers. The fifth rib in on each end of the AHM girders is double thickness. Cut on the outer edge of this double-thick rib.

H. Six long girder sections are needed. Only the tapered end pieces need to be sawed away on those sections. Leave the vertical rib standing on the end of each girder.

I. Remove the molded ladder rungs from the O scale signal bridge uprights by slicing with a single-edge razor blade.

J. File the surface of the signal bridge legs smooth so no traces of the ladders remain. Finish the job with fine wet-or-dry sandpaper.

C. Make deep knife cuts along the inside edges of the simulated wood walkways on the bottom of each AHM girder bridge.

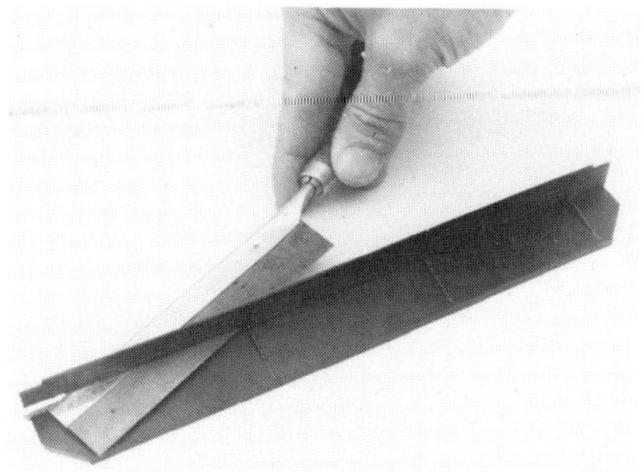

E. Slice the wood walkway from each girder. File the bottoms of the girders flat and at a right angle.

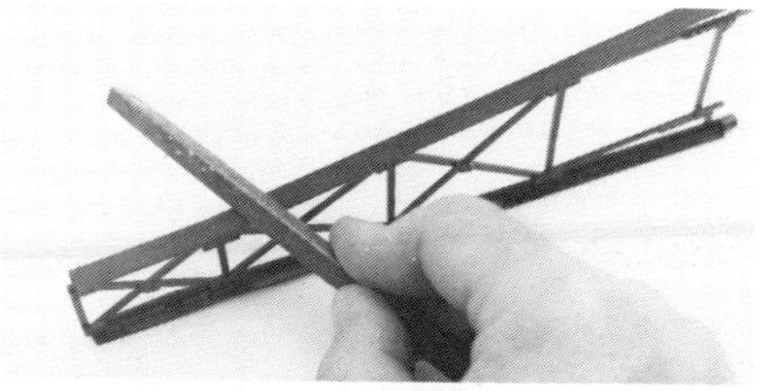

Molding your own parts. You can make duplicates of parts by using synthetic rubber molds and epoxy casting resins. This process can be used to "lift" details such as vents, fans, and louvers from one model for application to another. This is not a way to save money, in fact, it's quite expensive and time consuming compared to cutting up plastic parts. It can help when a locomotive body isn't available separately, or in the odd case where you have just one of a body type that is no longer in production.

To make a mold, coat the model in the

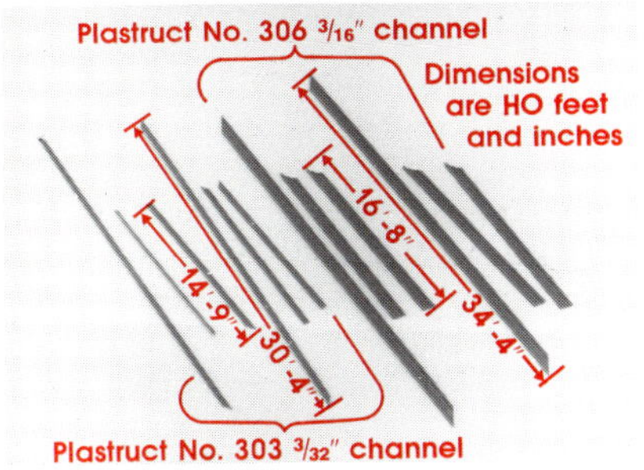

K. Cut all crossbrace pieces at once. The short pieces will be butted against the center of the long sections and the joints covered with riveted gusset plates.

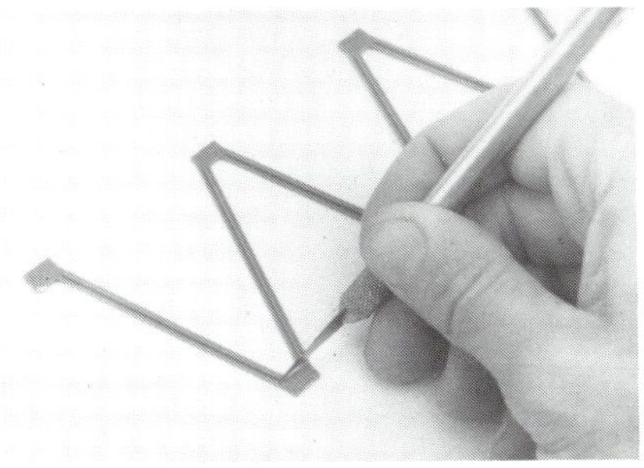

L. Make the cross brace gusset plates either by embossing rivets into .020" sheet styrene or ABS or by cutting appropriate riveted detail from parts of an existing kit.

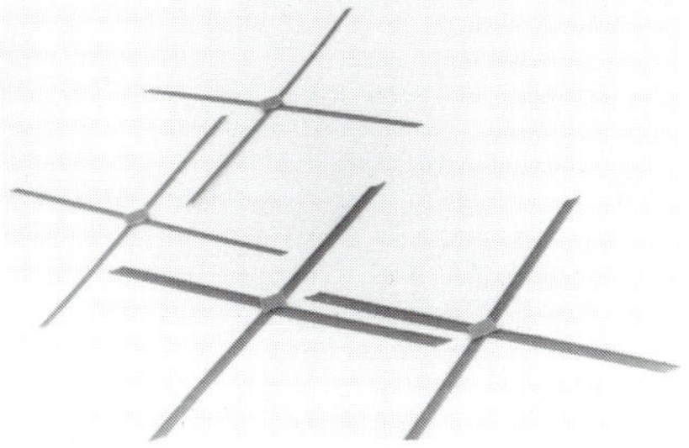

M. These gusset plates are from a Kibri truss bridge. Vollmer also makes a structural shapes assortment (No. 5021) which includes gussets that can be used here. Bond the gussets to the cross bracing.

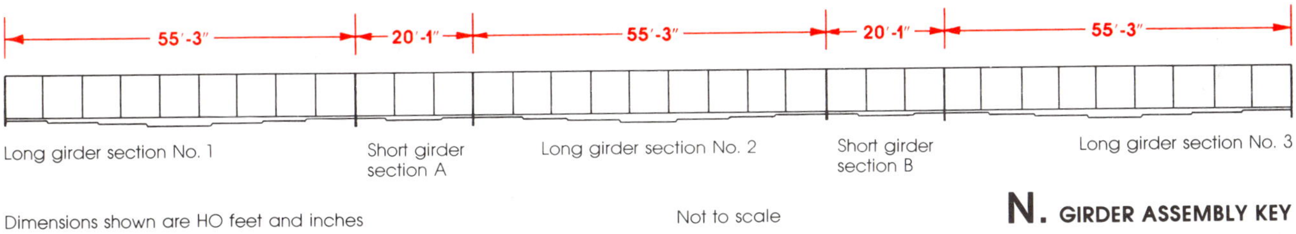

N. GIRDER ASSEMBLY KEY

O. Start assembly by cementing the girders together and to the track sections. Snap the track sections together and center the girder sections under them. Paint the signal bridge bases concrete and use them to hold the uprights while you cement the crossbraces in place. The center-to-center spacing of each pair of uprights should be the same as the length of a short bridge girder. When the cement has dried, remove the concrete bases and paint the towers.

P. A simulated concrete footing is required for each bent.

Q. Ensure the tower uprights align with the ends of the short girders.

R. The completed tall steel trestle is an excellent example of how you can use parts from one scale to make modeling in another scale easier.

Plastic body shells can be accurately sectioned using a small lathe or milling machine. With a Unimat, the first step is to mount the headstock on the vertical post and align it at a precise right angle to the lathe bed.

Murray Sincoff adapted a .010″-thick jeweler's slitting blade to the saw arbor of his Unimat. The handwheel feeds allow control of cutting that is not possible with a razor saw.

area you want to duplicate with a molding rubber such as Flex-Mold or Ruba-Mold. These are available at art and craft shops, or through industrial molding materials supply houses. Work the first coat of rubber into the surface of the model with your fingertip and allow it to dry for 30 minutes. Add a second coat and allow it to cure overnight.

The Flex-Mold or Ruba-Mold dries clear, but you can see its edges. Back the molding rubber with a layer of silicone adhesive, silicone caulking compound, or silicone molding and encapsulating rubber. Dow Corning makes a silicone rubber adhesive that works well, as do the rubbers in the General Electric Silastic RTV/LTV series. GE RTV-31 is a good choice. The GE rubbers are usually available through electronic parts distributors; check the Yellow Pages. Add several layers of silicone rubber to build up the mold to a thickness of at least 1/8″. Let this backing cure as directed on the package, then carefully peel the mold from the model.

Treat the mold with a release agent (several should be available from the place where you purchase the casting resin), and spoon epoxy casting resin into the cavity using a Popsicle stick or a tongue depressor. Spread the resin, and work it into all the nooks and crannies in the mold cavity. There are several casting resins you can use to make parts. Those shown in the photos were made with Marblette Maraset No. 13N epoxy resin and No. HH5 hardener. You can also use the two-part aluminum-filled epoxy auto body resins sold in hardware and auto stores. Do not use polyester resins; they will not cure over silicone. When the resin has hardened and cooled, peel back the mold, releasing the part. The molds can be used over and over again—a feature that is particularly handy when you need to mass-produce a particular item to give several models a family resemblance.

If you find lumps in the surface of the casting, they are probably caused by trapped air bubbles. Sand the casting to the correct contour and fill the exposed air pocket with filler putty. Where openings are required, they can be started with a drill and completed with saw and files. Large amounts of material can be removed quickly with a milling bit in a hand-held motor tool.

Developing "kitbasher's eye." The final area in which you can improve your plastic modeling skills is difficult to define or describe. The distinction between advanced kitbashing and scratchbuilding begins to blur as you tackle more-difficult projects. For example, the steel trestle project in this chapter is kitbashed, but it includes cross bracing constructed almost wholly from scratch. The key to changing the way in which you approach kitbashing projects is to force yourself to evaluate every kit in terms of what parts it can provide for something that you want to model.

You'll find that looking at kits as parts often leads you across scale lines. The HO scale steel trestle project is based on pieces from an O scale signal bridge, and a similar N scale model could easily be made with HO signal bridge parts. Heavy wagon wheels in HO become cart wheels in S or O. The trick—if there is a trick—is to train your eye to evaluate every piece you see, and not to dismiss anything for any reason until you've given it careful consideration. Check out every model by asking yourself how it could be stretched, shrunk, widened, or narrowed.

Finally, remember that kitbashing, while it is easy and fun and a great way to build models quickly, is far from the only way to build the models you want for your pike. Don't take on cut-and-fit jobs so extensive that you'll do more work than you would to scratchbuild the same model. The challenge—and one goal—of model railroading is to make your layout as much like real life as possible. Don't neglect any material or technique that can help you meet that challenge and achieve your goals. Good luck!

Sawing is done at low speed, and repeated applications of Vaseline are made to the blade to reduce friction and heat. This first cut removes the top of the short hood of an Athearn HO GP9 to start a low-hood conversion.

The third cut is made at a shallow angle to match the slope of the short hood on the prototype unit.

The second cut slices out a section of the hood to provide a single headlight on the kitbashed engine.

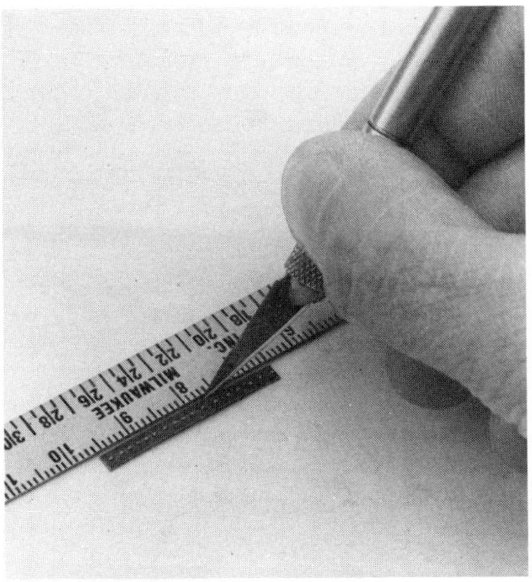

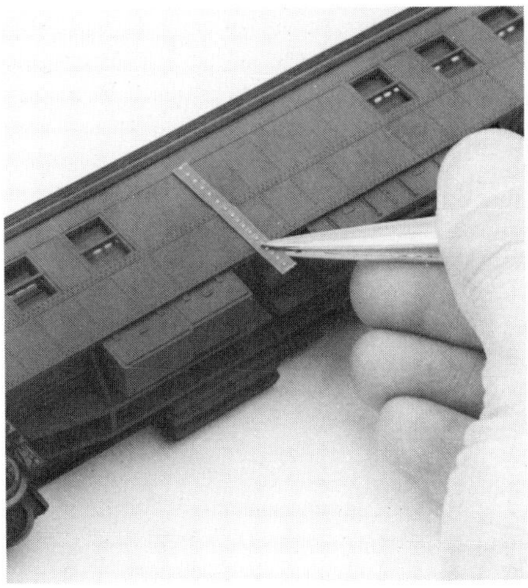

Where thin strips of rivets are required, cut them from the edge of a sheet after they are embossed. Such strips can be used to cover unsightly seams.

Murray Sincoff needed several louvered grills such as those on the Tyco HO GP20 (above) to kitbash Athearn GP9's into GP18's. When he couldn't locate enough spare Tyco shells, he made a rubber mold and used it to cast duplicate grills (below) in epoxy.

When the face coat of thin rubber has dried thoroughly, apply a flexible backing such as this silicone adhesive.

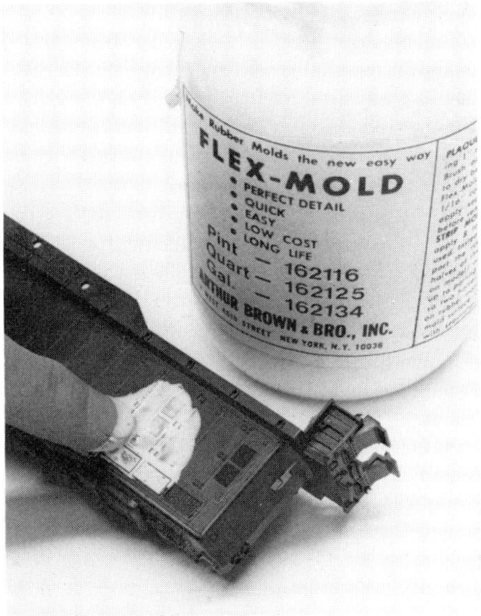

The working surface of the mold is a flexible rubber capable of picking up fine detail. This is backed with a heavy coat of stiffer rubber to strengthen the mold.

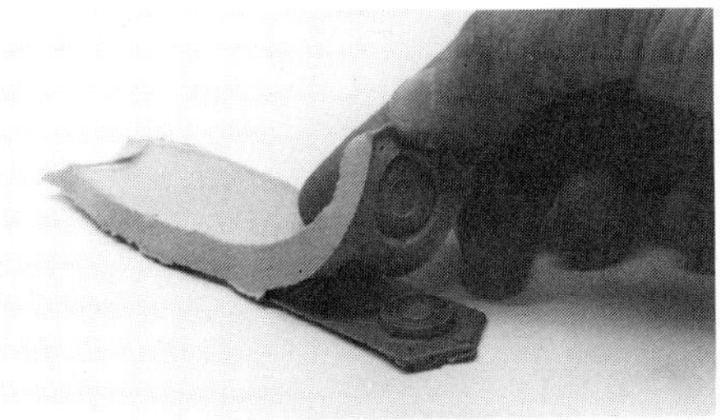

Use one of the many suitable epoxy casting resins to make duplicate parts in the rubber mold. Force the mixture into the mold cavity and allow it to harden according to the instructions. After peeling the mold from the casting, cut and file away excess material to make your required parts.

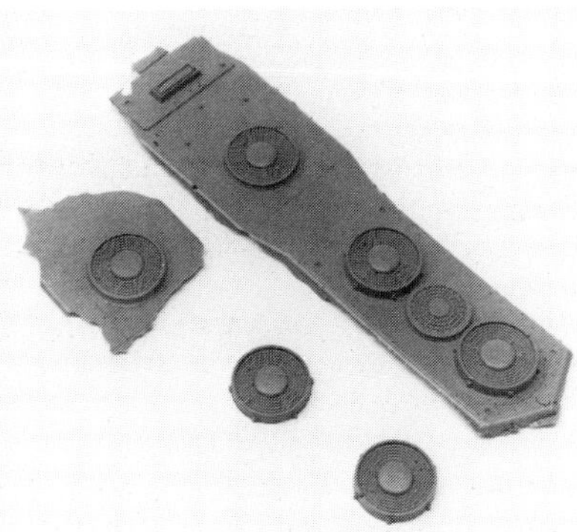

Cast epoxy parts can be trimmed, drilled, or tapped with either hand or power tools. After checking the part for overall fit, trim it to size and cut a matching opening. Cement epoxy parts in place with ACC or 5-minute epoxy.

Glossary and index

ABS: a resilient plastic similar to styrene, but more resistant to chemicals and solvents. Available in sheets, strips, and structural shapes. One brand is Plastruct. **37**

ACC, alphacyanoacrylate, cyanoacrylate, "super glue": a one-part liquid adhesive that combines great holding power with extremely fast setting. Recommended for nonporous materials, but some brands are also formulated to bond wood and paper. ACC bonds skin and must be used with care. Joined fingers may be separated using acetone or nail polish remover.

Acetate: a plastic available in several forms. In modeling it is commonly used in thin clear sheets for window glazing.

Adhesives, types, **7**

Airbrush: a miniature paint sprayer used by modelmakers and artists. An airbrush is variable in both air pressure and paint volume, produces a fine atomized spray, and requires compressed gas for operation. **87**

Airbrushing, **87-92**

Americanizing European structures, **80-84**

Assembly:
- Basic tools, **6**
- Kits, **7**
- Kitbashed structures, **84,85**
- Temporary, **43**

Blending structures into the layout, **85**

Bracing, **79**

Capillary action: the tendency of a thin fluid to flow along and be drawn into a crack or joint.

Cement:
- Applicators, **13,14**
- Plastic, types, **7**
- Stand, **7**
- Tube-type, **14**

Cementing, **13,44**

Clear plastic glazing: thin transparent plastic used to simulate window glass, usually acetate or clear styrene .010″ or .020″ thick.

Clear plastic parts, **9,15,57**

Clerestory: a raised section in a passenger car roof that includes windows to admit light and air for ventilation.

Covering poor joints, **81**

Crazing: the formation of minute cracks on the surface of plastic due to incompatible solvent action. The etched, orange-peel effect can be avoided by using plastic-compatible paints. **16,91**

Cutting:
- Body Shells, **56,57**
- General, **8,9,36,37**
- Notches, **37**
- Openings, **37**

Decals: a type of transfer lettering where the characters are printed or screened onto a clear film on a special backing paper. After soaking in water the film is released from the paper and applied to the model.
- Application, **27,28**
- Mistakes, **31**
- Pricker tool, **29**
- Scratchbuilding, **34**
- Setting fluids, **26,27**
- Striping, **30**

Delrin: a tough, flexible plastic used for injection molding. Often used for gears, truck sideframes, and handrails, it is difficult to paint or cement effectively because of its slippery nature.

Disassembling models, **41**

Doors, **79-82**

Drilling, **52,53**

Dry transfers: lettering and designs made of thin flexible plastic backed with a pressure-sensitive adhesive and supplied on a waxy carrier sheet that releases the letters when rubbed, transferring them to the model.
- Application, **32**
- General, **30**
- Removing, **32**

Eliminating repeated details, **75**

Enamels: plastic-compatible paints, usually thinned with mineral spirits and relatively slow-drying. Common brands are Humbrol, Pactra 'Namel, and Testors Pla.

Epoxy: a two-part resin-and-catalyst adhesive suitable for a wide variety of porous and nonporous materials. Epoxies cure rather than dry, and make strong bonds. Most epoxies are thick, do not shrink as they cure, and are waterproof after curing. The most useful epoxies for modelbuilding set in five minutes. **7**

Family resemblance (locomotives), **73**

File card: a short-bristled wire brush used for cleaning material from the teeth of files.

Filing, **48**

Filler putties, **45-47**

Flash: thin ridges of plastic on the edges of injection molded plastic parts. Flash is extra plastic, most often caused by molten plastic seeping into the gaps between the mated sections of the mold. **9-11**

Flats (structure), **77**

Fluting scraper, **55,56**

Free-lance model: a model without a prototype. Free-lance models usually incorporate features from several prototypes, or conform to standard practices and dimensions for similar prototype items.

Grab irons:
- Bending, **51**
- Replacing, **51**
- Table of sizes, **50**

Gussets, **45,46**

Hot knife, **68,69**

Injection moldings: parts made by forcing molten plastic into hollow dies or molds. Most plastic kits are manufactured by injection molding. **3**

Jigs, **47,49,51,53,60**

Kitbashing, kitlancing, kitmingling, or cross-kitting: combining parts from kits to produce models unlike the straight kitbuilt versions. **36**

Knives, modeling, **8,9**

Laminating, **95,97**

Lathe, **95,100**

Lengthening cars, **55**

Lighting, **85**

Liquid plastic cement: a solvent used to cement plastic by dissolving a thin layer of each surface to be joined. When the solvent evaporates the surfaces are fused together. Applied with a brush or needle applicator, liquid plastic cements have no body. They distribute themselves along joints by capillary action, leaving very neat results. Common brands include Testors Plastic Cement, Plastic Weld, and Micro Weld. **6,7**

Locomotive tender modifications, **65**

Low-relief buildings, **76,77**

Masking, **21-23**, **92,93**

Modular structures, **75,76**

Molding parts, **99-101**

Motor tools, **95-97**

NMRA: the National Model Railroad Association, a worldwide organization of model railroaders who exchange information and promote creative development and fellowship in model railroading. The NMRA researches and establishes standards and recommended practices that ensure the compatibility of mechanical and electrical components from different model railroad manufacturers.

Paint:
  Additives, **17**
  Clear finishes, **17**
  Incompatible types, **16,17**
  Mixing, **92-94**
  Plastic-compatible, **16,17**
  Preparing (for airbrush), **89**
  Protective coatings, **17**
  Storing, **93,94**

Painting:
  Advanced techniques, **87-92**
  Basic, **16-23**
  Before assembly, **12**
  Brush, **19,20**
  Highlighting handrails, **94**
  Holding fixtures, **19**
  Multicolor schemes, **21**
  Preparing the model, **18**
  Priming, **19**
  Spray-can, **20-22**

Parting lines: thin ridges left on injection molded plastic parts where the sections of the mold join together. **9,11**

Pin vise: a hand-held chuck used to grasp small-diameter drills while drilling.

Planning cuts, **56,57**

Plastic-compatible paint: paint that will not etch or craze the surface of a plastic model regardless of the method of application. These paints include enamels such as Humbrol, Pactra, and Testors, and water-soluble acrylic finishes such as Polly S.

Plugging holes, **39**

Primer: a specially formulated paint or coating that prepares a bare surface for additional paint coats. Primers are used to seal porous surfaces, to increase the holding power of subsequent coats, or to reduce the number of color coats required to achieve complete, opaque, coverage. **19**

Prototype: the original full-size object on which a model is based.

Reinforcement, **45,46,58,73**

Removing lettering, **86**

Removing paint, **86,87**

Removing unwanted detail, **38,62,63**

Reporting marks: the lettering on the sides and ends of freight cars that indicates who owns or operates the car.

Rivet detail, **95,97,98,101**

Runner: see *Sprue*.

Sawing, **38,40,41,60,100**

Scale rule: a ruler graduated in feet and inches for a modeling scale such as O, S, HO, or N.

Scraping technique, **11**

Scratchbuilding: building models from stock materials without using commercial parts other than motors, gears, couplers, light bulbs, and wood, metal, or plastic shapes.

Scribing, **42,43**

Sectioning body shells, **56,57**

Shortening cars, **55**

Sprue: the treelike molded framework to which injection molded plastic parts are attached. Most plastic kits include several sprues, each with several parts attached.
  As bracing, **79**
  Stretching, **43,44**

Stain: a thinned paint or pigment in a vehicle. Stains are absorbed into the surface of porous materials or settle on the surface of nonporous materials, modifying or dulling the base color. Most stains are made by thinning model paint.

Styrene: a soft, grainless thermoplastic that can be easily formed and fabricated with hand or machine tools. Styrene is the material for most injection molded model railroad equipment, and is also available in clear and opaque sheets, precut strips, milled structure siding, rods, and tubes.

Templates, **45,47,49,56**

Truing cut body shells, **60**

Ultrasonic cleaners, **87**

Undecorated equipment: models supplied without paint, lettering, or decals. Undecorated equipment is best for kitbashing projects because the modeler need not remove old paint.

Warped parts, fixing, **12**

Weathering: building, painting, and finishing a model to simulate exposure to weather, dirt, and wear.
  Cars, **24**
  General techniques, **23**
  Locomotives, **24**
  Stains and washes, **24,25**
  Structures, **24,25**

Wet-or-dry sandpaper: sandpaper made with waterproof backing and adhesives. Used wet, it produces a very smooth finish.

White glue: a polyvinyl acetate resin adhesive that is water-soluble and milky white in liquid form, but dries clear. White glue is suitable for porous materials, but has only limited holding power on metal and plastic. It is handy for attaching painted detail parts on plastic models and for gluing parts that may be removed later, such as structure roofs. Common brands are Elmer's Glue-All, Ambroid Se-Cur-It, and Slomon's Sobo Glue.

Windows:
  Altering arrangement, **58-61**
  Americanizing, **81**
  Cutting millions, **81**
  Filling in, **79,80**
  Narrowing, **79**
  Opening, **80**
  Replacing with door, **79**

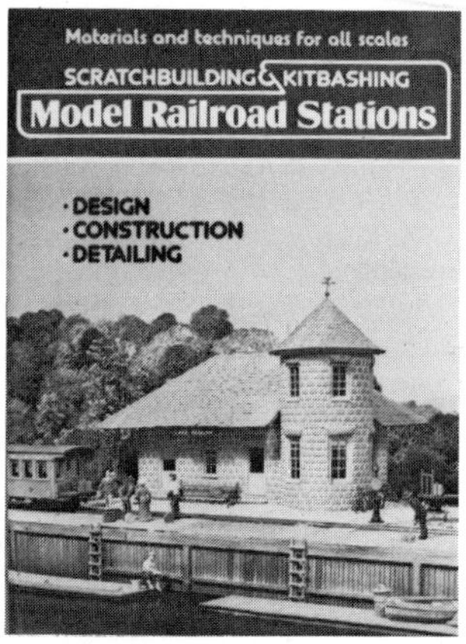

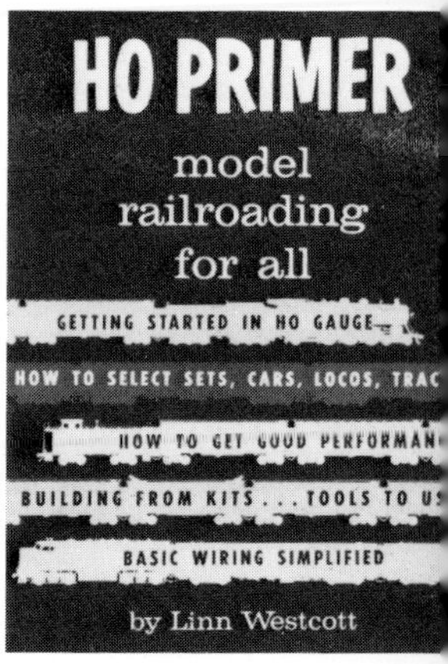

Whether you're a beginner or seasoned modeler, you'll discover tl
and enjoyment you get from model railroading. Select the books y